The Complete Bar/Bat Mitzvah Book

Everything You Need to Plan a Meaningful Celebration

By
Patti Moskovitz

CAREER
PRESS
Franklin Lakes, NJ

THE COMPLETE BAR/BAT MITZVAH BOOK
Cover design by Hub Graphics
Typesetting by Eileen Munson
Printed in the U.S.A. by Book-mart Press

To order this title, please call toll-free 1-800-CAREER-1 (NJ and Canada: 201-848-0310) to order using VISA or MasterCard, or for further information on books from Career Press.

The Career Press, Inc., 3 Tice Road, PO Box 687,
Franklin Lakes, NJ 07417
www.careerpress.com

Library of Congress Cataloging-in-Publication Data

Moskovitz, Patti
    The complete bar/bat mitzvah book : everything you need to plan a meaningful celebration / by Patti Moskovitz.
        p. cm.
    Includes bibliographical references and index.
    ISBN 1-56414-463-1 (paperback)
    1. Bar mitzvah—Handbooks, manuals, etc. 2. Bat mitzvah—Handbooks, manuals, etc. I. Title.
BM707.2 .M67 2000
296.4'424—dc21   99-059748

▲

To Rebecca and David,
with love
from Bubbi.

▼

Acknowledgments

Many people have contributed to this book. Without their shared wisdom and support of this project, it would not be a reality. My sincere and heartfelt thanks to all of them:

Joseph Aaron and Sara Belkov, *Chicago Jewish News*

Rabbi Elka Abrahamson

Noah Abelson

Gila and Mark Abelson

Rabbi Alan Berg

Rabbi David Cohen

Jacqueline Cutler

David, Ina, and Mikhail Drabkin

Stacey Farkas, Managing Editor, Career Press

Linda Feldman, Union of American Hebrew Congregations, Pacific Central West and Pacific Northwest Councils

Pamela Folbaum, Jewish Reconstructionist Federation

Howard Friedman, Director of the Battat Resource Center, Bureau of Jewish Education of San Francisco, the Peninsula, Marin and Sonoma Counties

Ron Fry, President, Career Press

Franci Goldberg and Diane Townsend

Rabbi Marvin Goodman

Barbara Ribacove Gordon, North American Conference on Ethiopian Jewry

Laurie Harper, Sebastian Literary Agency

Rabbi Jan Kaufman, Director of Special Projects, Rabbinical Assembly of Conservative Judaism

Caren Levine, Jewish Educational Service of North America (JESNA)

Marlene Levenson, LCSW, Jewish Family and Children's Services of San Francisco, the Peninsula, Marin and Sonoma Counties

Larisa Margulis, Bay Area Council for Jewish Rescue
    and Renewal

Rabbi Dan Moskovitz

Rabbi David J. Meyer

Gerald Posner, *The Jewish Journal North of Boston*

Karen Prager, Editor, Career Press

Rabbi Gerald Raiskin

Leslie Reisfeld

Mitch Reitman, United Synagogue of America

Leslie Sachs

Sally Samuels

Bernie Scharfstein, KTAV Publishing House, Inc.

Rabbi Mark Schiftan

Cantor Ellen Schwab

Cantor Doron Shapira

Betsy Sheldon

Lauren Silver

Eileen and Steve Silver

Rabbi Rick Steinberg

Jane Stern

Rabbi Elliot Stevens, Director of Publications,
    Central Conference of American Rabbis

Rabbi Andrew Straus

Heidi Sussman

Yelena, Larissa, and Eugene Taraschansky

Howard Wallach

Kimberly Wallis

Phyllis and Bob Wallis

Miriam Weissman, Director of the Bar/Bat Mitzvah Twinning
    Project, North American Conference on Ethiopian Jewry

Shari Anne Wiezbowski

Bob Wolfe

And special thanks to all my students and their families, from whom
    I have learned so much.

Contents

Introduction

If you are reading this introduction, you, your child, or someone you know is becoming a Bar/Bat Mitzvah. This book is for you!

I wrote it to help you over the long and often bumpy road of Bar/Bat Mitzvah planning. It is a practical and friendly guide for Bar/Bat Mitzvah students and their families, with suggestions for making this a meaningful and memorable milestone both emotionally and spiritually.

A step-by-step approach to all the major elements in the Bar/Bat Mitzvah process will enhance the experience so you can avoid undue stress and enjoy this once-in-a-lifetime event. Rabbis, cantors, and families who have gone through it share their insights. There is specific information to help with the preparation, the service, and the celebration that follows. There are also suggestions for becoming an adult Bar/Bat Mitzvah and for enriching and strengthening Jewish identity beyond the Bar/Bat Mitzvah moment. A glossary and appendices of resources and are also included.

For Jews, the Bar/Bat Mitzvah is a peak experience. It involves everyone in the family, forms and intensifies Jewish identity, and creates powerful Jewish memories. At whatever age it occurs, it can provide a springboard for further activity in Jewish life.

I hope you will find this book a helpful resource as you consider all the aspects of a Bar/Bat Mitzvah for your child, yourself, or someone you know. May it assist you in creating a significant moment in your lives.

One tip before you start reading: The term "Bar Mitzvah" or "Bat Mitzvah" refers to the child who is being celebrated, as well as to the celebration itself.

Enjoy, enjoy!
Patti Moskovitz
Foster City, California
March, 2000
Adar I, 5760

PART ONE:

PREPARATION

Chapter 1

What the Parent Needs To Know

Mazel-tov! Your child is beginning a formal journey to Jewish adulthood: becoming a Bar or Bat Mitzvah! It is an exciting time for you and your family, publicly acknowledging that your son or daughter is an adult in the eyes of the Jewish community. With this status come privileges and responsibilities. This moment is the culmination of years of study, and it initiates new opportunities for participation in Jewish life.

What is a Bar Mitzvah?

The Talmud uses the term Bar Mitzvah, which literally means "son of the commandment," to describe every adult Jewish male. According to Jewish law, boys become Bnai Mitzvah (plural of Bar Mitzvah) at age 13; from then on they are held personally responsible for their religious obligations. Your child is becoming part of a time-honored tradition. Boys have celebrated becoming Bnai Mitzvah for the last 600 years, although some scholars believe the custom is even older than that.

The Bat Mitzvah ("daughter of the commandment") ceremony for girls is actually quite recent. Growing out of the Reconstructionist movement, it began in the United States in 1922, when Rabbi Mordecai Kaplan's daughter, Judith, became the first Bat Mitzvah.

Today, even within Orthodox circles, there is usually some rite of passage celebration for a girl, though they take place when she reaches age 12, when according to Jewish law, girls reach religious maturity. She will not be called up to read from the Torah, but her coming of age is celebrated in some fashion. One who undergoes this alternative rite of passage is sometimes called a *Bat Torah* (a daughter of the Torah). Because in Orthodox Judaism gender differences are important, the term differentiates a girl's obligations from those of a boy and does not compete with the rituals observed by a Bar Mitzvah.

In Israel, too, girls have a different way of marking the 12th birthday: Instead of being called to the Torah, a girl might read from the prayer book or Bible, then present a *d'var Torah* (a commentary on the Torah portion), or at the very least, have a party to commemorate her new status as a Jewish young adult.

Bnai Mitzvah ceremonies have evolved over the centuries from the early custom of blessing a child who was 13 years old and had fasted on Yom Kippur (the Day of Atonement), to today's public ceremony of religious commitment and celebration. More than a party or gathering of gifts, this moment is primarily a religious event. The focal point of the occasion is the worship service and the preparation for it. This will be your child's first public reading from the Torah (the five books of Moses) and a *Haftarah* (a reading from the Prophets). He or she may also now be counted as part of a *minyan*, the quorum of 10 Jewish adults (or, for the Orthodox, men) necessary for certain parts of the congregational worship service. From this time on, one is permitted to recite *Kaddish*, the life-affirming prayer of praise to God, in memory of those who have passed away. At appropriate times he or she may wear a *tallit* (prayer shawl) and "lay" *tefillin* (don small leather boxes containing verses from the Torah). Your child is now considered an independent Jewish adult who is responsible for his or her own actions.

Usually, the Bar Mitzvah ceremony takes place on the first Sabbath following the 13th birthday (for a boy), or after the age of 12 (for a girl). However, one can become a Bar Mitzvah at any age following this birthday and the ceremony can occur at other times throughout the year, depending upon individual circumstances and the custom of your synagogue.

✡ ✡ ✡

Rabbi Andrew Straus: *"Every culture has its own puberty rite for a young person to 'perform,' proving that he or she is ready to be an adult in that culture. These rites generally reflect what the community values most. For example, many Native Americans in early U.S. history included puberty rites involving hunting and survival in the wild. Modern American culture has also developed puberty rites, which include (especially for males) driving, drinking, and loss of virginity. The Jewish community's puberty rite of Bar Mitzvah is based on a very different value system: We ask boys and girls to lead the congregation in worship and to teach Torah. Spiritual and intellectual/educational development are what we as Jews value most."*

✡ ✡ ✡

Deciding what kind of Jewish education is best for you and your family

The most important part of Bnai Mitzvah is the preparation that precedes them. It requires a Jewish education with a special focus on Hebrew. In general, Bnai Mitzvah must be able to lead the congregation in prayer; read from the Torah portion and *Haftarah*; and present a *d'var Torah*.

There may be several specific requirements connected with preparation for this milestone your child's life, depending upon your synagogue or the customs of your Jewish community. Preparation may also differ according to the kind of Jewish education available to your youngster. There are at least three kinds of Jewish instruction available: synagogue supplementary schools, day schools, and independent education/ private tutoring.

Synagogue supplementary schools

Synagogue supplementary schools, often called Hebrew schools, are the most common form of Jewish education in America today. Classes meet once or twice a week after public school hours and/or on weekends. Hebrew studies often begin when children are seven or eight. Studies in Jewish subjects (such as history, customs, ritual practices, and holiday observances) begin several years before the Bar Mitzvah. The lessons become more extensive and more frequent as one gets closer to the year of the Bar Mitzvah. In most synagogue schools, concentrated instruction for Bnai Mitzvah begins at least one or two years beforehand.

Jewish day schools

At day schools, the curriculum is more intensive. It includes daily instruction in Jewish subjects and Hebrew; students learn Hebrew grammar and conversation, the meaning of the prayers, and reading fluency and recitation of the service. Often Jewish topics are linked to the secular studies offered at the school.

If you are looking into a day school, you should inquire about its religious philosophy. There are many different kinds of day schools—Orthodox, Conservative, Reform, and non-affiliated community schools. If you choose a day school for your child, be certain that you are comfortable with the norms of that institution. Most day schools require some observance of *kashrut* (Jewish dietary laws) at the school, and some teach boys and girls separately. Others are egalitarian, and many offer alternative programs in a less structured atmosphere. In any case, be aware that if your child is enrolled in a private day school, you will be expected to embrace and uphold the philosophy of that school at home and in your religious life. To find out more about day schools in your area, consult your local synagogue or board of Jewish education.

In general, day schools do not offer programs of instruction to prepare children specifically for becoming Bnai Mitzvah. This they leave to the parent and/or the synagogue. So even if you are part of such a school, you may choose to structure an independent celebration or decide to affiliate with a congregation. Choosing to become part of a synagogue affords an opportunity for you, your child, and your entire family to become connected to a rabbi and to draw upon the spiritual support of a religious community. There are times in a Jew's life when a rabbi is needed. Affiliation with a synagogue allows you to have access to spiritual help, pastoral counseling, support, and association with clergy at critical moments throughout your life and that of your family.

Independent Bnai Mitzvah education

The third option is the independently structured Bar or Bat Mitzvah. This often takes place in small communities with no synagogue and/or rabbi or in families who want an alternative to synagogue or day school education. In this case, the family must create the program of study, oversee it, and assist with every aspect of the preparation. Although it is the norm, the presence of a rabbi or cantor is not required.

It is not an easy task to prepare for Bnai Mitzvah under such circumstances. One must obtain a Torah scroll and recite the proper blessings in the midst of a *minyan*. The family must enlist a teacher, create a religious and Hebrew curriculum, prepare the student, and embody the Jewish community in supporting the child's efforts. Such elements require a real devotion to this rite of passage and may take considerable time and planning. However, the sense of satisfaction that results from such an undertaking can be enormous and can have a lasting influence on the child and the family.

If you live in a small community without a rabbi, you can obtain help by contacting one of the major Jewish movements. They can help you formulate your own program of study, perhaps arrange for lessons with a part-time, traveling rabbi, and help you make your service a reality. (See Appendix A for information about contacting the major Jewish movements and Appendix F for an example of Bar Mitzvah requirements for students from communities with no synagogue, school, or resident rabbi.)

Choosing a synagogue

When you choose a synagogue, it is expected that you will join for more reasons than just the Bar or Bat Mitzvah. The synagogue has a three-fold function in Jewish life: It is known as a *Beit Ha-Midrash* (a house of study), a *Beit Ha-Tefillah* (a house of prayer), and a *Beit Ha-Knesset* (a house of assembly). For you and your family to call your synagogue home, it should ideally meet all of these criteria. It should be a place where study of Torah, texts and other Jewish matters occurs on a regular basis in an open and accessible environment. It should be a place where one can recite prayers in the requisite *minyan*, and it should be a place where you and your family can find a supportive community. If you are considering becoming a member of a congregation, you and your child should feel comfortable with the rabbi, cantor, and other staff, find the policies and philosophy of the congregation compatible with your own standards, and discover within the synagogue a variety of ways to tap into the richness of Judaism.

Here are some suggestions for choosing a synagogue:

- Begin to investigate the possibilities long before your child is of Bar Mitzvah age. Talk to others in the community, if possible, and find out about the congregation. It may take some time for you to make friends and find a niche for yourselves. Give yourself plenty of opportunities to do so.

- Go to services at the synagogue several times before making the commitment to join. Ask yourself: Do I feel comfortable with the *minhag ha-makom* (the custom of the place)? Does my family feel at ease with the rituals here? Will we be able to express our own concept of Judaism in this community? Is it an environment where *all* of us can feel at home? Are the people friendly? Are there activities for different age groups and interests, especially where the children are concerned?

- If you are a single parent, gay or lesbian, of an interfaith or blended family, or if you have other special family concerns, decide whether the synagogue is comfortable for your unique circumstances. Feeling at ease in the congregation will allow you and your youngster to become active members of the synagogue before the big day and for many years afterwards.

- Regarding the religious school of the congregation: Be clear as to its philosophy, and know the school's requirements and restrictions. Is it suitable for your family and especially for your child? Are there enough teachers for the classes? Are the teachers compassionate and caring? Can the school provide for special needs and abilities? Do they love children, and are they passionate about teaching the joys of Judaism? Is it a happy place? How does your child feel about the ambiance of the synagogue? Most important, are you comfortable with the philosophy and implementation of the Bnai Mitzvah program?

- Make an appointment with the rabbi and the cantor. Be candid about your own goals for Jewish growth. Are they accessible to the members of the congregation? Do they have direct contact with the student during preparation? If not, who does? Meet with that person as well. Find out if the specific curriculum requirements for the Bar Mitzvah year are realistic for your child and compatible with your own Jewish family life.

- When you meet with the membership committee, clarify the financial requirements of the synagogue. Find out what additional monetary obligations there will be for the Bar Mitzvah program. If you have circumstances that require special attention, is the synagogue administration sensitive to your needs?

- Be sure that the congregation reflects the Jewish movement with which you are comfortable and with which you identify. Be clear about the differences between Orthodox, Conservative, Reform, and Reconstructionist Judaism and Jewish Renewal. Understand how these differences will affect your family. For example, if you expect to have your daughter called up to read from the Torah Scroll when she becomes a Bat Mitzvah, be sure that girls and women are allowed to participate in the service at the synagogue you are considering. If not, you may need to look elsewhere.

- If your family is interfaith, clarify the synagogue's policy toward participation of the non-Jew in ritual matters, in the service, and in the congregation itself. You may wish to discuss their definition of who is a Jew, as recognized membership within the Jewish community depends upon the movement with which one affiliates. According to *halacha* (Jewish law) one is considered a Jew if born to a Jewish mother. The Orthodox and Conservative movements adhere to this definition. In Reform Judaism, ever since the resolution of "Patrilineal Descent" was established in 1983, a child is considered Jewish if either parent is Jewish and if there are public and timely acts of observance. Reconstructionist Judaism issued its statement as early as 1968 that one is Jewish if either parent is Jewish, with no other limitations. The Jewish Renewal movement is inclusive in its philosophy regarding status.

Note that although all movements recognize conversion to Judaism, the standards for becoming a Jew differ from movement to movement. If there has been a conversion in your family, be certain that you are in agreement with the synagogue's policy. These are sensitive matters and should be addressed in private conversation with the rabbi and/or membership chairman before affiliation.

Furthermore, some congregations hold Bnot Mitzvah (plural of Bat Mitzvah) on Friday nights only, while Bnai Mitzvah can take place on Saturday mornings, or even mid-week on Mondays or Thursdays. Some congregations require that both boys and girls wear a *kippah* (skullcap) and a *tallit* (prayer shawl) on the *bimah* (raised platform from which the service is led); others do not. Even within the movements there are differences, so be certain you are comfortable with the stance of your particular congregation.

What the synagogue may require in preparation

The preparation within a synagogue religious school varies from place to place, from movement to movement, and from congregation to congregation. It helps to be very clear about the expectations of the school in preparing for this event. Some synagogues have a contract that is signed by both the student and the rabbi, cantor, or Bar/Bat Mitzvah specialist. (For an example, see Appendix B.) Others have handbooks that delineate the responsibilities and expectations of both the school and the student. (You will find a sample in Appendix C.)

Depending upon the curriculum of your congregation, there may be additional requirements besides the in-class instruction. These may include: regular attendance at Sabbath and holiday services, performance of some of the *mitzvot* (commandments), a commitment to doing *tzedakah* and *chesed* (benevolent giving and acts of kindness within the community), involvement in youth activities at the synagogue, and performing daily rituals of Jewish life. You will want to know these before you begin your preparations.

Each congregation also has different expectations regarding how much of the service is led by the student. In some congregations, he or she will conduct the entire service. In others, there may only be a Torah reading and/or *Haftarah*. In almost every case, the student will be expected to give a *d'var Torah* on the week's Torah portion, relating it to his or her own life and to this special day. Be aware that the school may also set post-Bar Mitzvah privileges and responsibilities.

Gift-giving

It is customary to give gifts when people celebrate a birthday. Because Bnai Mitzvah are not ordinary birthday celebrations, the gifts your child receives should be connected to the religious significance of the event. Here are some questions for the gift-giver to consider:

- What is my realistic budget for a gift?
- What are some Jewish things I would like the celebrant to have and keep as reminders of this day?
- What special talents or interests does the child enjoy that could be cultivated through the gifts I give?
- What are the important Jewish values I would like to foster through the giving of this gift?

Here are some suggestions:

✡ Jewish books are always appreciated. Because Judaism stresses learning, any of the following volumes will make a good Bar Mitzvah gift:

- A *Siddur* (the prayerbook for weekdays, *Shabbat*, and festivals) or a *Machzor* (the prayerbook for the High Holy Days). There are different prayerbooks published by the different Jewish movements, so be sure to purchase one that is appropriate for the movement with which the youngster is affiliated. (Examples: The *ArtScroll Siddur* is Orthodox; *Gates of Prayer* is Reform; *Siddur Sim Shalom* is Conservative; *Kol HaNeshama* is Reconstructionist.)

- A *Tanach* (Jewish Bible). There are several versions available, including *TaNaKH*, by the Jewish Publication Society, and *The Jerusalem Bible*, published by Keren Press. You can purchase these in English, Hebrew, or a combination of both.

- A *chumash* (Torah, *Haftarot* and commentaries). You will find many different versions, including: *The Living Torah*, by Aryeh Kaplan, or *The Stone Edition of the Chumash*, by Nosson Scherman (both Orthodox), *The Torah: A Modern Commentary*, by W. Gunther Plaut (Reform), *The Pentateuch and Haftorahs* (with commentary), edited by J.H. Hertz (Conservative), and *The Jewish Publication Society Torah Commentary*, a five-volume set edited by Nahum Sarna and others. There are a variety of *chumashim* from which to choose, depending upon your budget, the student's affiliation, and his/her scholastic capabilities.

- Individual volumes or collections of the writings of the prophets and the psalms. There are collections published by both Mesorah Publications, Ltd., and The Soncino Press.

- Rabbinic commentaries on Torah and Talmud. Possibilities include: *The Kitzur Shulchan Aruch*, by Joseph Caro, *The Mishneh Torah*, by Maimonides, and *Chumash with Rashi*, edited by A.M. Silbermann. You might also select scholarly books by Nehama Leibowitz or *The Talmud*, by Adin Steinsaltz.

- Collections of *Midrashim* (legends, stories, and exposition of Torah and Talmud). Three of the finest collections are: *The Legends of the Jews*, by Louis Ginzburg, *The Midrash Rabbah*, edited by H. Freedman, and *The Book of Legends (Sefer Ha-Aggadah)*, edited by Hayim Nahman Bialik and Yehoshua Hana Ravnitzky.

- Other Jewish reference books, such as *The Encyclopedia Judaica*. There are also many useful and popular one-volume references available. Some possibilities are: *Jewish Literacy*, by Joseph Telushkin, *The Encyclopedia of Jewish Concepts*, by Philip Birnbaum, and *The Jewish Catalogue*, by Richard Siegel, Michael Strassfeld, and Sharon Strassfeld.

- Books on areas of Jewish interest, including history, observances, values, biographies, novels, and books about Israel.

While the suggestions above are by no means exhaustive, they should give you a place to start. You may obtain books and other gift items directly from Jewish publishers, Jewish gift and book stores, your synagogue gift shop, or even online through such sources as amazon.com or barnesandnoble.com. You may also purchase gifts from Jewish mail-order catalogues. (For the names of some Jewish catalogues and other gift sources, please refer to Appendix A.)

✿ Ritual objects to be used throughout the young person's life: items for *Shabbat*—such as candlesticks, a *kiddush* cup, or a *challah* cover; a *Havdalah* set for the ceremony at the close of the Sabbath; a *tallit* and matching bag; a set of *tefillin* and a *tefillin* bag; or holiday items—such as a *chanukiah* (a *Chanukah* menorah) or a *seder* plate for Passover.

✿ Assorted Judaica gift items—including original pieces of art, lithographs, handcrafted stitchery or needlepoint, glassware from Israel, and CDs and tapes of Jewish music.

✿ Less tangible items, but ones that will stand the student in good stead in the future: Israel Bonds or U.S. Savings Bonds. These are not merely purchases, but rather investments in the country that issues them. Another tradition is to give checks for $18 or multiples of this amount, because 18 is the numerical value of the Hebrew word that means "alive," *chai.* State of Israel Bonds recently issued a new Chai Bond. Costing $136, it is a generous and appropriate gift. Another way to invest in the child's future is to start a savings account for him, or to purchase shares of stock, preferably in Jewish companies. All these are gifts that will benefit the student far beyond the day of the celebration.

✿ A video of your family's history, to be presented to the child at the reception following the ceremony. Such a gift will ensure that future generations will have a record of your family's roots. Oral and video histories are precious mementos that can never be replaced. (Information about having such a video made professionally may be found in Appendix A.)

✡ Scholarships to summer camp; outings to Jewish exhibits, programs, or concerts; trips to places of Jewish interest (historic Jewish cities like New York and Los Angeles offer a wide range of Jewish possibilities); or even a trip to Israel. In some Jewish schools parents combine their funds and present each child with a group gift from the rest of the students in the class. In this way, the funds add up to a substantial amount given in the form of an Israel Bond or money for a future trip to Israel. Many congegations, local Jewish community federations, or boards of Jewish education now have Israel travel funds, into which money can be deposited by family and friends on a regular basis from the time the child enrolls in religious school. By the time the Bar or Bat Mitzvah rolls around, the child should have quite a nest egg toward a trip to Israel! (For more information about Bar Mitzvah trips to Israel, please refer to Appendix A.)

Clearly, the only limitations are your imagination and budget.

The greatest gifts, however, may not be material goods. Some families choose *not* to have gifts given to the youngster and instead ask family and friends to contribute to a favorite organization for the betterment of others. There are countless opportunities for the student's personal development and maturation throughout the entire Bar Mitzvah process. Some of them are discussed below.

Opportunities for spiritual growth

Preparation for Bnai Mitzvah does not involve merely learning Hebrew and being able to lead communal prayer. Though these are important and laudable skills, they are only part of the picture. There is a spiritual dimension to the process that is of great importance and that may be explored in different ways.

To be a true Son or Daughter of the Commandment, one should care for others. "You shall love your neighbor as yourself," is the Torah's highest command. It is a *mitzvah* (commandment) required of all Jews. This is a perfect time for your child to engage in acts of *tikkun olam* (repairing the world). Many congregations now incorporate *tikkun olam* activities during the year of Bar Mitzvah preparation. Make yourself aware of the requirements of your school and become involved along with your student. You may also request that in lieu of gifts, your guests make donations to organizations that will make the world a better place. It will enrich all of your lives, and you will know that you are doing your part in being a true partner with God.

"Twinning" the Bar Mitzvah

Twinning is a way of connecting to Jews in other countries and sharing the feelings of becoming a Bar or Bat Mitzvah in a powerful and personal way. Your child may choose to twin with Jews from the Former Soviet Union and Ethiopia. He or she may also twin with non-Jews who saved Jewish lives during the Holocaust.

Throughout the 1960s and 70s, many congregations established a tradition of twinning the student with a Jewish child in the Soviet Union. The Former Soviet Union held more than three million Jews and historically oppressed all those who practiced religion, but especially Jews. With Glasnost ("open-ness"), things changed, and nowadays people don't seem to think of ongoing crisis in connection with Soviet Jews.

The truth of the matter is that things are still difficult for Jews in the Former Soviet Union. Although many have left and are now living in safety in Israel and the United States, those who have stayed behind still face a perilous existence. Your son or daughter can still be involved in a twinning Bar Mitzvah sponsored by the Jewish Council for Jewish Rescue and Renewal. It is an act that reaches out to Jewish brothers and sisters who live in small communities in Russia and other newly liberated countries and who do not have the benefits of religious information that we enjoy in America.

It is also possible to twin with Ethiopian Jews who are now living in Israel. The North American Conference on Ethiopian Jewry (NACOEJ) has a program that enables children in the United States, Canada, and England to twin with their Ethiopian counterparts. Students exchange photos, letters, and other correspondence. The project also allows NACOEJ to raise funds for elementary schools in those towns in Israel where most Ethiopian immigrants live. These children generally live in impoverished areas, and the money provides needed additional educational supplies. For a $180 donation, the American student receives a beautiful certificate suitable for presentation and a gift.

Another way to share the spirit of the Bar or Bat Mitzvah day is to become involved with the Jewish Foundation for the Righteous, which provides ongoing financial aid to more than 1,500 poor and aged Christians who saved Jews during the Holocaust. Your child can be twinned with one of these Righteous Gentiles, communicate over the phone or by letter, and develop an ongoing relationship with someone who was engaged in acts of *tikkun olam* at a time when such acts were most desperately needed.

(For information about "twinning" with the organizations mentioned here, please see Appendix E.)

✡ ✡ ✡

Noah: *"I celebrated my Bar Mitzvah in connection with Alexander Roslan, a native of Poland who saved several members of a Jewish family during the Holocaust. All of the people did acts that deserved honoring, but his was the most righteous and special to me because he took care of three young Jewish boys who were ill. He even sold his house in order to take care of the boys' sickness! There are no words to describe the importance of what he did. It is just amazing!"*

✡ ✡ ✡

Acts of kindness and righteousness

Acts of *chesed* (loving kindness) and *tzedakah* (righteousness)—the giving of aid to those less fortunate—may be accomplished in many ways. Some activities require little time; others are more ambitious. All are worthwhile. Find something you and your family are passionate about, and give of yourselves at whatever level is possible. Your child may wish to incorporate into the *d'var Torah* some information about the organization with which you have all become involved. Your family and friends may also want to learn how to help. The lessons you and your child will learn from charitable acts will last well beyond lessons from a textbook. Here are a few examples of opportunities for involvement:

∠ Give to a local Jewish organization that helps the needy. Often, the best place to start is the Jewish Family and Children's Service. This is the trouble-shooting arm of the Jewish community, giving immediate and long-term assistance to emigres, the homeless, the aged, and the infirm. They can always use help making meals for people with AIDS, providing clothing for those in need, cooking kosher meals for indigent Jewish families, collecting toys for needy children at Chanukah, and putting together kosher-for-Pesach baskets of food at Passover.

∠ Volunteer at the local Jewish home for the aged. Lonely seniors appreciate anyone who comes to visit, and young people who spend time with the elderly often form strong friendships with them. Some synagogues put on yearly concerts for residents of old-age homes. Others regularly send students to do such small activities as playing Bingo, reading the newspaper aloud, helping with art projects, and so on.

∠ Tutor at a local elementary school, preferably one in a less affluent part of town, where children may need extra attention. Often, children who do not enjoy the benefits of a stable home will warm to another youngster who reaches out to them. Find out what is needed in your community, and offer to help.

∠ Become a candy-striper at your local hospital. Spending time on a regular basis assisting in the gift shop or the cafeteria may help lighten the load for others. Even more important is visiting children with chronic illnesses or those who have no one else to visit them. To do such caring work, you should speak to the volunteer director at the hospital or clinic, who will place you where you are needed most.

∠ Become active at your community's food bank. If you set aside just a few hours a week to collect and/or distribute canned food, you will be doing a *mitzvah*. You can supplement your time there by regularly cleaning out your kitchen cupboards and gathering up extra food-stuffs at home and with friends. Another way to help is to buy a few extra groceries each time you go to the supermarket. Set these canned goods aside, and bring them to the food bank every time you go to help. You will be doing a double *mitzvah*.

✡ ✡ ✡

Gary: *"Every year at the High Holy Days, everyone at our synagogue brings cans of food for our local food bank. Last year, we collected over three thousand cans of food on Rosh Hashanah and Yom Kippur. We also have a box in the foyer for ongoing donations of canned food. And every Bar Mitzvah student also gives money to the homeless shelter and food bank. It is a good feeling to know that I am doing my part to help. It makes my Bar Mitzvah even more meaningful to me."*

∠ Give to such organizations as Mazon—A Jewish Response to Hunger. If you give just 3 percent of the total cost of your celebration to Mazon, you will be helping to feed someone in need. Mazon sends money to the many hunger projects across the United States.

As the great sage Hillel once said, "If I am not for myself, who will be? And if I am for myself alone, what am I? And if not now, when?" The Bar or Bat Mitzvah year is the perfect time for a youngster to make efforts to make the world a better place. Engaging in acts of kindness and righteousness is essential in becoming a Jewish adult. Your child will reap great rewards from learning how to give with an open hand and an open heart. (For the names and addresses of suggested *tzedakah* organizations, see Appendix E.)

Long-range preparation

A word to the wise: The more you learn, and the sooner you learn it, the better! The Bar Mitzvah day is but one milestone in a Jewish life. In truth, preparation for this event may begin in early childhood, and the impact may continue long after the actual occasion ends.

✡ ✡ ✡

Rabbi Rick Steinberg: *"The familial aspects of becoming a Bar Mitzvah most capture me as a rabbi who works with children every day in this process. Theoretically, when a child is born into a family, that infant is born a free human being with the right to choose to do anything he or she pleases. But realistically, a baby cannot make any choices. The parents' role at this point is to take away that freedom and hold it for the child until he/she is able—and old enough—to reclaim it and start making his or her own decisions. At age 13, the age of Jewish responsibility, we see that freedom begin to transfer back from the parents to the child.*

Becoming a Bar Mitzvah is about more than reading from the Torah or leading the service. It is about the way families interact. It is about the responsibility children take on in their families, their communities, and especially for themselves at this time of growing maturity. And it is about the parents allowing their children to recapture the freedom granted them at birth. Bar Mitzvah, much like the story of the Exodus from Egypt, is about seizing the freedom that is granted to every human being."

✡ ✡ ✡

In an ideal situation a child is exposed to Jewish rituals in the home, recites prayers, learns to read Hebrew, and observes holidays with family and community from a very early age. In this environment, Bnai Mitzvah events become a natural outgrowth of living an all-encompassing Jewish life. While some preparation of Torah and *Haftarah* is necessary, it is not overwhelming to the student or the family because it has been part of their lives for a very long time.

But in the real world of most liberal Jews, things are often different. We live in a less intense Jewish environment where there may be infrequent synagogue attendance, little familiarity with basic prayers, and observance of only a few Jewish holidays and festivals. It's often unlikely that concentrated Jewish involvement permeates every part of the child's life with daily prayer, fluency in Hebrew, and ongoing observance.

Therefore, some intensive preparation must take place within a year or two of the celebration. As the time approaches, the family becomes centered on this life passage, and the focus can become quite daunting to the parents and the child. It requires a new adjustment of time, energy, and attention. Other activities, usually taken for granted heretofore, are suddenly set aside to make way for this important milestone. Allow plenty of time for preparation and for conversations with your child about the event. The more you involve the student, the more vested he or she will be in the process. Furthermore, you may require some juggling of other commitments, creative time-management and a setting of priorities to adequately complete all that is required. It will be much easier for you to work together on these matters than for you to arbitrarily impose such decisions on your youngster in an authoritative fashion, possibly causing dissension and resentment.

A realistic suggestion: Consider your goals. If you want this to be truly meaningful, begin to incorporate Jewish rituals into your family's life early on. Such observances will enhance your Jewish life and need not be difficult or time-consuming. Reciting *Sh'ma Yisrael* (the central Jewish monotheistic affirmation) both at bedtime and again upon arising, lighting candles on Shabbat, saying the proper blessings, going to age-appropriate Jewish events and worship services, and enrolling your child in religious school—none of these require excessive amounts of time. They *do* require a commitment, however, to the long-term goal of fostering Jewish identity. Such commitment will have results well beyond the actual day of the Bar Mitzvah. It will help to create and strengthen affinity for Jewish living and will enable the student to integrate the Bar or Bat Mitzvah into the entirety of his or her life.

Here are some suggested pre-Bnai Mitzvah experiences for you, your youngster, and the rest of the family to enjoy together:

∠ Begin incorporating small teachable Jewish moments into your family's life. Such activities as lighting Shabbat candles on Friday nights, putting money into a *tzedakah* box, baking *challah* (the braided bread for the Sabbath), and marking the close of the Sabbath with *Havdalah* (the ceremony separating the Sabbath from the rest of the week)—all are Jewish moments that can ignite a spark of interest and fan the flame of Jewish involvement.

∠ Begin to live in Jewish time. Get a Jewish calendar and refer to it. This will put Shabbat and the holidays into a clear perspective, enable you and your child to feel the rhythm of the seasons in a unique way, and help to place the upcoming Bar Mitzvah within the context of a Jewish year.

∠ Celebrate the holidays with friends and family. The High Holy Days, Sukkot, Chanukah, Purim, and Passover all help build Jewish identity. The impressions they make are joyous and lasting, especially for the young. Just as important is the concept of forming a community of Jewish friends with whom to observe these special days. Powerful Jewish memories can come from Shabbat and holiday celebrations. Celebrating with people who are important in our lives makes the events all the more meaningful. And after all, hopefully, these will be the people helping you celebrate. How fortunate you will be to draw upon a network of Jewish friendships established over time!

∠ If possible, arrange to send your child to a Jewish summer camp. Camp memories are irreplaceable, and often the influence of peers creates a greater impetus for becoming a Bar or Bat Mitzvah and for adult Jewish involvement. There are excellent Jewish camps all across the country—both sleep-away camps and day camps. For information, contact your local Jewish community center, synagogue, or Jewish youth organizations.

∠ Start a Jewish library in your home, and include a variety of Jewish resources: magazines, music, videos, and books. All will enhance your Jewish life, stimulating further interest and expanding your child's Jewish learning.

∠ Go to places of Jewish interest in your local community, so that you and your child can experience being part of something larger than just your own immediate family. The richness of Jewish life extends backward in time and outward to the larger Jewish world. How exciting to discover one's place within it!

∠ Attend services at many congregations so that you will experience Shabbat and the holidays in several different places. This is especially important with regard to preparing for a Bar Mitzvah, for it not only enlarges the scope of the family spiritually, but it also enables the student to become acquainted with the service and makes the learning process easier for everyone. The prayers and rituals become old friends wherever you are—comfortable and comforting, sweet and familiar.

∠ Engage in some sort of Jewish study. This can be done on a congregational level, as many synagogues have ongoing classes in various aspects of Jewish life. It can also be done on a less formal basis, with individual and/or family efforts to learn more about Judaism. A particularly helpful task would be for you as the parent to become familiar with some Hebrew before the Bar Mitzvah year. You do not need to become fluent in conversational Hebrew, but an ability to decode the letters and to read and recognize prayers in the service will go a long way to assist you and your child.

∠ Travel to Israel as a family. This is probably the most powerful learning experience you can have. It will open up untold vistas of Jewish knowledge and possibilities for you, your child, and your whole family. There are many opportunities for family trips to Israel—both before and after the celebration. Many synagogues offer family tours to Israel. These are usually scheduled during the summer months and are led by the rabbi, cantor, or principal of the religious school. The age limitations and particulars of these trips are set by each congregation. Consult your local synagogue or Bureau of Jewish Education for details about trips in your area.

Short-term timetable

Preparation that focuses on Bnai Mitzvah usually begins at the end of sixth grade, or the year before the event. If you are a member of a synagogue, there are several resources available, including instruction offered by the rabbi, cantor, or Bar/Bat Mitzvah specialist. (Please refer to Appendix D for an example of a Bar Mitzvah timeline.)

The general Hebrew program may range from three to five years, depending upon the synagogue's policy. The curriculum in the earlier years gives the youngster the basics of reading Hebrew, building up to competency in reading the Shabbat service. In most congregations there is a student evaluation of skill level before beginning the Bar Mitzvah year, and steps are taken to ensure that the youngster has the necessary basic prayer-reading Hebrew skills to proceed with learning the Torah and *Haftarah* in the months ahead. While the exact schedule may vary from synagogue to synagogue and from movement to movement, the time frame looks something like this:

Before fourth grade: The student is enrolled in religious/Hebrew school and by sixth grade is becoming proficient in basic Hebrew skills. The complete Hebrew curriculum leading toward Bnai Mitzvah may vary in length from three to five years, although in special circumstances it may be less. Let the school know about your specific needs.

By fifth or sixth grade: The family meets with the rabbi and/or cantor to select a date. The date chosen will not be earlier than the child's birthday of the Bar Mitzvah year, but it may be on any Shabbat thereafter. In some congregations the date is set the year before the event, but in some synagogues the family must choose a date two, or even three, years ahead of time, due to the large number of students. Be sure to allow yourself enough time to make this decision.

By the end of sixth grade: There may be an evaluation of the student's Hebrew skills by the school before entering the Bar Mitzvah program. Those who need to be brought up to grade level may be offered tutoring or time with the cantor, rabbi, or other specialist. (For more information about tutoring, please see Chapter 3.)

Twelve months before: Parents may be invited to attend a Bar Mitzvah series or class. At the same time, the student should be beginning his/her Bar Mitzvah project, if such an activity is required by the school.

At least six to nine months before the Bar Mitzvah: The components of the service—the basic prayers and blessings—should have been mastered.

At least six months before: The student may begin learning his or her Torah portion. If the portion is to be chanted, your child may need a bit more time to learn the *trope* (the melodies for Torah/*Haftarah* chanting). If a child is having difficulty, or if there are special circumstances, he or she may begin sooner than this. Discuss your particular situation with your youngster and with the school.

On the average, four to six months before the Bar Mitzvah: Students may begin intensive instruction on the Torah portion and *Haftarah* with the rabbi, cantor, or other Bar Mitzvah specialist in the school. Some congregations begin this part of the process as early as one year ahead of time. Others do so much closer to the date.

Four months before: The student should be concentrating on becoming more proficient at reading the Torah without vowels. Here again, the time frame may vary from synagogue to synagogue and from student to student. Be aware of the policy and your own child's needs.

Two or three months before: Work with the rabbi on the *d'var Torah.*

At least one month before the Bar Mitzvah: The student should have everything learned, although some final polishing may still be needed. There may be an initial run-through of the service at this time.

The last two weeks prior to the service: The student has final meetings and rehearsals with the rabbi, cantor, or Bar Mitzvah specialist. The final rehearsal will involve the rest of the family members taking part in the service.

The Friday evening before the Bar Mitzvah day: The student often takes part in the *Kabbalat Shabbat* (the service to welcome the Sabbath), chanting the *Kiddush* (the blessing over the wine) and *Ha-Motzi* (the blessing of the bread), and perhaps leading some other parts of the service.

The day of the Bar Mitzvah: Come early, and "*shepp nachas!*" (Take pride in your child's accomplishments!)

The better prepared you are for this important event, the more significant and less stressful it will be. Your goal should be to share a life passage with your child and the other members of your family in a way that is rich in meaning. Prepare well, and you will be able to enjoy this moment and its memories for a lifetime.

Chapter 2

Getting Started

Now that you are ready to get down to basics, the biggest question seems to be, "What to do first?"

There are at least two practical matters to attend to immediately:

1. Choose the date, time, and place of the service. This is done in consultation with your rabbi and/or cantor and requires some special consideration.

2. Choose a place and time for the celebration following the service. Begin to consider musicians and caterers, if appropriate, as these must be booked well in advance. (For more about this, please refer to Part 3: The Celebration.)

Choosing the date

Choosing a date depends on many things: your child's birthday, the restrictions of the Jewish calendar, what dates are available at your synagogue, which day of the week and what time of day you would like to schedule the service, the *parashah* (Torah portion) and *Haftarah* for the week, and other practical issues.

Your child's birthday

As indicated earlier, the Bar Mitzvah date is usually set for the Shabbat immediately following the 13th birthday, while the Bat Mitzvah service may be held after the age of 12. Most liberal congregations nowadays do not differentiate and schedule both Bar and Bat Mitzvah services on or after the 13th birthday. You should contact your synagogue to be sure of the particular policy of your congregation.

It has been said that one must be a mathematician to understand the Jewish calendar! It is rather complicated, but here goes: One may calculate the child's birthday by either the Hebrew date or the secular date. In many congregations, the Hebrew date is preferred, so that it will coincide with the Torah portion and *Haftarah* for that week. You will need to know your child's year of birth, according to the Jewish calendar, as well as the day of the Hebrew month. To compute your child's Hebrew birthday, you should remember that the Jewish calendar is based on lunar months, but with accommodations to the solar year. Therefore, the secular date will vary from year to year.

Also, remember that according to the Jewish calendar, days begin at sundown of the night before. This means that if your child was born after sundown on a certain day, then his or her birthday is actually on the following day, according to the Jewish calendar. To determine a Hebrew birthday, consult with your rabbi or refer to a Jewish calendar. You may also refer to the perpetual Jewish calendar in the *Encyclopedia Judaica* or buy one in Jewish bookstores. (A five-year calendar of Shabbat Torah readings is included for your reference in Appendix G.)

Concerning the Jewish calendar

There are additional considerations having to do with appropriate dates, depending upon the restrictions of the Jewish calendar. Bnai Mitzvah services are not held on Rosh Hashanah (the Jewish new year), Yom Kippur, or the 10 days between them. Nor are they scheduled on the first two days of Passover or on fast days, such as Tisha B'Av (the 9th day of the month of Av, which marks the destruction of both Temples in ancient days). Bnai Mitzvah are also not held on modern Jewish days of mourning, such as Yom Ha-Shoah (Holocaust Remembrance Day) and Yom Ha-Zikaron (Memorial Day for Israel's fallen soldiers). There are other restrictions during the period between Passover and Shavuot, so consult your rabbi. However, it is possible to hold Bnai Mitzvah on other holidays, including Sukkot, Chanukah, and Purim. The joyful themes of these holidays add to the richness of the day, and often the youngster can incorporate these ideas into the Torah commentary or sermon.

You may choose a date based upon the content of the Torah portion or *Haftarah*. There may be several reasons for this: If one *parashah* is particularly meaningful to your child, you might decide to schedule the service around that portion. Some people decide on a specific date to mark an earlier milestone in the life of their family. One family from Iran scheduled their son's Bar Mitzvah to coincide with the anniversary of the date they immigrated to the United States. Or perhaps you would like your child to have the same Torah portion that you had, or that your grandparent had. This can be easily arranged if that date is available. Be aware that in addition to the vagaries of the Jewish calendar indicated above, there may be some differences in the Torah and *Haftarah* portions scheduled for each Shabbat by Ashkenazim and Sephardim, in Israel and the Diaspora, and by Reform and traditional Jews. Again, you should clarify these factors with your rabbi. (For a listing of the Torah portions and *Haftarot* for the Jewish year, please refer to Appendix G.)

Finding an available date

Many synagogues are so busy that families must schedule Bnai Mitzvah very far in advance. As indicated in Chapter 1, some congregations make plans two or three years before the event. Naturally, your choice of a date will be affected by the availability of the synagogue and the rabbi. So, it is helpful to have that information ahead of time, if possible.

Another factor to consider is that some synagogues in large Jewish communities schedule so many Bnai Mitzvah that sometimes it is not possible for every student to hold his or her ceremony alone; each child shares the *bimah* and the service along with at least one other youngster. Although it is not always the first choice, such combined ceremonies can foster strong feelings of camaraderie and friendship between the students and their families. In fact in some instances, it may be helpful to hold a combined service, especially when the family or families have few members present for the occasion. Joining with another family encourages a feeling of inclusiveness, and encourages more people to come and share the joy of the moment.

Combined services can also cut down considerably on the costs of the flowers, photography, and even the rabbi's and/or cantor's fees because two families are sharing the expense. They do make for a larger crowd in the sanctuary, and the service must be tailored to fit the special circumstances. Sometimes, it lightens the load for each student, as they may divide a Torah portion and a *Haftarah* and take turns leading the service. Each may give his or her own *d'var Torah* and enjoy individual honors for his or her family while on the *bimah*. If this will be the situation in your own congregation, discuss the arrangements with your rabbi, cantor, or Bar/Bat Mitzvah specialist in order to plan it appropriately.

On Shabbat—or another day?

Because Shabbat is the holiest day of the week, it is fitting that one becomes a Bar or Bat Mitzvah on that day. However, it is not mandatory to schedule the service on Shabbat morning. (Some traditional congregations, where girls are not called up for an *aliyah* and are not counted as part of a *minyan*, hold Bat Mitzvah services on a Friday night, when there is no Torah service.) Generally speaking, however, it is common practice to hold the service on a day when the Torah is read in the presence of a *minyan*, and these are not only on Shabbat.

The days of public Torah readings were set many centuries ago in Jewish history, after 586 B.C.E., when the First Temple in Jerusalem was destroyed by King Nebuchadnezzer of Babylonia. The Jews were sent into exile in Babylonia and remained there until King Cyrus of Persia conquered Babylonia in 550 B.C.E. and allowed them to return to Jerusalem. In the days following the exiles' return, it became customary to read from the Torah three times a week—Mondays, Thursdays, and Saturdays. On each of these days there would be enough people in the Temple to comprise a *minyan*. Mondays and Thursdays were market days, and Saturday was Shabbat; so it was easy to assemble the requisite number. As the tradition evolved, there were never more than two days intervening between Torah readings, and the same Torah portion would be studied during the entire week.

In all Orthodox and in many Conservative congregations today, the Torah is still read three times a week. Therefore, one may hold Bnai Mitzvah on any of those three days. In most Reform and Reconstructionist congregations, where there are not usually daily or mid-week services, the Torah reading takes place on Shabbat morning. Therefore, that is when most Bnai Mitzvah services are held. However, some Reform synagogues have a Torah service on Friday evenings as well. If you prefer a Friday night service, it is a good idea to check with your synagogue to see if that is possible.

About *aliyot* and choosing the day

Another reason for holding the service on Shabbat is that it is the day when there are the most *aliyot* (the privilege of being called up to recite blessings over the Torah), and therefore more members of the family can be honored in this way. The honor of an *aliyah* (meaning "ascending") is given to adult Jews only. In Orthodox synagogues only men are called up to the *bimah*, while in liberal congregations both men and women are given this privilege. (The *aliyot* and the Torah service are discussed in detail in Part 2.)

Some practical considerations concerning the date

Besides the religious aspects of the date, you may want to consider some practical matters. For example, if you have family coming from far away, you may want to take into account the time of year the service is to be held. If you live in an area with snow and ice, you may want to schedule the gathering for a more temperate season. This is especially true if you have elderly parents or grandparents in attendance. It is complicated if they live elsewhere and are flying in to be with the family. It may be difficult for them under the best of conditions, but to have them battle a winter blizzard in order to attend may be a bit too much to expect. The same may be said of hot and humid summers, where people not used to the climate may literally pass out in a packed synagogue without air conditioning. (At the very least, it is bound to put a damper on the festivities!)

Be alert to other events occurring at the same time. Programs taking place in your synagogue, the larger Jewish community, or your municipality may have an effect upon your plans. Hotel reservations, availability of reception sites, ease of transportation—all of these can become complicated issues.

Finally, the time of year will be affected by school and vacation schedules and other holidays on the calendar. Planning your child's Bar or Bat Mitzvah the same week as final exams puts undue pressure on everybody. Scheduling the service on a Shabbat that coincides with a secular holiday may result in fewer guests being able to attend.

Deciding on the time of the service

Not all Bnai Mitzvah services must be held in the morning. While this is the usual time for such a ceremony, the service may take place at any time when the Torah is read. In congregations with a daily *minyan* there may be services three times a day. This is unusual in Reform, Reconstructionist, and Jewish Renewal congregations, but is more common in Conservative and Orthodox synagogues. These three services are: *Shacharit* (the morning service), *Mincha* (the afternoon service), and *Ma'ariv* (the evening service).

The services are structured in remembrance of the times of the various sacrificial offerings in the Temple in ancient days. *Shacharit* comes from the word *shachar* (dawn). It may take place anytime after dawn until about noon. Most morning services begin between 9:30 and 10:30 a.m. and end between noon and 12:30 p.m. A service with a full Torah and *Haftarah* reading most commonly takes place during *Shacharit.*

On Shabbat mornings, Rosh Chodesh (the new moon celebration) and festivals, there is an extra set of prayers and blessings following *Shacharit* and the Torah service. This is the *Musaf* (additional) service, which takes its name from the additional sacrifices brought in the Temple on those occasions. It is not part of the Reform or Reconstructionist worship service. But if your child is becoming a Bar or Bat Mitzvah in a Conservative or Orthodox synagogue, he or she may be expected to lead the *Musaf* service in addition to parts of *Shacharit* and Torah and *Haftarah* chanting. *Musaf* makes for a longer morning service and includes repetition, additions, and variations of certain prayers.

Mincha (offering) gets its name from the afternoon sacrifice that was made during Temple days. This afternoon service usually takes place just before sundown. It can come before 5 p.m. during the winter months, but may be much later when the days are longer in the summer. This will have an impact on the timing of your post-ceremony celebration. Some Conservative congregations may have a combination *Mincha-Ma'ariv* service, which is a kind of double-header. It is a back-to-back afternoon/evening service, with a Torah reading during the *Mincha* portion. (Traditionally, there is no Torah reading in the evening, although as we have noted, many Reform and Reconstructionist congregations now include a Torah service as part of their Friday night *Kabbalat Shabbat* service, when most of the congregants are in attendance.)

In some congregations, one may schedule Shabbat afternoon Bnai Mitzvah as part of *Mincha.* The Torah is read during this service but a *Haftarah* may not be included. It is a shorter service than the one in the morning.

Services also may be held at a time to include *Havdalah* (the short ceremony that takes place at the close of Shabbat, marking the separation of the Sabbath from the rest of the week.) In this case, arrangements are made to have a special Torah reading at that time, since one does not usually take place at that ceremony. Often, the congregation will structure *Havdalah* Bnai Mitzvah to take place in conjunction with the *Mincha* service late on a Shabbat afternoon, to be followed by *seudah shlishit* (the third meal), a light supper to mark the close of the Sabbath.

Rosh Chodesh is also a good time for Bnai Mitzvah services. Additional prayers are recited on Rosh Chodesh, and it has become a popular time for Bnot Mitzvah ceremonies in particular because, traditionally, Rosh Chodesh is seen as a half-holiday for women, affording them an opportunity for additional study of Jewish texts. Because there are no travel restrictions on this day, people who normally do not drive on the Sabbath can still attend.

As you decide upon the most appropriate time and day for your service, degrees of Sabbath observance become an important issue for you and your guests. One who is *shomer Shabbat* (literally, "guardian of the Sabbath") will not cook, drive, or handle money on Shabbat. This is true from sundown on Friday night until after sundown on Saturday night, following *Havdalah*. Consequently, you should take this into consideration when deciding when to hold the service. If there are specific travel arrangements that must be made for family and friends who do not drive on Shabbat, the service may be scheduled for a weekday, such as a Monday or Thursday, when the Torah would normally be read and travel is allowed.

✡ ✡ ✡

Adam: *"I remember my son's Bar Mitzvah date very well. We decided to hold it on Thanksgiving day because many of the people who were invited did not drive on Shabbat. This was the perfect alternative! Everyone was together, and there was a Torah reading on Thursday. Because it was a weekday, our son could lay tefillin for the first time, something that is not done on Shabbat. The guests could all drive without compromising their level of observance, and everyone had a wonderful time. It was a very special Thanksgiving; we certainly had a lot to be thankful for."*

✡ ✡ ✡

Some alternatives to the traditional synagogue service

Although the traditional and most preferred site for Bnai Mitzvah is the synagogue, some people have reasons for holding them elsewhere. (Please see Chapter 10.)

Why hold Bnai Mitzvah
in a synagogue?

Although the service and celebration can be held in a variety of places, most Bnai Mitzvah are held in a synagogue, for many reasons.

First of all, the synagogue is the home-away-from-home for the Jewish people. Because Judaism is a home-centered way of life, much of what is important in a Jewish life takes place within the confines of one's own house. However, the Bar or Bat Mitzvah involves the community. People will come from near and far to share this moment and to embrace your family and your child within the arms of the entire Jewish community. It is fitting to do this in the sanctuary, the center of the synagogue, which is itself the heart of Jewish communal life.

Secondly, the Bar or Bat Mitzvah service is a *religious* event. The public worship service is the central core of the occasion, and as such it usually takes place in a synagogue. Also, it is easiest to hold the service in the synagogue. The staff there are accustomed to handling the multitude of details connected with Bnai Mitzvah, and they have the means to facilitate the event.

Finally, the synagogue is the place where you and your family will form a relationship with your rabbi and/or cantor and create bonds with the larger Jewish community. Within its walls you may make lasting friendships with your extended Jewish family. If your youngster was educated within this congregation, it is a familiar environment for him or her. If you have been connected with your synagogue for many years, it is a place where you have attended Shabbat services repeatedly. You will have been to High Holy Day services here and marked other moments in your Jewish lives in its sanctuary. Perhaps your child will read from the same Torah scroll that you, the parent, read from when you became a Bar or Bat Mitzvah. It is here that you have the opportunity to forge strong links in the chain of Jewish life. Ideally, your child may be married in this same sanctuary, on the same *bimah*. What a wonderful way to establish Jewish family traditions!

Once you decide when and where to hold the service, you will have taken the first steps in making your plans a reality. And you can then begin to concentrate on your plans for the rest of the celebration. Once you have taken care of all the preliminary considerations and feel you are ready to move ahead, the next step is to find out more about the worship service itself and your child's specific responsibilities. (Please see Part 2: The Service.)

Chapter 3

Family Matters

Now that you have decided to celebrate your child's Bar Mitzvah with a formal service and celebration, your work has just begun! There are countless details to organize and many decisions to make. Some of them will be easy, but others will require some thought and sensitivity. Whether or not you have planned a Bar Mitzvah before, celebrated one as a child, attended many others with friends and family, or are a first-timer, it will be an emotional experience filled with anticipation and excitement. There will be highs and lows ahead, and sometimes you and your son or daughter will find the ride a little bumpy as you navigate the road to the big day.

The ABCs of preparation

To minimize the stress a bit, you might take a moment to consider the ABCs of Bar Mitzvah preparation. They are **Attitude**, **Balance**, and **Communication**. All three have an impact on this important event.

Attitude

The secret of enjoying a positive and powerful Bar Mitzvah experience lies in your attitude and that of your child. If you want this moment to reflect a sense of joy and accomplishment, engaging the student in the process and entering into the spirit of the occasion is the first step. If the whole affair becomes a tug-of-war between you and your son or daughter, then some of the sweetness of the event is lost.

There is an interesting tension here: The Bar Mitzvah may celebrate the coming-of-age of your child, but it is not for your child alone. It is a family event. And because an important part of being Jewish is belonging to an extended family, everyone who cares about the boy or girl who is becoming a Bar or Bat Mitzvah has a stake in it. That's all well and good. But in the end the responsibility for leading the service, learning the Torah portion, and writing the *d'var Torah* rests upon the shoulders of the Bar or Bat Mitzvah student. For some children, this is more than a little intimidating. Others take it all in stride. Their response to the challenge depends on their own feelings of confidence and competence—and the cues they take from the people around them, especially Mom and Dad.

As a parent, there are things you can do to foster a positive attitude in your child. Here are few suggestions:

Clear the decks. Afford your child the opportunity to study and prepare. Set a regular time for practice, and stick to it.

Get involved. Be willing to listen to your youngster read or chant the prayers for you. Even if you don't know one word of Hebrew, the fact that you're supportive is important. If you do know Hebrew and can help in that way, your knowledge will be a source of support to your child.

Be encouraging. Things may seem a bit overwhelming at times—both for you and the student. If you have a positive attitude, it will carry over to your child. Make your comments constructive and upbeat, so that you foster a real sense of joy in Jewish learning.

Be realistic. If your expectations are too high, the student will not be able to meet them. If they are too low, he will not realize his true potential. Recognizing your child's aptitudes and limitations will enable you to set reachable goals. For example, if Hebrew does not come easily to your child, you might plan to supplement his or her in-class Hebrew studies with private tutorials. As another example, if your child panics when speaking before large groups of people, you can arrange opportunities for practice in front of family and friends before the big day. This will help ease the anxiety and instill confidence.

Set the tone. Talking to your child about the Bar or Bat Mitzvah with joyful anticipation will go a long way toward establishing a sense of purpose. If you make it seem like a burdensome task, he or she will reflect that attitude. Inviting your teenager to become part of the planning and to have a vested stake in the outcome will ensure cooperation and a sense of purpose.

Share the load. Involve other people in your immediate family whenever possible. Perhaps they can help by driving your child to Hebrew lessons, writing the program for the service, or assisting you with the hundreds of little details that suddenly appear during the planning. The less stress you feel, the more relaxed your child will be.

Be sure you and your child are clear about the expectations of the rabbi, the cantor, and the school. If you are all on the same page, things will go smoothly.

Joyce: *"When Michael became a Bar Mitzvah, it was a battle from day one. He didn't want to practice and I wanted him to. He didn't want to write his speech, but I kept after him. By the time of the service we were both frazzled beyond belief. Luckily, about a month beforehand, we had a long talk and both of us changed our attitudes: I backed off, and he took over his own part of the responsibility. Things went much easier after that!"*

✡ ✡ ✡

Balance

Your participation in this process is very important. Emotional support, practical assistance with transportation, a willing ear for student practice, and an eagerness to work out the details of the service and the celebration following all help your child prepare for this important moment.

But at times, a parent—even with the best of intentions—may find the whole process difficult. If you are stressed about your child's progress, uncomfortable with the demands being made on both of you, or ambivalent about the very idea of Bnai Mitzvah, problems can arise. Sometimes, a parent doesn't understand the level of commitment necessary to master all the prayers and blessings, the Torah portion, and the *Haftarah*. In such a situation, allowances are not made for the increased time commitment placed on the child. As a result, the student and family become overloaded and frustrated. In other cases, a parent sometimes goes to the other extreme, taking over the celebration to relive his or her own childhood. As a result, the child may not have the opportunity to shine by himself. This can also be a hindrance.

Along with the religious growth and the rites of celebration comes the important element of gaining independence and maturity. Taking the initiative for learning the prayers, practicing the Torah portion and the *Haftarah*, writing the *d'var Torah*—all of these are exercises in growth and maturation. They foster responsibility and commitment. The Bar Mitzvah is also a powerful tool for teaching time-management and priority-setting. In order for a child to truly become an adult, he must learn to become accountable for his actions. Allowing your child to shoulder the responsibility for completing the required portions of the service lets him or her move from childhood to young adulthood, as the Bar or Bat Mitzvah is intended to symbolize.

At the same time, while the celebration of this moment is important to the whole family, it is uniquely and especially your child's moment. So as a parent you might feel pulled in two directions: On the one hand, this is an opportunity for you to *kvell* (feel proud of and gratified at your child's accomplishment) and to share that joy with all who are part of your life. But on the other hand, you must step back to allow your child to have his or her own *kavod* (honor). It is a bit of a balancing act, and keeping all the balls in the air is the trick to helping your youngster take this step into Jewish adulthood. In some ways, Bnai Mitzvah are symbolic of this transition—letting go of the child in order to acknowledge the young adult in your family.

There are many practical matters to keep in balance, too. Time is often the most difficult to control. Other commitments, school activities, hobbies, homework, sports, social obligations, family relationships, and Hebrew school requirements—all of these are everyday demands on your child's time. They do not disappear just because he or she is becoming a Bar Mitzvah. Trying to balance all of these will sometimes seem like a superhuman effort.

✡ ✡ ✡

Pam: *"I can remember one day shortly before my son's Bar Mitzvah. It had been a long holiday weekend, and I came into the rabbi's study in tears because Ricky hadn't wanted to practice at all that week. Instead, he wanted to go to the movies with friends and sleep overnight, go to the beach, and go fishing. I told the rabbi that I felt none of this was important. The rabbi said, 'Everything in life is important. Relax! He'll study again next week.' And sure enough, he did! I learned from that experience that balance is the thing."*

✡ ✡ ✡

Do the best you can. When things get overwhelming, take a deep breath. Go for a walk with your child, go out together for an ice cream cone, or just sit quietly for a few moments and revisit the reasons you are doing this in the first place. Then go one step at a time. It is not all going to be learned in one day, or achieved in one week. But setting your priorities together and being realistic about what you really can accomplish will go a long way toward keeping things in perspective.

Communication

The Bar or Bat Mitzvah experience is a process filled with myriad details, different people's needs to balance, and many competing tasks to accomplish. It may take weeks, or even months. Just as your child is learning to pace him or herself throughout the process, so must you as the parent. It is easy to become bewildered by the demands made upon you and your child. Communication between you, your child, and the synagogue is extremely important to help you through the ups and downs.

Communication between you and your child. When your child becomes a Bar or Bat Mitzvah, your relationship undergoes a subtle transformation. Your youngster is no longer a little child, but an adult in the eyes of the Jewish community. What you decide to do on this day, and how you decide to do it, will depend in large part on the shared communication between you and your son or daughter prior to the moment of celebration.

It is often helpful to remember that no one knows your child's capabilities, limitations, and particular style of learning quite the way you do. Even though teachers, scholars, rabbis, and cantors deal with many Bnai Mitzvah during the year, their perspective is different from yours. It always helps to have input from the professional staff, but in the long run you are the most valuable source of information for, and about, your child.

It is critical for you to work together as a family to set some realistic goals. Remember that your child's Jewish education doesn't end with the Bar Mitzvah and that this event is but one step along the path of Jewish knowledge and observance. It serves as a jumping-off point for further learning. After all, this is not meant to be just a once-in-a-lifetime performance. It is meant to be a chance to share the learning of pre-Bar or Bat Mitzvah training, to establishing a place in the adult Jewish community, and to provide an opportunity for further involvement.

✡ ✡ ✡

Rabbi Mark Schiftan: *"Before a child reads from the Torah, he or she must embrace it and hold it close to the heart for all the congregation to see. But even before that may occur, something else must happen, or else the Torah may never leave the Ark: The parent must first choose to take the Torah in his or her own arms, to embrace it publicly for the child to see, and only then may the child cradle it and be prepared to read from it. This is the true moment of choice: the moment the child accepts the scroll from the parent, and from a source more ancient still. This is what the choice is all about—about that single moment, the split second of trust, confidence, and pride, when both sets of arms embrace the same Torah, as one generation passes its most cherished possession to the next."*

✡ ✡ ✡

With this in mind, here are some things to ask yourselves and to discuss together:

- Why does your child want to become a Bar Mitzvah?

- Why do you want this for your child?

- What meaning does this moment have for each of you?

- What is the attitude of the rest of your immediate family? Are they supportive, neutral, or negative? How can younger siblings play a part in getting ready for the celebration—and anticipate their own? What can older siblings do to help—especially if they have already celebrated becoming Bnai Mitzvah?

- How would you categorize your family—nuclear, extended, single-parent, blended, interfaith, or other? What effects might your family situation have upon you and upon the learning experience of your son?

- What is the level of your child's proficiency in Hebrew reading and comprehension? Is there anything you can do to help your child increase his or her skill levels, either within the school curriculum or with a private tutor?

- How familiar is your child with the prayers and blessings of the service? What can you do to facilitate this?

- What are your child's feelings about religious school and/or Hebrew school? What can you do at this time of his life to enhance the educational experience?

- What aspects of Judaism are most enjoyable for your child? Least enjoyable? How can you help to make this a wonderful experience for all of you?

- What is your youngster's workload for homework and special assignments in regular school? How can you accommodate these demands on your child's time and energy and still include time for Bar Mitzvah obligations?

- If your child attends a Jewish day school, does he enjoy the kind of Jewish education offered there? Why or why not? What does she enjoy most? And what is his or her level of proficiency in Hebrew and Jewish studies?

- What is your child's learning/study style (auditory, verbal, visual, kinesthetic, and so forth)? How will this affect his preparation for the Bar Mitzvah? How can the school accommodate your youngster in this regard? What can you, the parent, do to assist your child?

- What other obligations does your child have (such as sports, music, drama, etc.)? Are there any that can be set aside for this one year? Find out which are the most important to your child, and discuss how to best include these in a balanced and realistic way.

- What other adjustments and compromises in your child's commitments might be made during this year in order to devote sufficient time to preparation?

- What skills do you have that might help prepare your child? (These might include, among others, knowledge of Hebrew or *trope* or familiarity with the Torah text and the service.)

- What concessions—in both time and money—might you have to make during this year to devote to preparation? Will there have to be some adjustment in your own schedule—work, recreation, leisure-time—to allow for these extra commitments? If you child needs private tutoring or additional study, how will you best facilitate this, both financially and practically?

After you have taken time to share your plans on a family level, you will better comprehend ways to implement them. If everyone knows what is expected of him or her, goals become realistic and the atmosphere becomes one of joyous anticipation. After your family discussions, it will be helpful to share your plans with the synagogue's professional staff.

Communication with the school. Often, synagogues hold parent orientation programs as part of the Bnai Mitzvah preparation, at which time they set forth their rules, standards, requirements, and goals. It is important for you to attend such workshops and to read the literature the school distributes so that you are all clear as to what will be expected of you and your child. Since synagogues often change their programs from year to year, it is a good idea to be aware of the current policies and programs that might affect your youngster.

If there is a private consultation scheduled at the beginning of the year, take advantage of the opportunity to sit down with the rabbi, cantor, or Bar/Bat Mitzvah specialist and discuss your own situation. This way, you will be aware of what is expected of you, and the school will be clear about the needs of you and your child.

Here are some possible areas of discussion:

- Make the school aware of any special circumstances in your family—interfaith marriage, divorce, custody concerns, a death in the family, and so on. (For more information about this, please read further along in this chapter.)

- If your child has any learning disabilities or special needs, let the school know at this time. They cannot make adjustments in teaching approach without knowing this, and the sooner, the better. In return, find out what resources are available to you within the synagogue and in the larger Jewish community. (More on learning disabilities later in this chapter.)

- Share with the school your child's special interests or talents. Perhaps there are ways to incorporate such skills into the service and/or celebration.

- Together, consider ways to extend the Bar or Bat Mitzvah experience beyond academic study. Explore avenues of community service or social action.

- Find out what your responsibilities will be for the service and the reception, as far as the synagogue is concerned.

- Discuss the Bnai Mitzvah program in general. Find out what additional requirements the school has for your child and your family during the year.

- Explore some ways to continue your family's involvement in the Jewish community after the big day.

Knowing your child's Hebrew name

However you decide to proceed, you will need to have some information on Hebrew names—yours, your child's, and those of your parents and grandparents, if possible. The Hebrew name gives you a definite place within the Jewish community, not only geographically, but spiritually. It is like having your own bookmark on a special page in a very, very long volume of names with tiny print. Once you know your Hebrew name and your child's, you and your son or daughter will always know where you fit in the chain of Jewish history. The Hebrew name embodies the qualities your family wished for you when you were born. It ties you to the generations that came before you, and will link you to those that come after you.

This is the name by which you are known in Judaism. It follows you all the days of your life. It is the name which is written on all religious documents, including the certificate of *brit milah* (the covenant of circumcision, which takes place for a Jewish boy on the eighth day after his birth), the baby-naming certificate (for boys and girls in liberal Jewish communities), the Bar or Bat Mitzvah certificate, the *ketubah* (marriage contract), and even the *get* (Jewish bill of divorce). It is also written on one's gravestone. If you are a Jew-by-choice, your Hebrew name has been chosen by you and appears on your conversion certificate and may also be on your certificate of *mikvah* (immersion in a ritual bath).

With regard to Bnai Mitzvah (or any service, for that matter), knowing your Hebrew name is important because in most congregations one is called to the Torah by his or her Hebrew name. There are many variations to this custom. Often, one is called along with the number of the *aliyah* assigned. The young person is called by his Hebrew given name, followed by "son of" his father's Hebrew name and then his mother's Hebrew name. (For example, the boy's name might be: David ben Moshe v'Sara—David, son of Martin and Sandra. The girl's name might be: Devora bat Shmuel v'Leah—Deborah, daughter of Samuel and Linda.) In congregations where the hierarchy of *kohen/ levi/ yisrael* is taken into consideration, the name might be extended to include that status, as well, such as Menachem ben Yosef ha-Kohen v'Rivka—Michael, son of Joseph the *kohen* and Rebecca. In other communities, one is called up with reference only to the father's name, and not the mother's.

In Ashkenazic Jewish households (whose forbears are from Central or Eastern Europe), children are named after those who have passed away. Among Sephardic and Mizrachi Jews (those whose ancestors came from Mediterranean and Middle Eastern countries), children may be named after the living. Names are chosen based upon the Hebrew version of a given name, upon names in the Bible, or upon names of people the family wishes to honor.

If you didn't receive a Hebrew name as a child, or if you haven't chosen a Hebrew name for your son or daughter, you should speak to your rabbi before the Bar Mitzvah date for help in choosing one. It should have meaning for you and your child, as it will be a name he will be known by in all Jewish documents for the rest of his or her life—and beyond.

Special situations

The synagogue and religious school will want to do whatever they can to make this experience wonderful for you. If your family and your child have special situations and needs, alert the school accordingly. In recent years, Jewish communal institutions have expanded their efforts to meet the needs of families that may fall outside a stereotypical model. It is wise at the beginning of the Bar Mitzvah process to be alert for possible special concerns. Let us take a moment and consider some of them.

Additional help for your child

Not all children meet their full measure of success in Hebrew school. For some, the classroom setting is just not enough. Perhaps they would do better in a small-group learning environment, or with a private tutor. The first step is to discuss your child's situation with your rabbi, cantor, or Bar Mitzvah specialist. Then, find out if the school has a Hebrew specialist on staff. If there is one available, it may be that just a few meetings will help your child over the hump of Hebrew. If more help is needed, speak to the professional staff about peer tutoring in Hebrew school, either during school hours or in addition to them. If there is no appropriate additional help available, you may wish to find a private Hebrew tutor for your son or daughter.

A Hebrew tutor can provide just the added boost of confidence and support your child needs. Usually, the sessions are one-on-one, and they may be an added resource for you throughout the months of preparation. A good tutor will work hand-in-hand with the school, inform them of your child's progress, and will also keep in touch with you on a regular basis. The hours spent in private instruction with a Hebrew tutor can do wonders to help a child. The individual attention, support, and genuine interest in each child make a tutor an important additional resource for you.

Private Hebrew tutors can be recommended by your synagogue or local board of Jewish education. Often, they are professionals who teach in Jewish religious schools or who are on the faculty of day schools. Sometimes, they are rabbinic students or others with strong Judaic backgrounds. Private tutors are usually paid by the parent. Their fees vary from community to community. Some will come to your home; many will ask that you come to theirs. Sometimes they will come to the synagogue for lessons.

Children and their families often become quite attached to their Hebrew tutors, forming long-term friendships that last over the years.

✡ ✡ ✡

Ben: *"I will never forget my Bar Mitzvah tutor. He was a gentle man who came to my house every week, rain or shine. He never got impatient, and he never disapproved of my efforts, even though there were times when I didn't do as well as I could have. It is because of his patience and his confidence in me that I did such a good job at my Bar Mitzvah. That was over thirty years ago, and I still remember him. We were in touch for years. I only wish he could have been around to tutor my daughter when it was time for her to study for her Bat Mitzvah."*

✡ ✡ ✡

Children of interfaith families and conversionary households

Since the 1960s, the intermarriage rate between Jews and non-Jews has grown considerably. What used to be unusual has come to be familiar in many Jewish families. In the April 1999 issue of *Moment* magazine, Dr. Egon Mayer of the Jewish Outreach Institute at the City University of New York estimates that 52 percent of Jews who have married since 1985 have married non-Jews. The numbers will probably continue to climb, as every generation of Jews has been intermarrying at a higher rate than the generation before. According to Reform movement statistics, more than 50 percent of children in Jewish religious schools will come from a home where one parent was not born Jewish.

This trend has enormous ramifications for synagogues, religious schools, and the parents and children who are part of them. One cannot assume that children of interfaith marriages will have Bnai Mitzvah, although many non-Jewish parents would support such a celebration. Intermarriage forces the Jewish parent to become more involved in the child's Jewish education, and thus in the Bar Mitzvah itself. (After all, it is not easy to plan this event, and if one is not Jewish and knows very little about Judaism, then the Jewish partner must take on a larger part of the responsibility.) Nonetheless, the non-Jewish parent also becomes involved, and it is often that parent (usually the mother) who drives the child to and from Hebrew school, attends school events when the other parent cannot, and so on.

Today, conversion to Judaism is also a growing phenomenon, with approximately one out of every 35 Jews in this country identifying as a Jew-by-choice, according to the National Jewish Population Survey of 1990. A conversionary marriage is not the same as an intermarriage. Once a person converts to Judaism, he or she is considered fully Jewish in the eyes of the Jewish community, and it is not proper to ever again remind him or her of any former status.

It is important for you, as the parent, to be very clear about the policy of your congregation when embarking upon a Bar or Bat Mitzvah. If you have any questions about your child's status in the eyes of your synagogue, make it a point to sit down with your rabbi well ahead of time to make certain that you can proceed without any difficulties. If there are formal rites of conversion to be performed before your child becomes a Bar or Bat Mitzvah, allow time for these. For example, for a Bar Mitzvah in a Conservative synagogue, it may be necessary to arrange for *hatafat dam brit* (a ritual drawing of blood from the penis) if no *brit milah* (ritual circumcision) was performed earlier, as well as for immersion in the *mikvah* as part of a formal conversion to Judaism. Be aware that these rites are more than just physical acts; they require psychological and spiritual preparation by the youngster and the parents. Your rabbi can be a big help to you in this process.

Clarifying the Jewish status of other family members will also be helpful when you decide who will receive pulpit honors on the big day. Those who are not considered Jewish may be given some recognition on the *bimah*, but are denied access to certain ritual observances. In some congregations, the non-Jewish parent may read some of the prayers, but not anything that includes the words, *"asher kiddishanu b'mitzvotav v'tizivanu"* ("who has sanctified us by His commandments and commanded us"), as this statement would require the non-Jew to attest to something he had not formally taken on as an obligation. In other synagogues, a non-Jew may not participate in the ceremony of passing the Torah down through the generations. In most congregations, a non-Jew cannot be called for an *aliyah*. If you are concerned about these or other matters, discuss them with your rabbi. It will eliminate any surprises and alleviate some of the tensions that might arise as you proceed with your plans.

Children with special needs

Throughout Jewish writings, reference is made to the wide range of children's learning abilities. We read about the Four Sons—one wise, one wicked, one simple, and the other unable to even ask questions—at the Pesach *seder* (the festive Passover meal). And the rabbis speak of the "giving" of the Torah at Mt. Sinai, rather than the "receiving" of it, because we are taught that each of us received God's laws according to our own individual needs and abilities.

It is written in Isaiah 44:13, "And all your children shall be taught of the Lord; and great shall be the peace of your children." One interpretation of this verse is that all children are entitled to the privilege and joy of an education. Jewish instructional institutions, therefore, have a mandate to provide religious training to every child, regardless of his or her abilities. If you have a child with special needs, your responsibility is to make the school aware and to discover what resources the school and the larger Jewish community have for you.

If you are fortunate enough to live in an area with a large and functioning Jewish community, your task is easier. Usually, if you live in a city where there is a sizeable Jewish population, the local board of Jewish education can give you names of special educators and schools with programs for children who need special consideration. Your synagogue, day school, or Jewish community center will also be helpful to you. However, even if you live in a small town with a less structured Jewish community, there are resources available to you. The best overall resource is the Jewish Education Service of North America, Inc. (JESNA).

For families living in Israel, there is only one Bar Mitzvah program for disabled children. "The Bar/Bat Mitzvah Program for the Disabled Child" was introduced in 1994 by the Masorti/Conservative movement, and is directed by Judith Edelman-Green. By the end of 2000, it will have enabled almost 100 disabled children to have Bnai Mitzvah, usually celebrated in group ceremonies. (For detailed information about this program, JESNA, and other resources for Jewish children with special needs and their families, please refer to Appendix A.)

Because disabilities can range from mild to severe, the more information you can provide the school, the better prepared they will be to meet your needs. Following are some things you might consider discussing with the appropriate professionals at your synagogue or Hebrew day school in this regard as you prepare for the Bar Mitzvah.

- The motivation of your youngster: What is his attitude toward the upcoming event? Does he look forward to this event, or does it promote some anxiety? How can the school help?

- The mental requirements of your child: Know the style of learning that works best for your child. Can she work within a standard classroom setting? If not, what does your child need in order to learn? Find out if a home tutor or a tutor at the school can help your child prepare.

- What limitations does your child have? Some specific areas of concern might be: ADD (attention deficit disorder), inability to sit for long periods of time, lack of visual acuity, hearing loss, difficulty with motor function, speech impediments, mental retardation, and other psycho-social or medical conditions that might impede his learning ability. In light of your child's unique requirements, what can the school do to help? Is the school accessible for physically impaired students? (This would include ramps and walkways, wheelchair access, TTD telephones for the hearing impaired, and easy access to the building, especially the sanctuary.)

- If your child is learning disabled, discuss the school's ability to meet his or her special needs. Are there special education teachers on the faculty? Is the administration sensitive to your child's limitations of attention span, physical and mental fatigue, possible increased susceptibility to infection, or other unique circumstances? How are they able and willing to help you?

● Once you have evaluated the learning situation, you can decide what to adjust to meet your child's needs. You may reduce the length of the Bar Mitzvah service and/or the amount of Hebrew instruction required, get interpreters to sign for the deaf, procure Jewish texts in Braille for the visually impaired, and supplement or replace classroom instruction with tutors and/or small-group learning.

Be aware of your responsibilities as the parent of the Bar Mitzvah. Here are some things you can do to help:

∠ Give the school as much information as you can. In return, be willing to accept the assistance the school can give you. If you work together, your child will surely benefit. Also, ask the school to keep you informed of your child's progress on an ongoing basis. Children with special needs should be monitored steadily. If there is a difficulty, you want to know way ahead of time. And if things are going well, the school should inform you of that too. This way, there will be no surprises as you get closer to the Bar Mitzvah day.

∠ Help your child strive for success by setting realistic goals and giving yourselves plenty of time. Don't overload your youngster or exert undue pressure. Minimize additional stress and frustration wherever possible. Make this a win-win situation so that your child can come through this experience with a sense of victory.

∠ Tailor the Bar Mitzvah to fit your child. It is not cast in stone that you must schedule the date around the 12th or 13th birthday. If your child needs six more months, or an extra year, plan ahead to arrange this. Also, in consultation with the rabbi, cantor, or Jewish educator, you may wish to choose a date on which the Torah portion and *Haftarah* are short. If your child is not able to do a full Torah reading, choose one short section that he or she can master. If you do not feel comfortable having your child do both a Torah portion and *Haftarah*, choose whichever will be easier. Choose those prayers and blessings that have meaning for the student, but eliminate portions of the service that might be too much. A good rule of thumb:

Better to do it short and well than long and with mistakes. A child who is only able to chant only a few prayers, but who does so with feeling and comprehension, is going to feel good about himself. A child who struggles through a long service is not going to feel confident and may always look back on the Bar Mitzvah as a time of apprehension and anxiety.

∠ Encouragement and praise will do wonders to help a child with special needs. If a youngster can see success through his own efforts, then the Bar Mitzvah is worthwhile. Any child will blossom if he receives positive feedback along the way. And children with special needs thrive on praise. Be sure that you and the school make it a point to commend your son on each victory, large and small. It will do wonders for your child—and for you!

∠ If your child has special abilities that will help in mastering the Hebrew and/or the service, make the most of them. For example, if music is something your youngster has a flair for, then the chanting of the blessings and the Torah portion will come more easily. If your child is able to read with some fluency or has a strong auditory memory, adapt the teaching approach to serve that strength. While this is true for all students, it is especially helpful to those who may require extra time for learning. In every case, encouragement, patience, and reinforcement of the material will enable each child to meet with success as he or she prepares for this important moment.

✡ ✡ ✡

Lauren: *"I didn't think I could ever do this. In the beginning I was really nervous, but I worked for over a year with my tutor. We spent a lot of time chanting the prayers. I loved the music. Once I could remember the melodies, it got easier for me, and in the end I loved doing it! My parents were very proud of me, but I was especially proud of myself because I realized could achieve it. Now, I think I can do anything."*

✡ ✡ ✡

∠ Remember that gifted children also have special needs. If you have a child who knows Hebrew already, can chant without difficulty, or is extremely bright and can do the entire service, be sure the school and the professional staff are aware of this. Enlist their expert help to engage your child and make the day memorable, no matter what the level of ability. Rely upon them to avoid the cookie-cutter Bnai Mitzvah syndrome, in which every child does exactly the same thing, regardless of his capabilities. This is an opportunity for every child to shine and to own the Torah in her own way.

Single-parent families

Life-cycle celebrations often exacerbate whatever problems a family may have, according to Marlene Levenson, a licensed clinical social worker with the Jewish Family and Children's Services in the San Francisco Bay Area. She notes that one of the most emotionally charged events in a Jewish family can be the Bar Mitzvah. When there has been a divorce, concerns about money, differences in degrees of religious observance, and differing feelings about parental participation may all raise red flags. Levenson goes on to say that fostering good communication during and following a divorce is important in defusing problems down the line.

As a divorced parent, you might want to consider:

- Do you, as the custodial parent, understand the demands to be made upon you in preparation for this day? While they are not different from those of non-divorced parents, they may be complicated by a divorce. You may very well be putting out all the time, money, and effort by yourself.

- If you have extended family or close friends living nearby, they can be of great help in driving your child to and from Hebrew school, taking care of details before the celebration, and giving additional attention to your child. They can take some of the pressure off of you and can be a source of support in many ways. Such secondary relationships also allow the child to vent his or her emotions to people not quite as tightly enmeshed in the situation as the immediate family.

- Custody contests complicate things. If your ex-spouse has equal rights to the children, visitation can become an issue during the period of preparation. School attendance may be affected, depending upon where the child lives half the time. Performance may have its ups and downs, depending upon the attitude between you and your ex-husband or wife. And if yours was an intermarriage, the difficulties and challenges may grow exponentially. (Does your partner agree to such a ceremony and celebration? Does his/her family plan to attend? How do you feel about that? How does your child deal with the tension between parents who have agreed to go their separate ways?)

- There is also the question of non-Jewish siblings in the family. What is their role? What can they do to participate in the preparations? What if more than one religion is practiced in the home? How does that affect your child? How does it affect you and the religious school/synagogue?

- And then, there is the matter of money. In a divorced family, "Who's going to pay for this?" can become a monumental question. The question of money being spent on Jewish life may even begin years earlier with the question of synagogue affiliation and then continue as the child gets closer to becoming a Bar Mitzvah. It helps if you can talk candidly and in a non-threatening way with your ex-husband or wife. If matters become tense, depending upon the level of communication between you and your ex-spouse, you may want to seek some professional advice from a family counselor at this time. Following that, if and when it is appropriate, share with your child those things that will ease tension and draw on the love both parents feel for their child. It may help to remember that whatever transpired between the two adults, the love you both feel for your child is true and all-important, especially when embarking upon such an important life passage.

If one parent is deceased, there are other issues. Loss, grief, and anger may all affect the child's relationship to the Bar or Bat Mitzvah experience. Such an event also affects you. You become the articulator of the wishes of your spouse, even though he/she is no longer present. If the loss is a recent one, you may want to reconsider the timing of the celebration or make it a smaller, simpler affair. Here again, you will want to speak to your rabbi about your feelings and those of your child. Be sure that the school is aware of your situation. Once the teachers know what to watch for, they can structure the program in the most sensitive manner to make things easier for your child and for you.

Gay/lesbian families

If you are in a domestic partner relationship, have had a commitment ceremony, or are in a long-term loving relationship with someone of the same sex who is Jewish, the religious issues are similar to those in any Jewish relationship. If you are committed to someone who is not Jewish, the interfaith issues are also present. You already may have discussed the implications of establishing a Jewish home. In addition to the questions and concerns indicated earlier, there are other factors to consider as well:

- Have a private conversation with the rabbi, cantor, or other professional in charge of the Bar or Bat Mitzvah. Be sure that the school is sensitive and sympathetic to your situation. If the school does not have a positive philosophy about gay/lesbian issues, you may want to look elsewhere for one that does.

- Go to synagogue frequently with your child not only to become familiar with the service, but also so that the members of the synagogue get to know you and welcome you and your family with sincerity and ease. If you are in the process of choosing a synagogue, you have several options. There may be liberal congregations in your area, composed mainly of heterosexual families but also welcoming gays and lesbians. To find these, word-of-mouth is often the best resource. If you seek a traditional congregation, you may wish to do some research on your own, as each community will have its own policy and practice. If you would prefer a congregation of primarily gay/lesbian families, you may want to contact the local office of the Union of American Hebrew Congregations (Reform). Several established gay/lesbian synagogues across the country are affiliated with the UAHC, and you might find that atmosphere most comfortable for you and your child.

- Choosing a Hebrew name for your child is something you may have done just after his or her birth. If not, this is a good time to consider it because your son will need that name when called to the Torah. Some questions to consider: Will both parents of one gender be included in the name (e.g. Shoshana bat Sarah v'Rivka) when the child is called to the Torah? If not, how will she or he be called? (For more about Hebrew names, please see Chapter 2.)

- Review the protocol for such passing the Torah down through the generations and sharing other pulpit honors. How comfortable will you be with this? How comfortable will your child be? What about the congregation?

Perhaps the most important considerations are your feelings of comfort and those of your child within the community you choose. Whether the synagogue is Orthodox, Conservative, Reform, Reconstructionist, or independent, you and your family should feel welcome and at home. The people should be warm and sympathetic, accepting and knowledgeable—not only for your sake, but for the sake of your child.

For all families

Clearly, there is a lot to think about. If all of this seems overwhelming, try to relax a bit. Ideally, things will go smoothly for you and your child. This section has touched on some of the matters that may affect you as a family. Consult your local Jewish organizations for more information as needed. It is better to be informed and thus prevent possible difficulties early on than to wait and be surprised later. Make use of all the professionals available to you. They will be more than happy to help you with your decisions so that you will be able to enjoy the day of the Bar or Bat Mitzvah with a clear mind and a smile on your face.

Part Two:

The Service

Chapter 4

THE

BASICS

The prayer service is the most profound moment of the Bar Mitzvah experience. You will find the service more meaningful if you understand the significance of your surroundings, the words spoken, and the rituals enacted.

✡ ✡ ✡

Rabbi David J. Meyer: *"There are three prevalent misconceptions regarding Bat Mitzvah, which I would like to clarify: First, there is no such thing as a private Bar/Bat Mitzvah service. As with all Jewish life-cycle ceremonies, it is a community celebration, more than a family event. Second, Bar/Bat Mitzvah does not mark an ending of anything. On the contrary, it signifies many important beginnings, especially personal responsibility and continued study. And thirdly, the Bar/Bat Mitzvah service does nothing to change one's Jewish status. It does not make one "more Jewish," but is an opportunity to verify a youngster's commitment to ongoing Jewish participation. Dispelling these three misconceptions deepens the experience and enriches its spiritual dimension."*

✡ ✡ ✡

The geography of the synagogue

When you begin your planning, the physical layout and terminology of the synagogue can be a bit bewildering. If you have never planned a Bat Mitzvah before, and if you are new to Judaism or to organized Jewish life, you will need to know:

- What is a synagogue?
- How are all synagogues alike, and what may we find there?

What is a synagogue?

The word "synagogue" comes from the Greek *synagogia* (a place of gathering). Jews may pray anywhere, in elaborate buildings or in simple, unadorned rooms, though there may never be any statues or icons. While it is highly meritorious to pray in a synagogue, it is not the place that makes the gathering holy, it is the presence of the sacred among those who are there. The synagogue should be a place where God can enter, and according to the sages, God is present wherever people let God in.

Some injunctions are given concerning decorum in a synagogue: One is forbidden to gossip, do business, or eat, drink, or sleep in places of worship. In earlier times, exceptions concerning food and a place to sleep were made in the case of scholars who spent a great amount of time there. (And it is permissible to have a sacramental meal in a synagogue, as long as there is no drunkenness.) There is also a requirement that a synagogue must have windows, a dictum based upon a passage from the *Book of Daniel* 6:11, which describes how the prophet Daniel prayed next to windows when facing in the direction of Jerusalem.

A synagogue is not the same as a Temple (with a capital "T"). There were only two Temples, both located in Jerusalem. Both of them were destroyed—the first one in 586 B.C.E., by the Babylonians, and the second one in 70 C.E., by the Romans. It was where the high priest, on behalf of the people, offered the *korban* (animal and agricultural sacrifices) as the ancient way of drawing near to God. The function of a synagogue is different from that of the Temple. No sacrifices are offered in a synagogue.

Traditionally, synagogues are built facing east, toward Jerusalem, the holy city, the site of the ancient Temple. When Reform Judaism came into being in 1750, however, the founders declared, "Any country we live in is our holy land, and any city we reside in is our Jerusalem, and any place we worship is our Temple." Therefore, Reform synagogues are often called "temples" and may be deliberately oriented away from the East! Although it is not a hard-and-fast rule, you can usually identify a Reform synagogue because many have the word "temple" as part of their names. Conservative and Orthodox synagogues usually have the word "congregation" as part of their names; synagogues are often called "Jewish communities" within the Jewish Renewal movement.

Sometimes, a synagogue is referred to as a *shul.* This is a Yiddish word, indicating a school or a place where people gather to study together. "Synagogue" and "*shul*" are often used interchangeably by Jews to describe the communal house of worship and study.

How are all synagogues alike, and what may be found in them?

All synagogues have certain things in common. Each one contains a light that is kept burning all the time. This is called the *ner tamid* (eternal light) and is reminiscent of the fire kept burning continually on the altar of the Temple in ancient days. It is located above the *aron ha-kodesh* (holy ark), which contains the *sifrei Torah* (Torah scrolls). There is a *bimah* (literally, "stage"), a raised area from which the service is conducted. And synagogues often contain a seven-branched *menorah* (candelabrum) to remind us of the one in the Temple, which symbolized the seven days of creation.

The seating may be arranged in rows, in a square, or in a circle or semicircle; and the reading desk may be in front, or in the middle of the room. There are always *siddurim* (prayer books) available, as well as *tallitot* (prayer shawls), *kippot* (head-coverings), and copies of the *chumashim* (volumes containing the Torah portions, *Haftarot*, and commentaries). The rabbi, cantor, and other leaders of the congregation are usually seated on the *bimah* during the service. The youngster who is becoming a Bar or Bat Mitzvah will also have a place of honor in front of the congregation.

Traditional items used in the service

Throughout the service several ritual objects are used. There is a Jewish tradition of *hiddur mitzvah* (beautifying the things we are commanded to do). From this, Jews are taught to elevate the rituals of Jewish life through the use of treasured objects. These are items that have been donated to the synagogue for congregational use or that belong to a family and are passed down from generation to generation.

The Torah

Dominating the *bimah* is the *aron ha-kodesh.* The most precious object in the sanctuary rests within the *aron ha-kodesh.* It is the Torah, a word meaning "instruction" or "direction." It refers to the first five books of the *Tanach* (the Jewish Bible), according to Jewish tradition given to Moses on Mt. Sinai and transmitted from generation to generation. Carried by Jews down through the ages, in times of prosperity and in times of trouble, the Torah is the Jews' most cherished possession.

There may be only one Torah scroll within the ark, or there may be several. Most synagogues have at least two because some of the portions that are read on special days require readings from two different places in the Torah. To save time, the scrolls can be pre-rolled to the correct places in the portion. If a congregation has been blessed with generous benefactors, it may own several Torah scrolls.

The Torah is written in Hebrew, on parchment—the skin of a kosher animal. It is inscribed with vegetable-dye ink using a turkey- or goose-quill pen. The person who writes a Torah scroll is called a *sofer* (a scribe). The *sofer* must be a pious Jew who prepares himself spiritually with immersion in a *mikvah* and careful meditation on holy matters before beginning his work. It can take about a year to write a Torah scroll. Nothing is written from memory. All writing is copied from an existing scroll, and each word is pronounced aloud before copying it. There can be no mistakes. If an error is made in writing God's name, the entire sheet of parchment is set aside and buried. Traditionally, Torah scrolls are written with three columns to every parchment sheet, and 42 lines in each column. The lines should accommodate 30 letters, although this may vary, depending upon the individual writing style of the *sofer* and the width of the Hebrew letters on any given line. If you were to look at a panel of Torah, you would see that there is no punctuation and there are no vowels. Some of the letters have decorative crowns on them. One of the challenges for Bnai Mitzvah is learning to read this text without punctuation or vowels. A book called a *Tikkun* is used to aid in this process.

The Torah scroll is attached to a wooden roller at each end, called an *etz chayim* (tree of life). The scroll is tied with a *gartl* (sash), to keep it from unrolling, and is covered by an elaborately stitched mantle, called a *m'eel*. Laying on the front of the mantle may be a silver breastplate, and on top of the rollers are placed silver finials called *rimmonim* (literally, "pomegranates"), or a large silver crown, called the *keter Torah*. These ornaments are usually adorned with little silver bells, reminiscent of those worn on the garments of the high priest in the days of the Temple. The reader uses a *yad* (pointer) to follow the text as he or she reads. The word *yad* means "hand" in Hebrew, and the pointer is often shaped like a little silver hand, with the index finger extended to point to the words being read. When not in use, the *yad* hangs down from one of the rollers on a silver chain.

For specific information about reading from the Torah, Torah honors, and the blessings associated with the reading of the Torah and *Haftarah*, please see Chapter 5.

The *kippah*

Traditionally, Jews wear head-coverings to show respect for God. In ancient days, the high priests wore head-coverings when serving in the Temple. In Orthodox circles, Jewish males wear skullcaps—*kippot* in Hebrew and *yarmulkes* in Yiddish—from the time they are born. (It's rather endearing to see a tiny little *kippah* on a Jewish baby boy's head at his *bris*!) It has become a custom in many liberal communities for girls to also wear *kippot*. The head-covering may be of any fabric, and just about any shape, although the round skullcap is most common.

It is customary for *kippot* to be worn in many synagogues. In some congregations, when one is called up to the Torah, one must wear both a *kippah* and a *tallit*. Therefore, such items are usually available in a large basket or cabinet at the rear of the sanctuary.

If you would like to order *kippot* in a certain color or with an imprint designating the date name of the Bar or Bat Mitzvah, you should do so early on in your planning, as they might take several weeks to arrive. Usually, the imprint will read as follows:

> Josh Goldstein's Bar Mitzvah,
> [secular and/or Hebrew date]

Or perhaps the family will choose this wording:

> Jennifer Levy, Bat Mitzvah,
> Torah Portion: Lech L'cha
> [secular and/or Hebrew date]

You can decide if you want enough just for the members of your family, for only the men, or for all of your guests. Your decision may depend on the custom of your synagogue and on your budget. If you are having a large celebration, this is an additional expense to take into consideration when you start planning.

Some Reform and Reconstructionist synagogues do not use head-coverings as a matter of religious principle. If it is customary in your synagogue for women to cover their hair during services, you may want to indicate that in your invitation. Sometimes lace head-coverings for women to use during services are also made available by the congregation.

For more information about *kippot*, consult *The Jewish Catalogue, Vol. 1*, by Richard Siegel, Michael Strassfeld, and Sharon Strassfeld (Philadelphia: Jewish Publication Society, 1973).

The *tallit*

A *tallit* is a fringed shawl traditionally worn by Jewish men over the age of 13 during prayer. Nowadays in many liberal congregations, women also wear a *tallit* during prayer. The word originally meant "cloak" or "gown" and referred to a large rectangular garment that men wore long ago. Jews attached fringes to the four corners based upon an injunction found in the Torah (*Numbers* 15:37-40):

> And the Lord spoke unto Moses, saying: "Speak unto the children of Israel and bid them that they make them throughout their generations *tzitzit* [fringes] in the corners of their garments, and that they put with the fringe of each corner a thread of blue. And it shall be unto you for a *tzitzit*, that you may look upon it, and remember all the commandments of the Lord, and do them; so that you do not go about after your own heart and your own eyes, after which you used to go astray; that you may remember and do all My commandments, and be holy unto your God."

The most important part of the *tallit* are the *tzitzit* on the four corners. These serve as reminders of the 613 *mitzvot* given by God to the Jewish people. The fringes are knotted in a certain pattern to symbolize 613. The *mitzvot* thus become visual; every time one sees the fringes, one is reminded of the obligation to keep the commandments.

It is customary to wear a *tallit* only during the daytime, when it is light out, in order to see the fringes, because we are enjoined "to look upon them." However, a variation occurs in some Reform congregations where the Torah is read on Friday evening, and the *minhag ha-makom* (custom of the place) is to wear a *tallit* when called up to the Torah.

The customs concerning the wearing of the *tallit* also vary from Ashkenazic to Sephardic communities. According to the general Ashkenazic custom, children younger than 13 may wear a *tallit* according to their size. In the Polish and Sephardic traditions, only married men wear a *tallit*. In *Mizrachi* (Middle Eastern) communities, even unmarried men may wear one. During Reform services, it is the custom for the rabbi and cantor to wear a *tallit* even at night in their roles as service-leaders. In America, it has become a tradition that a Jewish boy is given a *tallit* upon becoming a Bar Mitzvah. In more recent years, with the popularity of the Bat Mitzvah ceremony, a girl is also given a *tallit* upon reaching this moment of maturity. The *tallit* is often presented to the child by the parents or grandparents during the service. In many families, it is customary to pass a *tallit* down from generation to generation. The prayer shawl then becomes a visible reminder of loved ones in the family who may no longer be here, but whose presence is felt, especially on this important day.

How to choose a *tallit*

You can purchase a *tallit* in any Jewish gift store or in your synagogue gift shop. Many families buy a *tallit* during a trip to Israel and present it to their child in honor of the Bar or Bat Mitzvah. When you pick out a *tallit* for your son or daughter, you should find one which is big enough to "grow" with your child. It should be large enough to wrap in, but not so big that the young person cannot handle it adequately. Also, you might take into consideration a choice between a half-*tallit*, or a traditional *tallit*, which is quite large and full. A half-*tallit* would not be considered adequate in an Orthodox synagogue. In more liberal congregations you will see both kinds. You should also inspect the *tzitzit* to be sure that they are correctly knotted and are not torn. This should be done each time one puts on a *tallit*.

The *tallit* may come with the blessing stitched along the *atarah* (the collar of the *tallit*), which is, although some *atarot* come just decoratively embroidered. The *tallit* is always worn with the *atarah* along the top. You might want to make your child's *atarah* by hand and embroider it.

Putting on the *tallit*

When donning the *tallit*, after carefully inspecting the fringes, it is customary to recite the following verses from Psalm 104:1-2:

> **"Bless my soul, Adonai, You are very great, clothed in glory and majesty, wrapped in a robe of light. You spread out the heavens like a garment."**

Holding the *tallit* open in front of you with the *atarah* facing you, the following blessing is recited:

Ba-ruch a-ta Adonai Eh-lo-hei-nu Meh-lech ha-o-lam, a-sher ki-d'sha-nu b'mitz-vo-tav, v'tzi-va-nu l'hee-tah-tayf ba'tzitzit.

Blessed are You, O Lord our God, Ruler of the Universe, Who has sanctified us by His commandments and commanded us to wrap ourselves in the *tzitzit*.

It is customary to kiss each end of the *atarah*. Then, swinging the *tallit* around, some enclose the head within the *tallit* for a moment before settling the prayer shawl upon the shoulders. *Tallit* clips may be worn to hold the *tallit* in place while wearing it. (Incidentally, these clips—in silver or ceramic—make beautiful Bnai Mitzvah gifts.)

When removing the *tallit*, one gently pulls it from the shoulders, kisses each end of the *atarah*, carefully folds the *tallit* and puts it away. When not in use, the *tallit* is usually kept in its own bag, along with the *kippah*.

This may be the first time your child wears the *tallit*, but it surely won't be the last. It may be worn again when your child gets married, and throughout his or her life. A person can also be buried in a *tallit*; at that time, one fringe is cut to show that the garment is no longer being used for prayer. The *tallit* is a treasured religious object throughout a Jew's adult life. It will be a significant moment for your daughter, and for you, as well, when you see the *tallit* worn for the very first time. May it be the first of many.

Tefillin

Tefillin are small square leather boxes, painted black, to which leather straps are attached. The boxes contain parchment scrolls on which are written the *Sh'ma* prayer, a statement of monotheistic belief and a reminder of the Exodus from Egypt and the commandment to lay *tefillin*. One box, the *shel yad*, is placed on the upper part of the weaker arm; the other, the *shel rosh*, is placed on the forehead between the eyes. The straps are used to hold the boxes in place and are wrapped in a ritual manner.

The injunction to put on *tefillin* is found in four places in the Torah, and laying *tefillin* is considered a most important religious obligation for traditional Jews. It should be approached with seriousness and *kavannah* (intent or concentration). The act of putting on *tefillin* is a powerful reminder of our deliverance from slavery in Egypt and serves to symbolically bind the Jew to God in holiness. There is even a statement in the Talmud (Berachot 62) that God also lays *tefillin!*

Putting on *tefillin*

One dons the *tallit* before putting on *tefillin*. Then, the *tefillin shel yad* is placed upon the upper arm. Once it is properly in place, the following blessing is recited:

> *Ba-ruch a-ta Adonai Eh-lo-hei-nu meh-lech ha-o-lam, a-sher ki-d'sha-nu b'mitz-vo-tav v'tzi-va-nu l'ha-ni'ach tefillin.*
>
> Blessed are You, O Lord our God, King of the Universe, Who has sanctified us by His commandments and commanded us to wear *tefillin*.

The *tefillin shel rosh* is put on, and after the box is adjusted on the forehead between the eyes and the straps properly set, the following blessing is recited:

> *Ba-ruch a-ta Adonai Eh-lo-hei-nu meh-lech ha-o-lam, a-sher ki-d'sha-nu b'mitz-vo-tav v'tzi-va-nu al itz-vot tefillin.*
>
> Blessed are You, O Lord our God, King of the Universe, Who has sanctified us by His commandments and commanded us concerning the *mitzvah* of *tefillin*.

The wrapping of the *tefillin shel yad* is then completed.

Remember that if you are planning a celebration on Shabbat, *tefillin* will not be worn during the service, as they are worn during the morning service every day except Shabbat and holidays.

It is common to include the laying of *tefillin* in Conservative and Orthodox worship. Therefore, if your child is becoming a Bar or Bat Mitzvah in one of those movements, you will want to be sure preparation for such a ritual is included in his or her training. Often, one is given the *tefillin* a few weeks or months prior to the Bar or Bat Mitzvah day in order to practice. While this ritual is traditionally performed by Jewish adult males, in some liberal congregations women also lay *tefillin*.

For specific information about the laying of *tefillin*, please consult your rabbi. Other good sources are: *Encyclopedia Judaica* (Jerusalem: Keter Publishing Company, Volume 15, pages 898-903); *Tefillin*, by Aryeh Kaplan (New York: National Conference of Synagogue Youth, 1975); *The First Jewish Catalogue*, by Richard Siegel, Michael Strassfeld, and Sharon Strassfeld (Philadelphia: Jewish Publication Society, 1973); and *To Be A Jew*, by Hayim Halevy Donin (New York: Basic Books, 1972).

Candlesticks

In the Jewish tradition, light is a symbol of God. On Friday evening, candles are kindled to inaugurate the Sabbath. In the home, according to Jewish law, candles are lit between 90 and 18 minutes before sunset. It is a tradition that women light the candles, but it is also acceptable for men to do so.

If you are having the service on Friday evening, candles may be lit in the synagogue at the beginning of the service or may be kindled without a blessing prior to the service. Then, when the service begins, the mother may come forward to say the blessing. Often, mother and daughter light the Shabbat candles together. In some congregations, even if the service will take place on Saturday morning, the mother of the youngster will be given the honor of lighting the candles on Friday evening.

You should use kosher candles for this purpose, avoiding those made of animal fat, which is prohibited by Jewish law. Shabbat candles will burn for approximately three and a half hours in still air—definitely lasting through the service. It is customary to have at least two candles. However, you may light more. Some families light one additional candle for each child in the household. (It is considered improper to diminish the fulfillment of a *mitzvah*. So, if you kindle additional lights, do so on a regular basis.) In the synagogue there are usually just two candlesticks, which are set in a place of honor on the *bimah*.

Most synagogues have their own candlesticks, although if you have special ones you would like to use for the Bat Mitzvah, you may certainly do so. Often, the women's group of the congregation will present a set of candlesticks to the Bat Mitzvah in honor of the occasion, while the men's group may give the Bar Mitzvah a *kiddush* cup.

Once you have lit the candles, cup your hands as "parentheses" on either side of the candle. Make circles around the light, drawing the light to you. It is customary to do this three times. Then, cover your eyes with your hands, and recite the blessing:

> *Ba-ruch a-ta Adonai Eh-lo-hei-nu meh-lech ha-o-lam, a-sher ki-d'sha-nu b'mitz-vo-tav v'tzi-va-nu l'had-lik ner shel Shabbat.*
>
> Blessed are You, O Lord our God, King of the Universe, Who has sanctified us by His commandments and commanded us to kindle the lights of *Shabbat*.

It is appropriate during the time we recite the blessing to meditate upon the events of the past week, recalling the people we love and the events that have blessed our lives. It is also a time for private reflection or special prayers to God. Following the lighting of the candles in the home, the family will kiss each other and say, "*Shabbat Shalom* [Sabbath peace]!"

As part of the Friday night service prior to a Bar or Bat Mitzvah, the person lighting the candles may also offer a special prayer, looking back on the past week and anticipating the beauty of this moment in the life of the family.

The *Kiddush* cup

The word *kiddush* means "sanctification." The *Kiddush* is a prayer recited over a cup of wine on Shabbat and festivals to sanctify the day.

In ancient times, pagan tribes knew that they could become inebriated by drinking wine. They could happily lose control and let go of their inhibitions. In contrast, Jews elevated wine, the symbol of joy, to a level of holiness by reciting a blessing over it, using it in moderation, and linking it to moments of sanctity such as Shabbat, the festivals, and *simchas* (celebrations) in life.

We recite the *Kiddush* on the eve of Shabbat and *Yom Tov* (holidays) because one is forbidden to eat on the Sabbath and the festivals until this is done.

It has also become customary to recite *Kiddush* after the Sabbath morning service. This is usually followed by refreshments or a luncheon, also called *kiddush*. In the case of a Bar or Bat Mitzvah the family is usually responsible for providing the *kiddush*. (More information on this in Part 3.)

The wine cup, usually silver, is placed on the *bimah* on Friday evening. It is traditional for kosher sweet red wine or grape juice to be used. If you like, you may purchase a new *Kiddush* cup in honor of your child's Bar or Bat Mitzvah for presentation before the service. Sometimes, a family will use a *Kiddush* cup that has been in the family for a long time and has great sentimental value. It may also be a cup for the child to keep and use one day at his or her wedding or at some other future *simcha*. If you are purchasing a *Kiddush* cup especially for the occasion, you might consider having the name of the child and the date inscribed on it as a keepsake.

Reciting the *Kiddush*

Raise the cup, recite the following blessing, and then take a sip of wine.

Va-ye-hi e-rev, va-ye-hi vo-kehr, yom ha-shi-shi.
And there was evening, and there was morning, the sixth day.

Va-yeh-chu-lu ha-sha-ma-yim ve'ha-a-retz ve-chol tze-va-am, va-yeh-chal Ehlohim ba-yom ha-she-vi'i me-lach-to a-sher a-sah. Va-yish-bot ba-yom ha-she-vi'i mi-kol meh-lach-to a-sher a-sah. Va-yeh-va-rech Ehlohim et yom ha-she-vi'i va-yeh-ka-deish o-to, ki vo-sha-vat mi-kol me-lach-to a-sher ba-ra Ehlohim la-a-sot.
Now the whole universe—sky, earth, and all their array—was completed. With the seventh day God ended the work of Creation; on the seventh day God rested with all the Divine work completed. Then God blessed the seventh day and called it holy, for with this day God had completed the work of Creation.

Ba-ruch a-ta Adonai, Eh-lo-hei-nu meh-lech ha-o-lam bo-rei p'ri ha-ga-fen.
Blessed are You, O Lord our God, King of the Universe, Who creates the fruit of the vine.

Ba-ruch a-ta Adonai, Eh-lo-hei-nu meh-lech ha-o-lam, a-sher ki-d'sha-nu b'mitz-vo-tav v'ra-tza va-nu, v'sha-bat kod-sho b'a-ha-va u-v'ra-tzon hin-chi-la-nu, zi-ka-ron l'ma-a-sei v'rei-sheet. Ki hu yom t'chi-la l'mik-ra'ei ko-desh, ze-cher li'tzi-at Mitz-ra-yim. Ki va-nu va-char-ta v'o-ta-nu ki-dash-ta mi-kol ha-a-mim, v'sha-bat kod-sh'cha b'a-ha-va u-v'ra-tzon hin-chal-ta-nu. Ba-ruch a-ta Adonai, m'ka-deish ha-Shabbat.
Blessed are You, O Lord our God, King of the Universe, who has sanctified us with His commandments and takes delight in us. In love and favor You have made the holy Sabbath our heritage, as a reminder of the work of Creation. It is first among our sacred days, and a remembrance of the Exodus from Egypt. O God, You have chosen us and sanctified us from all the peoples, and the Sabbath is made holy in the love and favor You have shown us. Praised are You, O Lord, Who sanctifies holy the *Shabbat.*

Following the recitation of the *Kiddush,* it is proper to take a sip of the wine to complete the blessing. When this is done, it is customary for the congregation to offer the toast, "*L'Chaim* [To life]!"

The *challah* and the *challah* cover

Challah is a braided egg-bread that is a special part of the Shabbat meal.

The braiding makes the *challah* beautiful and the three interwoven strands may symbolize either God/Torah/the people of Israel or the kohanim/Levites/Israelites (three ancient ritual classes of Jews). The mystics believed that the braids represent the hair of the Sabbath bride. *Challah* is often sprinkled with poppy or sesame seeds, which remind us of the *manna* that we gathered when wandering in the desert after leaving Egypt. (For more information about baking your own *challah*, read *The Challah Book*, by Frieda Reider [Hoboken, New Jersey: KTAV Publishing Company, Inc., 1988].)

What makes bread *challah* is separating a piece from the loaf before baking. If this is not done, along with its accompanying blessing, then you have ordinary egg-bread. (It may be delicious, but it has not been elevated with a special ritual and blessing.) The separation of the dough reminds us of the sacrifices made in Temple days when the priests were given this part of the *challah* to eat.

If you are baking *challah* you should recite the proper blessing upon the taking of the dough. To fulfill the requirement, you should take a piece the size of your thumb, or the size of an olive. This is done just before braiding the loaf and putting it in the oven. The little piece of dough you separate should be set aside and burned in the oven or in the fireplace, in memory of the burnt offerings brought in ancient days. Here is the blessing for the taking of *challah:*

> *Ba-ruch a-ta Adonai Eh-lo-hei-nu meh-lech ha-o-lam, a-sher ki-d'sh-a-nu b'mitz-vo-tav v'tzi-va-nu l'ha-freesh chal-lah.*
>
> Blessed are you O Lord, our God, King of the Universe, Who has sanctified us by His commandments and commanded us to separate challah.

It is customary to have two *challot* on the table. The second loaf reminds us of the extra portion of manna that was given to the Israelites on Fridays during the 40 days they were wandering in the desert. That extra portion was graciously given by God so that the people would not have to work on the Sabbath to gather their daily food.

In addition, the Shabbat table becomes like an altar. Because knives are used for killing, and because the Sabbath table is a symbol of peace, many people either cover the knives or wait until after the blessing to put them on the table. Therefore, when eating the *challah*, it is the custom among many Jews to tear the bread after reciting the blessing, rather than cutting it with a knife.

According to traditional Jewish law, one is obligated to ritually wash the hands before eating a meal with bread. This comes from the days of the ancient Temple, reenacting the priestly service in which the priest would wash before offering the various sacrifices to God. This ritual is performed by using any round container that does not have a spout. Pour cold water into the cup or pot to be used, and pour the water three times over each hand, then recite the blessing for washing the hands:

Ba-ruch a-ta Adonai, Eh-lo-hei-nu meh-lech ha-o-lam, a-sher ki-d'sha-nu b'mitz-vo-tav v'tzi-va-nu al n'tee-laht a-da-yim.

Blessed are you O Lord our God, King of the Universe, Who has sanctified us by His commandments and commanded us concerning the washing of the hands.

It is proper not to talk between the time we recite the hand-washing blessing and the recitation of *Ha-Motzi* (the blessing over the bread). Humming and singing wordless melodies, called *niggunim*, is encouraged. (These are not considered speech.)

Before taking the first bite of *challah* we often dip the bread in a bit of salt to remind us of the sprinkling of salt on the altar of the Temple in ancient days. Many families use kosher salt for this purpose. (On *Rosh Hashanah*, however, we dip our bread in honey for a sweet year.)

Ha-Motzi (the blessing over the bread)

Ba-ruch a-ta Adonai, Eh-lo-hei-nu meh-lech ha-o-lam, ha-mo-tzi leh-chem min ha-a-retz.

Blessed are You O Lord, our God, King of the Universe, Who brings forth bread from the earth.

In some congregations the *challah* is on the *bimah* during the service on Friday nights and on Saturday mornings. In other synagogues the *challah* is part of the celebration following the service. When this is the case, it is shared with all the guests at the *oneg* or the *kiddush* luncheon. Be sure to order a *challah* that is big enough to serve your guests—and more besides! You may order a *challah* from a kosher bakery, or if you are really ambitious you can bake your own. Your synagogue may have names of bakeries who can accommodate you. But if you want to bake your own, it will be even more delicious! (My family's personal *challah* recipe is here for you to try, and enjoy. Warning: It tends to be addictive!)

The Best C*hallah* Recipe

2 cups hot water	1 package dry (or 1 cake compressed) yeast
1 tablespoon salt	1/4 cup warm water
1 heaping cup granulated sugar	2 eggs, beaten (or 4 egg whites)
2 tablespoons vegetable oil	8 cups flour

Put sugar, salt, and vegetable oil in small mixing bowl. Over this, pour the hot water. In a measuring cup, pour the 1/4 cup warm water. Add this to the yeast. Dissolve the yeast, and stir. When lukewarm, add this to the sugar, salt, and oil. Stir well. Break the eggs into another measuring cup, and beat. Oil a large mixing bowl lightly. Gradually add to this large bowl the eggs, flour, and other ingredients.

Mix and stir well, then knead until smooth and elastic. Cover, and set aside in a warm place, away from drafts, until doubled in bulk. When the bread is ready for next step, punch the dough down. Remove a piece of dough no smaller than an olive, and after saying the proper blessing for the "taking of challah," burn this piece in the oven or fireplace.

Divide the bulk of dough in half. Put one-half on a lightly floured bread-board, and cut this half into three parts. Roll these each approximately 1 and-a-half inches thick, forming them into long, fat rolls. Twist these three into a braid; fasten the ends well, and place on a lightly floured cookie sheet. Repeat the process with the other half of the dough.

Return the dough to a warm place, and let rise for one hour, or until again doubled in bulk.

Preheat oven to 350 degrees. Brush the *challot* with beaten egg, and, if desired, sprinkle with poppy seeds, sesame seeds, raisins, or cinnamon-sugar. Bake for 30 minutes, uncovered, on the second-to-bottom rack. When done, leave out to cool, uncovered. When ready to transfer to serving platter, gently cut around *challot* with knife to free them from the cookie sheet, if necessary.

Keep covered until ready to serve. Yields two *challot*.

The *challah* cover

The tradition is that the *challah* should be kept covered out of respect because it has to wait patiently while the *kiddush* is recited!

For the Bar Mitzvah you may want to have a special *challah* cover. You can buy one at your synagogue's gift shop, in any Jewish store, or in Israel. You may be fortunate enough to have a *challah* cover that belonged to your grandmother or great-grandmother. Or if you like, you can make your own in honor of the occasion. You can use any fabric and decorate it with Jewish symbols or the blessing over the bread. It may be simple or elaborate. You may wish to embroider the name and date of the Bat Mitzvah on it. Anything you do will make it even more special because it will be made with love.

Books to be used during the service

There are two books used during the worship service. They are *siddurim* (prayer books) and *chumashim* (books of the Torah portions and *Haftarot*, often with commentaries).

Siddurim

The word *siddur* comes from the Hebrew word for "order," as the prayer book describes the order of the service. Each of the Jewish movements has its own *siddur*, and while there are differences, they have much in common. The synagogue will provide *siddurim*; just make sure you have enough for your guests. The prayer books are kept either in little racks in front of each seat in the sanctuary or on a table or cart at the back of the room. If they are not already at each person's seat, you may want to have someone hand them out to the guests as they enter the sanctuary. (You may also like to have two other people greeting your guests—one to hand out *chumashim* and another to give people programs for the service.)

An alternative to using the prayer books published by the Jewish movements is to produce your own. (This is discussed in more detail in Chapter 6.)

Chumashim

The word *chumash* comes from the Hebrew word for five. It contains the five books of the Torah: *Genesis, Exodus, Leviticus, Numbers,* and *Deuteronomy,* along with the accompanying *Haftarot* and commentaries. The *chumash* is usually kept on a cart or table at the rear of the sanctuary and is used on all days when the Torah is read. Therefore, if your child is reading from the Torah, the *chumash* will be used during the service. There are several *chumashim* in use today, depending upon the affiliation of the synagogue.

Chapter 5

Finding Your Way Through The Service

Now that you have a basic understanding of the synagogue and the things you will see there, it will be helpful to you to consider the service itself. The service is of great consequence for your son or daughter, your family, and the Jewish community.

It is important for your child because by participating in the worship service he fulfills the obligations that mark this transition from Jewish childhood to Jewish adulthood. It represents years of study, through which one learns that effort and sustained dedication do flower into real accomplishment. Leading the prayers, chanting or reading from the Torah and the *Haftarah*, and sharing a commentary on the lessons of the Torah portion—all of these are opportunities for the student to take hold of the moment and grow from it. Your child will never look at Judaism quite the same way again. From this point on, she will be a full adult partner in the ongoing Jewish way of life.

The service is important for your family because it represents generations of hopes and dreams, memories and legacies. The longings of grandparents, parents, and children are interwoven on this day. They come to fruition as your child steps forward to lead the service. It is a golden opportunity for you to come together and enjoy this moment in time, setting the tone for your child's future Jewish life, serving as an important stepping stone to further involvement and commitment.

The service is important to the larger Jewish community because coming together in public worship reaffirms the continuity of Judaism in a concrete way. Your child is living proof of the survival of the Jewish people. He is evidence of the realization of history, reminding us of the past, bringing optimism and hope to those who follow after us.

✡ ✡ ✡

Rabbi David Cohen: *"To the student: I know you want this morning to be a success, but remember that success isn't measured by how well you chant the prayers or lead the service, but rather whether you participated with all your heart and soul. Today is the real thing. Everything up to this moment has been preparation, but today it all becomes real. Your words are really prayers . . . make your words sing. Try to be fully present—for the Torah's sake and for your own. And most of all, try to capture this moment. Be conscious of the community gathered around you. Take a mental snapshot of all the people who have gathered to celebrate with you. You will have many pictures from today, but the picture you carry around inside of you will be the most important of all."*

✡ ✡ ✡

The service crystallizes the joy and sense of achievement of all those who take part in this moment. Above and beyond the parties, the new clothes, the gifts, the influx of friends and relatives, and even the excitement of the parents and family stands the worship service. Strengthening the sense of connection to the larger Jewish community in a public manner, it is the peak of the Bar Mitzvah experience and as such, requires that you have some knowledge of the following:

- The structure of the service and the significance of the prayers.

- The Torah, *Haftarah*, and rituals surrounding them.

- The ritual responsibilities of the Bar or Bat Mitzvah during the service.

The structure of the service and the significance of the prayers

As indicated earlier, the Jewish worship service is derived from the ancient offerings brought in Temple days. Even today, traditional congregations hold services three times daily in commemoration of the *Shacharit, Mincha,* and *Ma'ariv* services held in the Temple. Although there are some differences between the various services, they have certain elements in common:

- Judaism is not a religion expressed in solitude. Rather, it revolves around community and public, group worship. Therefore, all services derive their strength from the individuals who come together to form the community. Similarly, many of the prayers are said in the plural and on behalf of the community.

- As noted earlier, certain prayers require a *minyan*. These are prayers that require a communal response. In Orthodox Judaism, only men are counted for such a response. The prayers that require a *minyan* are: the *Bar'chu* (call to worship), the *Kedusha* (part of the standing prayer), the reading of the Torah, and the *Kaddish* (a prayer of praise to God that is associated with mourning, but which makes no mention of death).

- Portions of the service are recited while seated and others while standing. As a general rule, *b'rachot* (blessings) are recited while standing. Furthermore, even while standing, the worshipper frequently moves his/her body in a rocking motion, carried by the rhythm of the Hebrew and the ancient melodies. This movement is called *shuckling.*

In order to get the most out of any Jewish service, it is important to be an active participant. To most effectively take part, you should become familiar with the prayers, melodies, and rituals of the service. While there are differences from synagogue to synagogue and from movement to movement, once you feel at ease with the service itself, you can feel at home no matter where the service takes place. As the parent of a Bar Mitzvah child, you especially should be familiar with the service. The more comfortable you and your child are, the easier and less stressful the actual ceremony will be and the more meaning you will derive from it.

Outline of the service

If the structure of the service seems mystifying to you, perhaps you could use a sort of road map to help you find your way. Know that whether it is a weekday, Shabbat, High Holy Day, or festival service, the fundamental components remain the same. Depending upon the custom of your own congregation, the Bar Mitzvah may lead any or all of the prayers. As you will see, there are five major parts to the service.

I. Introduction

Introductory elements to help prepare the worshipper for prayer. These include Psalms from the Bible, *Pisukei D'Zimra* (songs of praise to God), meditations, a reading in English, or some preliminary blessings.

A *chatzi-Kaddish*, (Reader's *Kaddish* or half-*Kaddish*) is recited here to set off the completion of the preliminary prayers from the next section of the service. The *Kaddish* is a prayer of praise to God; it "rounds out" different portions of the service.

II. The *Sh'ma* and its blessings

This section includes the *Bar'chu* and prayers that surround the *Sh'ma* (the central prayer in Judaism, affirming a belief in one God). The *Bar'chu* will be repeated later in the service as part of the blessing to be recited before reading from the Torah.

The *Sh'ma* is preceded by two blessings, each with evening and morning alternatives, that address:

* **Creation**, or God in Nature: *Ma'ariv Aravim* (a prayer thanking God for bringing on evenings) or *Yotzer Or* (a prayer acknowledging God as the creator of light, recited in daytime).

* **Revelation**, or the gift of Torah as proof that God loves us: *Ahavat Olam* (evenings) or *Ahavah Rabbah* (daytime).

The *Sh'ma* itself is as follows:

Sh'ma Yis-ra-el, Adonai Eh-lo-hei-nu, Adonai Eh-chad.
Hear O Israel, the Lord is our God, the Lord is One.

This statement (taken from *Deuteronomy* 6:4) is so important in Judaism that it is recited every evening and morning of a Jew's life. It is the first prayer taught to children, and it is to be the last thing a Jew says before death. It is always to be recited or chanted with great *kavannah* (intent and concentration). Often, people cover their eyes to aid in intensifying their *kavannah*. Depending upon the custom of the synagogue, the *Sh'ma* may be recited either sitting or standing.

The *Sh'ma* is accompanied by another short statement that was later added to the liturgy by the rabbis. It reads:

Ba'ruch shem K'vod, mal-chu-to L'o-lam va-ed.
Blessed be His Name, Whose Glorious Kingdom is Forever and Ever.

Depending upon the custom of the synagogue, this sentence may be whispered, chanted in an undertone, or sung aloud after the *Sh'ma*.

The *Sh'ma* is followed by additional paragraphs from the Torah. In Reform Judaism only the first one, the *V'ahavtah* (*Deuteronomy* 6:5-9), is recited or chanted. In Orthodox and Conservative Judaism two more paragraphs are included, one that reminds the Jew to follow God's laws and not to go astray and worship alien gods, (*Deuteronomy* 11:13-21), and another that enjoins the Jew to wear *tzitzit*.

Included in this section of the service are a series of blessings on the theme of **Redemption**:

∗ *Emet v'Emunah* (recited in the evening) or *Emet v'Yatziv* (recited in the daytime). Both of these blessings include a prayer called *Mi Cha-Mo-Cha* ("Who is like you, O God?"), which was the praise sung by Moses at the Red Sea. The second paragraph varies, depending upon its recitation as part of a day or an evening service.

In an evening service, the *Mi Cha-Mo-Cha* is followed by a prayer called *Hashkiveynu* ("Allow us to lie down in peace and to arise in peace"). On Shabbat evenings a passage called *V'shamru* ("and you shall keep the Sabbath") is chanted (*Exodus* 31:16-17).

III. The Amidah/Shemonah Esray/Ha'Tefillah

This is the central prayer of the service. It comes from the word *la'amod* (to stand). During the week, it is known as the *Shemonah Esray* (18), because it consists of 18 benedictions, plus an additional one added in the Middle Ages. On Shabbat, it is called *Ha-Tefillah* (the prayer), because it is the core prayer of the service.

It is at this point in the worship service that there may be much individual movement. One "steps into" the *Amidah*, creating a private, sacred space within which to address God in a personal, intense manner.

At various points throughout the prayer the worshipper bows in reverence to God as in a private audience with a great monarch, and at the conclusion of the prayer he/she withdraws from God's presence by stepping backward and bowing with great respect.

Beginning with *Adonai S'fa-tai* (an introductory prayer that asks God to grant the worshipper the ability to pray), the *Amidah* has two initial paragraphs: the *Avot v'Imahot* (which speaks of the God of our ancestors) and the *G'vurot* (which reminds us that God is the source of life).

Following these two introductory paragraphs is a section called *Kedushat Ha-Shem* (The Sanctification of God's Name), which requires a *minyan*.

The blessings in the *Amidah* include the following specific requests when the prayer is recited during the week: for understanding, repentance, forgiveness, redemption, health, abundance, freedom, justice, righteousness, return to Jerusalem, deliverance, and acceptance of prayer. Some of these requests are for the individual, but the majority are for the community as a whole.

On Shabbat there is only one blessing included in this portion, and that is *Kedushat Ha-Yom* (the blessing for the Sabbath day).

The remainder of the *Amidah* includes the *Avodah* (a request that God accepts our prayers in love), and *Modim* (a prayer that expresses thanks to God for life, health, peace, beauty, and love.) The *Amidah* closes with a prayer for peace, which has evening and morning variations. In the evening, it is *Shalom Rav*; in the daytime, *Sim Shalom*.

Kaddish is again recited to mark the separation of this part of the service from the next section, the taking out and reading of the Torah.

IV. The Torah service

The Torah service is always important, but at a Bar or Bat Mitzvah it is of even greater significance, as this is where your son or daughter will lead the service and read/chant the Torah portion and the *Haftarah*. More specific information about the Torah service follows later in this chapter.

The *d'var Torah* is often presented at this point. For more about this, read further on in this chapter.

V. Concluding prayers

These include *Aleinu*, which is also known as the "dangerous prayer," because during the Spanish Inquisition it was recited on pain of death.

It reminds the Jew that God gave us a unique destiny, and it calls upon us to remain true to God's commandments and retain our identity, even in the face of persecution. It closes by looking ahead to the coming of the Messiah and a time of everlasting, universal peace.

The final prayer of the service is a *Kaddish*. It is known as the *Kaddish Ya-tom* (Mourner's Kaddish), because it is recited by those in mourning. It requires a *minyan* and is a prayer of praise to God, emphasizing life and its goodness. All forms of *Kaddish* have the same theme—thanksgiving for life.

Following *Kaddish* is a closing hymn, and the service is sometimes concluded with the priestly benediction from the Torah: "May the Lord bless you and keep you. May the Lord make His face to shine upon you and be gracious unto you. May the Lord turn His face unto you and give you peace (*Numbers* 7:22-27)."

In some congregations there is also a *Musaf* (additional) service. In Orthodox synagogues, *Musaf* can be rather lengthy, while in Conservative services it is usually shorter. Reform synagogues do not include a *Musaf* service. *Musaf* includes a repetition of the *Bar'chu*, the *Amidah*, and other accompanying prayers, and concludes with *Aleinu* and the Mourner's *Kaddish*.

The rituals surrounding the Torah service

This is the moment when all your child's hard work and study comes to fruition, for in being called to the public reading of the Torah as an adult member of the congregation, he or she is fulfilling the most visible pulpit obligation of becoming a Bar or Bat Mitzvah.

L'dor va-dor: Passing the Torah from generation to generation

In recent years, many liberal synagogues have incorporated a ritual that may take place before the *hakafot* (the Torah procession): The handing down of the Torah from one generation to the next. Those who are responsible for having transmitted the knowledge and love of Torah to the student are called to the *bimah* for this honor. The Torah scroll is physically passed from grandparents to parents to the Bar Mitzvah. It is an emotional moment, one often anticipated for years and looked back upon long afterward as a symbol of the continuity of the Jewish tradition within the family.

The policy of passing down the Torah varies from congregation to congregation. Some synagogues invite only parents and grandparents to participate. In other communities older siblings may also take part. In some smaller congregations the whole adult community, including the religious school and Hebrew school teachers, may participate.

This ritual can be emotionally laden for several reasons:

∠ In most families, this is a time for coming together and publicly acknowledging the contributions of all the immediate family members. Relatives come from far and wide to participate in this ritual. The grandparents, parents, and children stand proudly in front of the congregation and are honored through the act of handing the Torah down from one to another. It is a moment of recognition— of the hours spent in helping to bring the student to this day, of the years of effort and teaching that preceded it, and of the potential impact to be made upon the Jewish future as a result of this celebration. The ceremony also calls to mind those who have passed away and who had an influence upon the life of the child, but whose presence is felt at this moment.

✡ ✡ ✡

Shari: (from remarks to her daughter Ali at her Bat Mitzvah) *"As you know, we've lost several family members to early death. While they may not be here today in body, they are certainly all here in spirit. Despite the contradiction in terms, they were all survivors. Their legacy to you is your persistence, a will to succeed, and a desire to conquer all odds. From your great-grandparents you also have a legacy of survival—not of fighting disease, but of surviving anti-Semitism. Two of them escaped Nazi Germany, while the other two escaped the Russian pogroms in the early part of this century. Their legacy to you is your tenacity, the gift of finding solutions to problems and discovering the best in all situations. Yet, with us today is your grandmother, who stood with you on the bimah and was able to hand the Torah down to you for all the family members we have lost and who could not be here."*

✡ ✡ ✡

∠ In families where there has been a divorce, this ritual may be difficult. Sometimes, ex-spouses may not feel comfortable participating in it together. In some cases, the child is more connected to one parent than the other, and may have strong feelings about the other's participation. Sometimes, however, it reminds the couple that whatever their differences, they were able to successfully bring their son to this moment in time. Passing the Torah on to their child may be an opportunity to look beyond their own history as a couple, and to look to the future of their child as an independent and responsible Jewish adult.

∠ Where there has been a death in the family, the surviving members may feel the loss most poignantly at this time. It is fitting to remember the departed during the service, and especially during the passing down of the Torah scroll. Often, the rabbi will add a few words to the ceremony, reminding those in attendance of the contributions made to the Jewish education of the child by those who are no longer present to physically share in the moment.

∠ There is at least one other potentially sensitive issue concerning the passing down of the Torah: In some synagogues, non-Jews are not allowed to take part in this ritual. If your family situation is such that there might be a question about who may be involved in this part of the service, discuss this with your rabbi well in advance. It is important that this matter be handled with delicacy and sensitivity so that there is no confusion and so that no one's feelings are hurt. Your rabbi can be your best guide in this regard.

The procession of the Torah

During the Torah service, prayers of praise and honor to the Torah are recited before removing the scroll from the Ark. The *Sh'ma* is repeated in front of the open Ark, after which the Bar or Bat Mitzvah is handed the Torah and given the privilege of carrying it around the sanctuary before beginning the Torah reading. A procession is formed with the rabbi, cantor, student, parents, grandparents, and siblings. As they walk through the sanctuary carrying the Torah, members of the congregation greet them and wish them well. In many congregations people will touch or kiss the Torah as an expression of love for its teachings. It is a sweet moment for the family, allowing them to share their joy with all those dear to them. For the youngster it is a golden moment of recognition, approval, and anticipation.

Learning to read the Torah portion and *Haftarah*

It is not easy to read from a Torah scroll, because, as illustrated in Chapter 4, it lacks vowels and punctuation marks. Therefore, when a person learns to read from the Torah, he or she practices with a *Tikkun*, a copy of the Torah containing two columns of the same text on each page—one with vowels, punctuation, and *trope* (cantillation) marks, and one that looks exactly like a Torah scroll.

Besides the *Tikkun*, there are several other educational tools to assist your child in learning the Torah portion and *Haftarah*. Many Jewish publishing companies have such items available for purchase. They also will have ancillary materials explaining the meaning of the prayers, the structure of the worship service, and the significance of the weekly Torah portions and *Haftarot*. If your child is enrolled in a synagogue Hebrew school or Bnai Mitzvah program, the school will provide these for you. If you are doing the preparation on your own, you may want to contact the publishing companies directly and purchase the proper ones for your child. They can also be ordered through a Judaica gift store or obtained through your local board of Jewish education. For a listing of educational resources please refer to Appendix A.

In addition to the commercially produced learning aids, your rabbi, cantor, or Bar Mitzvah specialist will often provide your child with an audiotape of his portion. This is a valuable tool for ongoing reinforcement and familiarization with the text. The tape may also contain the entire service so that the student can master it. By listening and singing along, your child can become proficient in the prayers and can learn at his or her own speed.

The *Parashiyyot* (Torah portions) of the Jewish year

Originally, the Torah was read in its entirety over a period of three years (a triennial cycle). However, during the Babylonian exile it became customary to read through the entire Torah in one year, in 54 *parashiyyot* (portions). Because 54 portions have to accommodate the number of weeks in a Jewish leap year, as well as festivals that fall on Shabbat, portions may be doubled up.

In some synagogues the triennial cycle is still followed, requiring three full years to read the Torah. In these congregations, the portions are divided into thirds: The first year of the triennial cycle, the first third of each portion is read. The second year, the middle portion is read, and the third year the last third is read.

Other congregations read the Torah on a yearly basis. Some read the entire *parashah* each week, while others shorten the Torah portion in the interest of time. Depending on the ability of the student, the number of verses to be read may vary. Some students may read just a few lines, while others master lengthy portions. The length and organization vary from synagogue to synagogue, and you should find out the custom in your congregation when you begin your planning.

Please refer to Appendix G for a listing of the Torah portions and *Haftarot* for the Jewish year.

Special *Parashiyyot* during the year

Holidays and other observances have special Torah portions and *Haftarot*. They are:

- Rosh Hashanah (Jewish New Year).
- Shabbat Shuvah (the Sabbath between Rosh Hashanah and Yom Kippur).
- Yom Kippur (Day of Atonement).
- Sukkot (Feast of Tabernacles).
- Shabbat during the intermediate days of Sukkot.
- Simchat Torah (Rejoicing in the Law).
- Chanukah (Feast of Dedication/Feast of Lights).
- Shabbat Shekalim (the Sabbath before the first day of the month of Adar).
- Shabbat Zachor (the Sabbath before Purim, the Feast of Lots).
- Shabbat Parah (the Sabbath preceding Shabbat Ha-Chodesh).
- Shabbat Ha-Chodesh (the Sabbath before the first day of the month of *Nisan*).
- Shabbat Ha-Gadol (the Sabbath before Passover).
- Pesach (Passover).
- Shavuot (Feast of Weeks).
- Tisha B'Av (Ninth day of the month of Av).
- Parashat Pinchas (the Sabbath after the fast of the 17th of *Tammuz*).
- Special *Haftarot* for Sephardim (see Appendix G).

There may be other special occasions. Consult your rabbi to determine which rules will apply to you.

About the *aliyot*

Because one of the most meaningful parts of the service is the honor of being called up to the Torah, you may want to include a number of your family and closest friends. To help you decide which day might be the most fitting for your celebration, consider the number of *aliyot* given. The more *aliyot* there are, the more people you can involve. The number of *aliyot* depends upon the sanctity of the day:

- On weekdays and Shabbat afternoons, there are three *aliyot*.
- On Rosh Chodesh and on intermediate days of holidays, there are four *aliyot*.
- On holidays, there are five *aliyot*.
- On Yom Kippur, there are six *aliyot*.
- And on Shabbat, there are seven *aliyot*.

When you decide who will be called up for an *aliyah*, remember that although one must be a Jewish adult to receive this honor—that is, over the age of 13—other customs related to the *aliyah* do vary from movement to movement. In Orthodox congregations, only men are given the honor. Also, in Conservative and Orthodox Judaism, the first *aliyah* is given to a *kohen* (one of priestly descent), and the second to a *levi* (a descendant from the tribe of Levi). In Reform and Reconstructionist congregations, no such distinctions are made. If you have a question about the proper order and rank of a particular *aliyah*, ask your rabbi. And if you are not certain which category you and your family fall into, this should be clarified with your rabbi, as well.

It is customary to give *aliyot* to such family members as grandparents, aunts and uncles, cousins, brothers and sisters, and, of course, parents. Usually, the parents have the last *aliyah* before the Bar or Bat Mitzvah's.

What to do when called for an *aliyah*

Inasmuch as being called to the Torah is a great honor, there is proper etiquette to follow. Here is the basic procedure: When called to the Torah for an *aliyah*, one should approach the *bimah* by the most direct route to indicate eagerness to perform a *mitzvah*. As you face the Ark, the person given the honor of the *aliyah* stands on the left side of the *ba'al koreh* (Torah reader)—who is probably, in this case, the Bar or

Bat Mitzvah. The reader will indicate where the reading will begin, and the person having the *aliyah* then touches either his *tallit* or the back of the *siddur* (the prayer book) to that spot. It is customary for the Torah scroll to be rolled together and for the rollers to be gripped by the person given the *aliyah* while the blessings over the Torah are pronounced. This makes the individual and the Torah scroll one. The blessing is recited or chanted, and the reader then unrolls the scroll and commences with the reading. Following the reading, the person given the *aliyah* again touches the last word of the portion being read, waits as the scroll is closed again, and, holding onto the rollers, recites the blessing following the reading of the Torah. The person given the *aliyah* then moves to the right side of the reader and remains standing there while the next *aliyah* is chanted or read.

Often, following the reading and before commencing with the next *aliyah*, the rabbi will offer a blessing in honor of the person who was called to the Torah.

One then returns to his or her seat by the most indirect route, to show reluctance to terminate the performance of a *mitzvah*, and will be wished *"Yasher koach!"* ("May you be strengthened!") by members of the congregation. The proper response for such a wish is *"Baruch t'hiyeh!"* ("May you be blessed!")

This is the procedure for every *aliyah*.

If all this seems a bit confusing, don't worry. The rabbi or cantor will be happy to assist those who are honored with an *aliyah* so that the process goes smoothly.

Two bits of advice, however: First, if you are in charge of arranging people for *aliyot*, be sure to inform them well in advance. This is not something that should be left as a surprise. They will need time to prepare and should be clear about which *aliyah* will be theirs. Secondly, if you are given the honor of an *aliyah*, do plan to practice the blessings ahead of time so that you can recite or chant them with some measure of confidence. It is a bit disconcerting to witness someone unprepared to read the blessings. You can expect to be a bit nervous; after all, it is an important moment! But do your best to do it properly. It's advisable to keep your eyes fixed on the printed blessings in front of you; read slowly and carefully, and be respectful of the words you utter. Then, when you are finished you will truly feel worthy of a *"Yasher koach!"* from family and friends.

The Maftir

The *maftir* is the last part of the Torah portion. The word *maftir* is related to the word *Haftarah*, meaning "conclusion." The person who is given the last *aliyah* in the service is called the *maftir*, the one who concludes, and the portion he or she reads from the Torah is also called the *maftir*. Starting from the 14th century, it became customary to honor the Bar Mitzvah by giving him the privilege of reciting the *Haftarah*. This recitation took place after reading/chanting from the Torah and reciting the appropriate blessings. Specifically, it was done following the *maftir aliyah*, the last of the *aliyot*. However, this *maftir aliyah* is not counted as one of the required *aliyot*; it is an additional one, given so that the person honored with the *aliyah* can then chant or read the *Haftarah*. Nowadays, it is a common in liberal synagogues for girls to be given this same honor when they become Bnot Mitzvah.

Blessings to be recited/chanted with each *aliyah*

Before the Torah is read, the following blessing is chanted or recited:

Reader: *Ba-r'chu et Adonai ham-vo-rach!*

Congregation: *Ba-ruch Adonai ham-vo-rach l'o-lam va-ed!*

Reader repeats: *Ba-ruch Adonai ham-vo-rach le-o-lam va-ed!*
Reader continues: *Ba-ruch a-ta Adonai, Eh-lo-hei-nu meh-lech ha-o-lam, a-sher ba-char ba-nu mi-kol ha-a-mim, v'na-tan la-nu et Torah-to. Ba-ruch a-ta Adonai, no-tein ha-Torah.*

(The congregation responds, "Amen.")

Note: The translations below are taken from *Gates of Prayer for Shabbat and Weekdays*, Chaim Stern, editor, published by the Central Conference of American Rabbis, New York, 1994. Orthodox and Conservative translations may vary.

Praise the One to whom our praise is due!
Praised be the One to whom our praise is due, now and forever!
We praise You, Eternal God, Sovereign of the Universe: You have called us to Your service by giving us the Torah. We praise you, O God, Giver of the Torah.

The Reconstructionist movement uses a slightly different version of the second blessing recited before reading from the Torah. It eliminates the reference to "chosen-ness" and instead says that the Jewish people were "drawn to God's service."

After reading from the Torah, the following blessing is chanted or recited:

Reader: *Ba-ruch a-ta Adonai, Eh-lo-hei-nu meh-lech ha-o-lam, a-sher na-tan la-nu To-rat eh-met, v'cha-yei o-lam na-ta b'to-chei-nu. Ba-ruch a-ta Adonai, no-tein ha-Torah.*

(The congregation responds, "Amen.")

We praise you, Eternal God, Sovereign of the Universe: You have given us a Torah of truth, implanting within us eternal life. We praise You, O God, Giver of the Torah.

Honors given after the Torah reading

Following the reading of the Torah, two people are called up to the *bimah*—one to hold the scroll up to the congregation, the other to roll it closed and dress it. The honor of raising the Torah scroll high is called *hagbahah* (literally, "elevating"), and the person who has the honor is called the *magbihah*. To properly lift the Torah, the *magbihah* unrolls the scroll to a width of three columns and slides it down the reading table so the bottom rollers clear the table. Bending the knees and pushing down to tilt the scroll upward, the *magbihah* carefully lifts the Torah overhead and turns around so the written text of the Torah can be seen by everyone in the synagogue. The rabbi will instruct the *magbihah* to sit down at the proper time so that the Torah can be rolled and tied.

The second person, called the *golel*, performs *gelilah* (rolling the scroll together again). The left roller, where the Torah starts, should be placed over the right one so that the two parts of the scroll are nestled together. The *golel* also has the honor of dressing the Torah by putting on its ornaments. The rabbi assists in doing this properly.

Both *hagbahah* and *gelilah* are honors of great distinction. In more traditional congregations, only men are called upon to lift the Torah. (On a practical level, I suggest that you choose someone who is strong to lift the scroll, as it is quite heavy!) It is common in liberal congregations to see a man lift and roll the Torah and a woman dress it. The *magbihah* may be given the honor of sitting on the *bimah*, holding the Torah, during the *Haftarah* reading.

About the *Haftarah*

Besides the Torah portion, in most synagogues the Bar or Bat Mitzvah also reads or chants the *Haftarah*, a portion from the Prophets.

In 165 B.C.E., when the Jews were conquered by the Syrian-Greeks, it was forbidden to read from the Torah. To get around this injunction, portions from the later biblical writings were selected instead. These sections were coupled with each week's Torah portion and were linked thematically to them. (*Haftarah* portions that do not relate thematically to the Torah portion usually are tied to an upcoming holiday or historical remembrance.)

By the time it was permitted to read from the Torah again, the Jewish community had grown attached to the *Haftarah* readings, and so retained them. In Reform synagogues, selections from the third part of the Bible, *Ketuvim* (Writings), are used as *Haftarot* as well; Conservative and Orthodox congregations use only passages from the Prophets. The *Haftarah* generally has at least 21 verses, although many students do not read that many lines as part of their service. There is a different *trope* for the *Haftarah*, which the student learns to chant as part of the preparation.

Blessings recited/chanted before and after the *Haftarah*

Before the *Haftarah* is chanted on Shabbat, the following blessing is read or chanted:

Reader: *Ba-ruch a-ta Adonai, Eh-lo-hei-nu meh-lech ha-o-lam, a-sher ba-char bi'neh-vi-im tov-im ve'rah-tza b'div-rei-hem ha-ne-eh-mar-im b'eh-met. Ba-ruch a-ta Adonai, ha-bo-cheyr ba-Torah u-v'Mo-she av-do, u-v'Yis-ra-el ah-mo, u'vi-nev-i-ei ha-eh-met, va-tze-dek.*

(The Congregation responds, "Amen.")

We praise you, Eternal God, Sovereign of the Universe: You have called faithful prophets to speak words of truth. We praise you, O God, for the revelation of Torah, for Moses Your servant and Israel Your people, and for the prophets of truth and righteousness.

In the Reconstructionist movement the phrase *"u-v'Yis-ra-el ah-mo"* (and Israel Your people) is omitted.

The following blessing is read or chanted after the *Haftarah*. The version below is from the Reform *siddur*, *Gates of Prayer for Shabbat and Weekdays*, published by the Central Conference of American Rabbis, and is reprinted here with permission. The version used in Conservative and Orthodox congregations includes references to the coming of the Messiah and the rebuilding of the Temple, which are eliminated in the Reform version. There are also variations in the Reconstructionist blessings, which omit references to the throne and monarchy of David and emphasize God's house as a house of prayer for all people.

> Reader: *Ba-ruch a-ta Adonai, Eh-lo-hei-nu meh-lech ha-o-lam, tzur kol ha-o-lam-im, tza-dik be-chol ha-dor-ot, ha'Eil ha-neh-e-man, ha-o-mehr v'-o-seh, ha-m-dah-ber u-m'ky-yeim, she-kol d'var-av eh-met vah-tze-dek. Al ha-Torah, v-al ha-a-vo-dah, ve-al ha-neh-vi-im, ve-al yom ha-Sha-bat ha-zeh, sh'na-ta-ta la-nu, Adonai Eh-lo-hei-nu, li-k'du-sha v'-lee-meh-nu-cha, le-cha-vod u-l'tee-fahr-et, al ha-kol, Adonai Eh-lo-hei-nu, ah-nach-nu mo-dim lach, u'm-va-rech-im o-tach. Yit-ba-rach shim-cha b'fee kol chai tah-mid le'o-lam va-ed. Ba-ruch a-ta, Adonai, m'ka-deish ha-Sha-bat.*

(The Congregation responds, "Amen.")

We praise You, Eternal God, Sovereign of the Universe, the Rock of all creation, the Righteous One of all generations, the faithful God whose word is deed, whose every command is just and true.

For the Torah, for the privilege of worship, for the prophets, and for this Sabbath day that You, our Eternal God, have given us for holiness and rest, for honor and glory, we thank and praise You. May Your name be praised forever by every living being. We praise You, O God, for the Sabbath and its holiness.

There are additional variations of the blessings on the festivals.

Giving the *d'var Torah*

Following the chanting of the *Haftarah*, the student concludes the Torah service with the giving of the *d'var Torah*. This is the Torah commentary and is one of the most important aspects of any service. It is sometimes also called a *drash*, from the word "to uncover, expose, or expound." When one gives a Torah commentary, one is uncovering or exposing the hidden or more subtle meanings of the text.

Your rabbi, cantor, or Bar Mitzvah specialist will help your child write the *d'var Torah*. There may be a series of several meetings to discuss the content and organization. Your child will be asked to study the Torah portion and outline it to find the important points. After further conversations, he will be expected to write a commentary about the portion, explaining and relating it to his own life. The *d'var Torah* is an expression of the understandings gained from his or her religious education about the material included in the Torah portion. In addition, your child will be expected to do further research and study other Jewish sources to consider what other rabbinic scholars have written about the *Parashah*. Drawing upon the rabbinic wisdom from the sages, the Bar or Bat Mitzvah will be asked to apply the Torah's teachings to real life experiences and share what she or he has learned with the congregation.

Usually, the rabbi, cantor, or educational specialist will help your child with the mechanics of a proper delivery—clear enunciation, making eye contact with the congregation, speaking slowly and with expression. (This last is important because it doesn't matter how brilliant the speech is if no one can make out what's being said.) There may be one or two complete rehearsals before the big day to allow the student to feel comfortable speaking from the *bimah*. For some youngsters it is a bit intimidating to speak before a large group of people in such a setting. However, by the Bar or Bat Mitzvah day, your child should feel at ease and excited about this presentation.

Composing and delivering a *d'var Torah* is serious business because it allows the student to explore the true significance of what he or she has read in the Torah. The commentary may or may not be long, but it is an opportunity for the youngster to own the portion, to make it real, and to personalize it. If the process is approached with care and patience, your child will gain new levels of understanding that may have a real impact upon his or her life. Even more important than a proper delivery of the speech is the meaning behind it. If your child not only masters decoding the Hebrew and the *trope* of the Torah and *Haftarah*, but also truly understands and can interpret the text, then he or she has taken a big step toward assuming Jewish adulthood. And it is even more significant when the lessons contained in the Torah portion or *Haftarah* transfer into your child's life. Giving the *d'var Torah* becomes a moment to treasure and remember and is a highlight of the Bar Mitzvah experience.

✡ ✡ ✡

Michelle: *"My Torah portion was Parashat Shemini, from the Book of Leviticus. Part of the portion dealt with the laws of kashrut. Although my family did not keep kosher, my rabbi suggested that I try it for a couple of weeks as a way of learning more about the meaning of the portion. I did it, and it made a strong impression on me. Even though we do not have separate sets of dishes at home, I still keep a level of kashrut and will continue to do so. I am now more aware of the sanctity of life and of separating milk and meat because of my Torah portion."*

✡ ✡ ✡

Ritual responsibilities of the student during the service

The student will take an active part in the worship service in many ways, depending upon his or her capabilities and the customs of the synagogue.

Here is a list of some of the things the child may do:

- Lay *tefillin* for the first time.

- Wear a *tallit* for the first time.

- Light Shabbat candles on Friday evening.

- Chant the *Kiddush* and *Ha-Motzi* during *Kabbalat Shabbat* services.

- Read and/or chant the prayers and blessings during the preliminary service on *Shabbat* morning.

- Read and/or chant all the appropriate prayers and blessings during the *Shacharit* service.

- Be counted as part of a *minyan* for the first time.

- Lead or take part in those portions of the service that require a *minyan*, specifically: *Bar'chu, Kedusha,* the Torah service, and *Kaddish.*

- Have the honor of an *aliyah* for the first time.

- Read and/or chant a Torah portion and *Haftarah.* (This may be the *maftir* or a longer portion of the Torah.)

- Lead the *Musaf* service on Shabbat.

- Give a *d'var Torah.*

Be sure that you speak with your rabbi and/or cantor about the responsibilities your child will assume. In some congregations, the student only does certain prayers in the service. In others, he will lead the Torah service and then *Musaf.* And in other communities, she will lead the entire service. It is helpful to discuss the extent of your child's participation with her as you continue to prepare. In the beginning, it all may seem a bit overwhelming, but as time goes on, your child may want to take on more and more of the service.

The responsibilities your child assumes are important for the rest of his Jewish life. Leading the prayers, reading from the Torah, chanting the *Haftarah*, and giving a *d'var Torah* all are stepping stones to a competent and knowledgeable Jewish adulthood. Whatever your child is capable of doing as part of the service is meaningful. And all of it is a reason for rejoicing at this time of your child's life, as he truly becomes a Bar or Bat Mitzvah—a son or daughter of the commandments.

Chapter 6

Creating Memorable Moments In the Service

Every Jewish worship service is special. All the parts of the service—prayer, music, ritual, study, and meditation—make the experience meaningful and inspirational, if we only open ourselves to them. Even so, there are extra-special moments in the service that remain indelibly marked in our memories, months and even years later. And each celebration is unique, with its own elements that create powerful memories for the student, the family, and all those in attendance. In this chapter, we will consider:

- Keepsakes of the service.
- How to involve your loved ones in the service.
- Music as a key to spirituality.
- Some unforgettable moments.

Keepsakes of the service

There are some meaningful items you may create for your child's Bat or Bat Mitzvah service, which will be precious keepsakes of this occasion. They include:

- The service booklet.
- Your own prayer book or creative service.
- Personalized ritual items, such as *kippot.*
- Videography and cassette-recordings of the service.

The service booklet

It is always helpful for your guests to be able to follow along with the service, especially if they are not familiar with the liturgy. A service booklet or program will help them tremendously, explaining what is going on in the service and who has what honor. Although it is not required, it is a welcome addition.

Some congregations print up service booklets as part of their preparation for Bnai Mitzvah. The secretarial staff in the synagogue office may have a basic form explaining the synagogue and the service, which can then be personalized for each one. These are often kept as mementos, so if you decide to use such a form, be sure to let the office know how many guests you will have.

The information you will need for the service booklet includes:

- The English and Hebrew names of your child.
- The secular and Hebrew dates of the Bar Mitzvah.
- The Torah portion and *Haftarah.*
- The names of the people who are being given honors during the service. These include those who are lighting the Shabbat candles (if appropriate), passing down the Torah from generation to generation, receiving an *aliyah,* serving as *magbihah* and *golel,* reciting the *Kiddush,* making presentations to the Bat Mitzvah, and paying tribute to her through personal speeches.
- The names of deceased family members whom you wish to remember on this day.
- A personal message from you, the parents, to your guests, welcoming them to this special moment in your lives.

A sample of a service booklet is included in Appendix H.

Your creative prayer book

As mentioned in Chapter 4, you may find it meaningful to create your own service booklet, writing your own *siddur* and distributing copies to all of your guests as keepsakes. This takes time and effort, so plan ahead. You may wish to do this with your child.

You will need to use the basic structure of the Shabbat or weekday service as a guide. Be sure to include the following: Reader's *Kaddish*, *Bar'chu*, *Sh'ma* and the blessings surrounding it, the *Amidah* (silent prayer), the Torah service and *Haftarah*, *Aleinu*, Mourner's *Kaddish*, and opening and closing songs. (For details on each of these prayers, please refer to Chapter 5.)

Using a Hebrew font on your computer, you may wish to duplicate the prayers and blessings. For resources that will assist you in doing this, please refer to Appendix A. If you would rather not use a computer, use the old-fashioned cut-and-paste method. Simply make a copy of the parts of the service you wish to include, cut out the Hebrew and English portions, and tape them onto a blank paper. Then make copies of these. Be sure to cite the sources you use. To do this properly, write to the movement(s) whose prayer books you'd like to use for permission to duplicate the material. For information on how to contact the Jewish movements, please see Appendix A.

You may take the basic elements of the service and add to them by writing original prayers and meditations or incorporating suitable pieces from other sources. Writing your own material should not be daunting. Your words will be meaningful to those who read the service you create and will enable you to express your personal feelings in a unique way. You may also obtain professionally produced prayer books and personalized remembrance booklets. For such resources, please refer to Appendix A.

It is also appropriate to include specific wishes to the student. In a tribute to loved ones, some families also mention those who have passed away. Many times, the student will write a welcoming paragraph in the front of the booklet.

Often, copies of the child's Torah portion and *Haftarah* are incorporated as part of the personalized *siddur*. This will also help people follow along if there are not enough *chumashim* available for everyone.

If you do decide to create your own prayer book for this occasion, it is a good idea to discuss the project with your rabbi or cantor to be sure that you are not leaving out any important parts of the service and that the translation you provide is accurate and appropriately worded for the congregation.

✡ ✡ ✡

Leslie: *"Writing our own prayer book for Loryn's Bat Mitzvah was a labor of love. It took a lot of time to create, but it was worth every moment. Our whole family—and even Loryn's friends—wrote letters to her, which we incorporated into the book. We included English translation and transliteration under the Hebrew passages so that everyone could follow along. Loryn designed her own cover for the prayer book, and a friend of ours who is a graphic artist illustrated it beautifully. It is something Loryn and I will treasure always."*

✡ ✡ ✡

Photography, videography, and audio recordings of the service

Memories of the service are precious, and become even more so as time goes by. When you look back on the day and recall the people who were there, the feelings of joy and love, the words spoken and the prayers chanted so beautifully, it is heartwarming. The clearest recollections may come from photograph albums and videotapes or audiotapes of the service, if permitted by your synagogue. All of these make wonderful keepsakes. Copies can be made so that the whole family, wherever they may live, can enjoy the occasion over and over again.

Before you begin to arrange for a photographer, videographer, or someone to make a cassette recording of the service, be sure you understand the rules of your synagogue.

If you engage a professional photographer or videographer, that person should be available for the entire service and the celebration following. We will consider the photography/videography of the reception in Part 3, but for now, let us consider the service.

Photography. Some congregations will not allow flash photographs in the sanctuary at any time. Others will permit photography only before and after the service. If you are hiring a professional photographer, make sure he or she is familiar with the layout of the synagogue and the restrictions under which photos may be taken. Stipulate that the policy must be followed by whomever you engage for this purpose.

If you are not holding your Bar Mitzvah in a synagogue, you may be the one setting the rules. Remember that you want to maintain the decorum of the worship service. It is a good idea to request that the photographer be unobtrusive and to use natural light, if at all possible. (It will be less distracting to everybody—especially to your child, who will be in the spotlight as it is.)

Videography. Orthodox congregations do not permit photography or videography on Shabbat or during any services. In some Conservative congregations the policy may a bit more flexible. Generally though, these synagogues will only allow videography if the camera has been set on a timer and is positioned so that it does not interfere with the service in any way. The Reform movement is even more liberal. Many congregations have taping apparatus built in. If not, then arrangements must be made to record the service in the proper manner. Whatever the affiliation of the synagogue, it is important to use good judgment and to show respect for the place and the occasion.

You may wish to hire a professional to do the videography. There may be several fine videographers in your area. Be sure to interview them early in your planning. They are often very busy. And you may need to reserve your date very far in advance. It is also a good idea to get some references from other people. If the videographer is not familiar with the rituals in a Jewish worship service, you will want to take time to explain everything to him or her so that there are no surprises and so that everything goes smoothly.

Costs for photography and videography vary from region to region. They will also depend on the number of photos you want taken; there are often several different packages to choose from. You might also want to buy the proofs of the photos and an extra copy of the video. In some cases these are included in the price.

Here again, it is important that you clarify the policy and set-up of your synagogue with the rabbi, cantor, or synagogue administrator. Once you are clear about the requirements of your congregation, you can articulate them to your professional videographer. If videography and/or audiocassette recording are permitted, be sure to have enough film and tape to cover the entire service and reception.

If it is too expensive for you to include professional photography in your budget, you might ask a family member or friend to take pictures for you. These can be just as beautiful as those done professionally, and they cost far less. An additional advantage is that a friend or family member may be more familiar with the people involved and thus be able to catch people in candid moments.

Audio recording. If, for whatever reason, you choose not to use a photographer or videographer, consider tape recording the service. In most synagogues the recording can be wired into the sound system. Often, the cantor will be happy to oversee this part of the process for you. But be sure to alert the rabbi and/or cantor that you wish to do this. Give them plenty of notice, provide them with enough tapes, and don't forget to thank them afterwards.

How to involve your loved ones in the service

It is natural to want to include the people you love in this important life passage. It is especially important to your child to feel surrounded by love on this day. Through the years of growth that precede the Bar Mitzvah, you may have been given the loving support of many people—your parents, your spouse, your extended family, and your friends. The service is a fitting time to give *kavod* (honor) to those who have played a significant role in your life and that of your son or daughter. It is an opportunity for you to acknowledge their contribution and to say thank you.

There are private and public ways to do this. Here are a few suggestions:

Private acknowledgments

- Make a donation in their honor to the synagogue or some other Jewish organization.

- Send a note that expresses your thanks for the part they have played in the preparation for this day.

- Give each person a gift as a token of your appreciation. It need not be expensive or elaborate. The important thing is that you take the time to let them know how important they are in your life and that of your family.

Public acknowledgments

- List them in the service booklet as deserving of special thanks.

- Give them such pulpit honors as being called to the Torah for an *aliyah*, passing down the Torah (if appropriate), reading a special prayer or passage during the service, or presenting one of the gifts to your child on behalf of the synagogue.

- Publicly thank them during the service—either in the remarks you make to your child, or in the speech your child presents in the *d'var Torah*.

Remember that it is not only your own family and friends who are deserving of thanks. The rabbi, cantor, Hebrew specialist, and other synagogue staff would also appreciate a public acknowledgment. (There is an old saying, "If you want to know who really runs the synagogue, get to know the secretary and the custodian. They are the ones who make things happen!") Often, these people put in long hours of extra time on your behalf and work with no recognition at all. A few words of gratitude go a long way. As part of your child's becoming a Jewish adult, public commendation of others is more than just good form; it is an important part of being a *mensch* (a good person).

What can young children do?

Anyone who has had small children knows that Jewish worship services can seem interminable to a young child. Sitting for an hour and a half may seem like years, especially if there is no place to let off steam, move around, or keep quietly busy.

Some parents deal with this by arranging for some form of babysitting or day care for toddlers and pre-schoolers during the service. If this would be a help to you, speak to the synagogue staff about reserving a room or play area with supervision. Perhaps one of the teenagers in the synagogue youth group, a friend of the family, or even one of the teachers' aides in the religious school will watch the little ones for part of the service. Be sure there are quiet toys and books, and perhaps some non-messy snacks, if necessary.

By the time children are five or six, things get a little easier for everybody. They can sit for longer periods of time, are not as easily distracted, and have a better understanding of what is going on. If you wish to involve a young child in the service, there are several helpful things they can do. (One word of caution: Often they are so adorable, they may steal the show!) Here are some suggestions:

- Enlist their help in opening and closing the Ark doors at the appropriate times during the service.

- Use them as assistant ushers to distribute the service booklets, prayer books, *kippot*, and *chumashim* as people enter the sanctuary.

- Include them as part of the Torah procession.

- Enlist them to pass out candy to the congregants at the proper time during the service. (Originally a Sephardic custom, this is now done in many synagogues. Those in attendance throw candy at the Bar or Bat Mitzvah after he or she has concluded the blessings following the *Haftarah*. It makes for a bit of noise and confusion, but it is a fun-filled break in the seriousness of the occasion.) A bit of advice: Be sure to use individually-wrapped soft candy (fruit jellies are popular), and encourage the young children to come to the *bimah* to gather it all up off the floor after this part of the service.

- Call all the children up to the *bimah* to join in the traditional closing hymn—usually *Ein Keloheinu* or *Adon Olam*.

- Invite them to help hold the trays for *challah* or pass around small trays of cookies during the *oneg Shabbat* or *kiddush* following the service.

A word about decorum

It is a fact that babies often cry, toddlers get cranky, and even pre-teens and teenagers can get fidgety during a long worship service. This can be distracting to the student and the family, especially at pivotal moments of prayer, when a quiet and reflective atmosphere should be maintained. It is only natural for friends to want to sit together and chat, and we want to encourage Jewish youngsters to see the synagogue as a friendly and comfortable place. But there are tactful ways to ensure that during the service noise and disturbances will be at a minimum.

Here are some suggestions:

- Help your congregation establish an informal policy of conduct for the synagogue. While it is perfectly acceptable for people to greet each other and be sociable before and after the service, certain behaviors should be avoided. They include: chewing gum, eating in the sanctuary, writing, and making loud noise. Another suggestion might be to instruct people to turn off their cellular phones and pagers while in the sanctuary. If this all this becomes customary behavior over time, and those who attend on a regular basis are aware of it, they will help to pass the word along. Then proper demeanor at a Bar Mitzvah service will be *de rigueur* for everyone.

- If children are unable to sit through the entire service, plan their arrival for after the prayers begin. In many congregations people drift in at different times (before the Torah service starts) in order to stay attentive for the full service.

● Make it clear that it is customary not to walk in and out of the sanctuary while the Torah is being read.

● In some congregations, the rabbi or president of the synagogue will say a few words of welcome, setting out some basic rules of etiquette to assist people who are unfamiliar with the proper conduct in a Jewish house of worship. This way, everyone starts with the same information and feels more comfortable knowing what to do and how to behave.

● Request that those who bring infants or toddlers to the service take them out of the sanctuary if they cry or cause a disturbance. If appropriate, parents should be told nicely that they are responsible for their children's behavior and that crying or other noise makes it difficult for the person conducting the service to concentrate.

Such considerations should be handled well in advance. The better you plan for these things, the better the service will go and the lower the stress level will be for you and your child. At least one family fostered proper decorum by sending out a short letter to teenage guests and their families, clarifying the synagogue's policy on etiquette in the sanctuary. (The letter is included in Appendix I for your information.)

The music as a key to spirituality

Have you ever been in a place where the music moved you so deeply that you always remember that moment? Have you ever recalled melodies that ever afterward you associated with the happiest times of your life? Have you ever shared tunes with your children that date back to your own childhood, and that remind you of people and places dear to you? Most of us have had such experiences. They are sweet and poignant, bringing a smile to our lips and perhaps a tear to our eyes.

Jewish music has the power to touch us deeply in all these ways. It is rich and varied: melancholy Yiddish melodies from Eastern Europe, lilting Ladino tunes from Spain and Portugal, hearty Hebrew folk songs from Israel, awe-inspiring cantorial music, sweet lullabies, and ancient psalms—the list goes on and on.

Music raises the spirit, warms the heart and elevates the soul. Haunting melodies make the prayers come alive, give heightened meaning to the words, and allow us to go within ourselves to find the deeper significance of the liturgy and connect us to our past.

The traditional blessings strengthen our identity, and the familiar songs enable us to feel at home wherever we are, in any synagogue, anywhere in the world.

The power of music in Judaism goes back to the Bible, which documents David, the "sweet singer of songs," who calmed the agitated King Saul by soothing him with his voice and harp. Today, in the worship service itself, we sing several psalms, including Psalm 96, which exclaims, "Sing unto the Lord a new song: Sing unto the Lord all the earth," and Psalm 98, which exhorts us to "Sing praises to God with the harp...with the voice of melody...with trumpets and the sound of the horn." In many synagogues, the Shabbat morning service is not complete without the singing of Psalm 150, which mentions every musical instrument in the Bible that is used to praise God.

The person who is responsible for leading the congregation in song and prayer is the cantor, a word of Latin origin that means "singer." The Hebrew word for cantor is *hazzan*, from the word *hazah*, meaning "to see." The full title is *hazzan ha-knesset*, or "one who oversees the assembly."

The musical format of the Jewish worship service is governed by something called the *nusach*, a pattern or form of text. Historically, different groups of Jews in different places followed different *nusachim*.

Nusach also means a particular pattern or melody or prayer style that governs the chanting of the prayers. The *nusach* applies to almost every prayer in the service and may vary from *hazzan* to *hazzan*, from region to region, and from congregation to congregation. The *nusach* also depends upon the type of service; there is one for weekdays, another for Shabbat, and still another for the High Holy Days. Sometimes it is in a major key, and other times it is in a minor one. Even the rhythm of the music is dependent upon the *nusach*. For example, the rhythm of the Friday evening *Kabbalat Shabbat* service (to welcome the Sabbath) is in three-quarter time. The melodies sound almost like waltzes, fluid and lilting. The rhythm of the Saturday morning Shabbat service, on the other hand, is in four/four time. The beat is marked and strong, like a march.

Even if you do not have a formally trained cantor in your congregation, you may have a cantorial soloist or someone who is well versed in Jewish music. There are also many contemporary Jewish composers and artists whose music adds immeasurably to the beauty of the worship service. Check your local Judaica shop or synagogue gift shop for a list of popular Jewish artists. If you are affiliated with a more traditional synagogue, remember that no musical instruments are allowed on Shabbat. This will not stop you from enjoying beautiful Jewish music *a cappella*. Whatever you can do to include songs and uplifting melodies during the service will make the celebration that much more meaningful and memorable.

Here are some suggestions:

∠ As you begin your planning, arrange a meeting with your cantor or soloist. Do this early to allow plenty of time for your child to learn and practice the parts of the service to be chanted.

∠ Become familiar with the prayers and blessings that are traditionally included in the service. If you have a preference for certain melodies, discuss this with the cantor.

∠ Involve your child in the process of choosing extra music for the service, if possible. She may have favorite songs that are not usually part of the service. These can be inserted into the service as time permits and where appropriate.

∠ If a song will be unfamiliar to most of those in attendance, make copies of the lyrics and include them in the service booklet or your creative prayer book. This is especially true if the song is in Hebrew. You can always print a transliteration.

∠ Get a CD or cassette of the prayers and songs. Your cantor or cantorial soloist will often provide you and your child with a tape of the entire service. Use this as a primary learning tool. Play the music at home during the months before the Bar Mitzvah. In this way, you and your family will become very comfortable with the tunes well ahead of time.

∠ Be sure to arrange regular lessons for your child with the cantor throughout the preparation for the Bat Mitzvah. The cantor will schedule these in order to monitor your youngster's progress. To ensure that your child is polished and confident on the big day, make sure she comes prepared and doesn't miss these lessons.

Special moments during the service

Every element of the worship service is important, and everyone who attends will find his or her own connection to the occasion. But some things make the occasion especially memorable for you, your child, and for the whole family. They include:

- Presentation of the *tallit*.

- The student's *d'var Torah*.

- The parents' remarks.

- Recognition and honors given by the school.

- Expressions of gratitude on the part of the student.

- Remembering those who came before us.

Presentation of the *tallit*

A *tallit* is often presented formally to the student during the service. It is appropriate for the parents and/or grandparents to make a short public statement when presenting it. They may speak of what is unique about that particular *tallit*, and of the hopes and prayers that accompany it.

In one family, for example, the same *tallit* was passed down from one generation to the next, to be worn on the Bar or Bat Mitzvah day by each child in the family. In another family, the *tallit* was brought back from Israel especially for the occasion. Sometimes, the *tallit* is handmade. In every instance, the love that is expressed is clear and heartfelt. For a full description of the *tallit* and the rituals surrounding it, refer to Chapter 4.

The student's *d'var Torah*

As indicated earlier, one of the highlights of the service is the *d'var Torah*. The perceptions shared by the young person at this important moment afford us an opportunity to gain a new perspective on the wisdom of the Torah. They also allow us to learn more about the child who is delivering the message. It helps us to focus on the Torah portion through the eyes of the young Jewish adult who stands before us. The lessons offered by the student can be as perceptive and transforming as those of any rabbi or scholar. In fact, the youngster's remarks often allow us insights that we do not get from professional scholars. The comments offered by the student are fresh and honest, giving us new ways to embrace old truths.

Some families include the *d'var Torah* in the service booklet. Or you may want to include a copy in a scrapbook as a family memento. Along with the service booklet, a printed copy of the service itself, and some photos, a scrapbook creates vivid memories for years to come. You might also like to send copies of the *d'var Torah* to friends and family who could not attend the celebration.

Another plus of our technological age is the videotape. If you make copies of the service, you can give them to those who are unable to join you in person. When someone actually sees the child delivering the *d'var Torah*, the experience becomes more immediate.

For a full description on preparing the *d'var Torah*, see Chapter 5.

Murray: *"The videotape is a wonderful invention! When our son celebrated his Bar Mitzvah, my parents were many miles away. Both were elderly and in poor health, and they could not take the long flight to be with us. Just as soon as the day was over, I mailed them a copy of the videotape. They were just thrilled! They were especially moved by Allen's* d'var Torah. *They kept replaying it over and over, drinking in every word. You would have thought he was Moses himself, speaking to them!"*

✡ ✡ ✡

The parents' remarks

There are many highlights of the Bar or Bat Mitzvah service, but especially moving is the message you will give to your child. It is an opportunity to include all those who are important in the lives of your family and to embrace everyone with your words. It is a time to *shepp nachas*.

For you, the parent, it calls to mind the many hours spent in carpools, the weekly or twice-weekly Hebrew lessons, and the days when this commitment took precedence over other activities. You may have asked yourself from time to time, "Is it worth it?" And there may have been instances when you questioned the outcome. But at this moment, in the circle of family and friends, you realize that it truly was worth all the effort. And this is your chance to let your child know how you feel.

This is a moment when you have permission to acknowledge and celebrate your child's uniqueness, to smile a lot, to cry a little, and to speak words that will be remembered for years to come.

Here are a few suggestions for making a speech to your child:

Be honest. Your remarks will be meaningful only if you speak them from the heart.

Be prepared. This is not the time to wing it. Write your remarks down ahead of time.

Be positive. If there were difficult moments along the road to this day, you might mention them in passing, but only if you think it will not hurt your child's feelings. Otherwise, stick to the happy memories.

Be short and to the point. The service tends to be long, and the parents' message to the child usually takes place toward the end of the morning. If your remarks drag things out too long, people will lose their concentration and will miss the impact of what you say.

Make it relevant. Many parents tie their comments to the message of the Torah portion. This is important because then the *parasha* is always remembered in conjunction with the memory of this moment.

Keep it simple. Grandiose speeches are best left to politicians. Parents' statements are most moving if they are clear and easy to understand.

Remember that you are speaking to your child. Even if the room is filled with hundreds of important guests, no one there is more important than your child. This is an opportunity to publicly express your love for your child directly, simply, and with grace.

Recognition and honors given by the school

One of the most remarkable elements of Bnai Mitzvah is the abundance of presents. They are unlike any other birthday, and your child will probably receive gifts from everyone who is part of the occasion. In addition to the presents given privately by family and friends, the representatives of the congregation will also offer gifts publicly to the student.

Usually at the conclusion of the service, the dignitaries of the congregation will make presentations to the student. These individuals may include the rabbi and/or cantor, the president of the congregation, the president of the brotherhood and sisterhood, the religious school principal, and a representative from the Bnai Mitzvah class. In addition to making short speeches honoring the celebrant, they may give him or her such ritual items as Shabbat candlesticks, a *Kiddush* cup, or a copy of the *chumash*; make donations to *tzedakah* organizations; or plant a tree in Israel in the student's honor.

Your child may not be asked to formally respond to such gifts from the *bimah*, but in any case it is appropriate to write thank-you notes to the various representatives within the following week, if possible.

It is possible for your youngster to give *tzedaka* to the synagogue or other Jewish organization. The contribution should be money that the student has raised. If this is presented formally during the service, it may be done during the *d'var Torah*, or during a few moments at the conclusion of the service set aside to allow your child to say a few words.

Some families wish to show their appreciation to the synagogue in concrete ways. Here are a few suggestions:

- Plant a tree in Israel in honor of the congregation.

- Make a donation in honor of your synagogue to the governing board of the movement with which you are affiliated.

- Add a gold leaf to the "Tree of Living Gifts" if your congregation has such a fund. If not, offer to help start one.

- If your synagogue has one, write your family's name in the congregation's book of celebrations as a permanent record, along with a monetary gift. If there is not one already established, you may wish to initiate such a project, with all the proceeds from Bnai Mitzvah going to the religious school.

- Start, or contribute to, a scholarship fund at your synagogue.

- Contribute to the library fund.

- Contribute to your community's camp fund or other worthy cause.

- Ask that guests bring with them a "gift of Elijah"—food for the hungry. The next day, take it to a homeless shelter.

By giving something back, you, your child, and your entire family will gain a sense of satisfaction. You will have shown by your actions that *tzedakah* is a meaningful part of your lives. And you may inspire others to do the same, exemplifying the adage that "One *mitzvah* begets another."

Zichronam L'vracha: remembering those who came before us

Zichronam L'vracha means "May their memories be for a blessing." Because Judaism depends to a great extent upon connection to the past, those who have died never really leave us. At every happy occasion, we include them.

There are several ways to do this:

- The names of those we wish to remember could be included in a special section of the program to be distributed at the service.

- Their names may be read during the course of the prayers.

- The student might speak of them during his/her speech.

- The student and the family may make a donation to a Jewish *tzedakah* organization to honor their memory.

- In some congregations there is an empty chair set aside on the *bimah* to represent their presence.

- If a grandparent had a favorite Jewish melody, it might be included as one of the songs during the service, and noted as such.

- During the celebration following the service, a candle might be kindled in remembrance of them as part of the candle-lighting ceremony.

Such reminders do not dampen the joy of the occasion. They enrich it and make it more meaningful for the child, the family, and all who attend the service.

✡ ✡ ✡

David: *"In my Bar Mitzvah speech I dedicated my Bar Mitzvah to the memory of two people whom I knew well, my grandparents Judith Drabkin and Ilya Eydinzon. Their spirits and the love they had shown me will always stay with me. I also dedicated my Bar Mitzvah to the memory of many members of Drabkin, Levin, Eydinzon and Veyberman families whom I have never met. They were killed in ghettos and concentration camps, in Babi Yar, and on the battlefields of the Second World War. Memories of them connect my family's past to the present."*

✡ ✡ ✡

The information offered in this chapter should help to make your Bar or Bat Mitzvah service more meaningful. As you plan for this important occasion, give considerable thought to other ways you might make the service even more significant by adding your own personal rituals, prayers and meditations. Such efforts will serve to lift the service into the realm of the holy through your *kavannah* (serious intent).

Part Three:

The Celebration

Chapter 7

The Nuts and Bolts of Planning The Party

The Bar Mitzvah is not only a religious event, it is also a *simcha* (a celebration). Because it is such an important occasion, the preparations can become overwhelming, and the party planning can easily get out of control. Nowadays, the festivities often have a tendency to take over the whole occasion and the underlying meaning of the moment may be buried under a mountain of balloons, tinsel, loud music, and popping light bulbs. As you read the rest of this chapter, you may find that one of your biggest challenges will be to keep everything in proportion. Try to incorporate the important elements of *tzedakah*, *chesed*, and *tikkun olam* into every part of the day, including the celebration.

✡ ✡ ✡

Cantor Ellen Schwab: *"I worry that so often our commitment to mitzvot such as* tzedakah *is not at all evident at most celebrations. I remember being so happily surprised when a family recently included in their decorations a card announcing a donation to Mazon in honor of each guest. More often than not, a great deal of money is spent on disposable party favors and decorations. Our synagogue urges families to use canned goods, books, toys, or other items that after the celebration could be a donation to a charitable cause."*

✡ ✡ ✡

119

Even with this in mind, when planning your celebration there are so many details and so much to do that you may not know where to start. Hopefully, the information offered here will help you get over your fears and jump-start your motivation.

As a first step, there is an important preliminary decision to consider. That involves deciding just what kind of party you want. Once you come to some conclusions about this, everything else seems to fall into place.

Deciding what kind of party you want

As you begin your planning, sit down with your spouse and your child, and discuss what the celebration means to each of you. This is a good time to reach a general agreement about what each of you envisions. Two or three years prior to the Bar Mitzvah is not too soon. You can decide the details later, but initially you should at least be able to agree on the size and "flavor" of the event. Here are some questions you should consider:

∠ When will you be celebrating? On, or close to, your child's birthday? If not, when?

∠ Would you like to hold the service at a synagogue or in another place?

∠ Do you want the service on Shabbat evening, Shabbat morning, or another day?

∠ Do you want to have a party, or would you rather extend the celebration in some other way, such as a family trip to Israel? (For Bar Mitzvahs and celebrations in Israel, please see Chapter 10.)

∠ Do you want to mark the occasion with just the worship service? Or do you want to go all out, with a Friday evening Shabbat dinner for family and out-of-town guests, a *kiddush*-luncheon following the Shabbat morning service, a *Havdalah* service for the close of Shabbat, and a brunch or luncheon on Sunday?

∠ Do you prefer a simple *oneg Shabbat* or *kiddush*-luncheon, or do you want a formal dinner and evening of festivities?

∠ Do you want a small, intimate gathering, or would you like a larger, more inclusive celebration?

∠ Do you wish to have a family-and-adult luncheon, followed by a supervised kids' party in the evening?

∠ How can you celebrate in a meaningful way, retaining the religious significance of the event?

Considerations for party planning

Once you have a clear idea of the kind of celebration you want, you can decide on the following specifics:

- Budget.
- Guest list.
- Caterer or hotel.
- Invitations.
- Music.
- Flowers and other decorations.
- Photography and videography.

Setting the budget

In drawing up a budget, consider:

- Invitations.
- Postage.
- The site.
- Food and beverages.
- Music.
- Additional entertainment and activities.
- Flowers.
- Balloons and/or other decorations.
- Photography/videography.
- Party favors.
- Fees to the synagogue and clergy.
- A gift for the Bar Mitzvah child.
- A *tzedakah* donation.

The amount of *tzedakah* should be built in, along with the other given expenses. If you are giving to Mazon—A Jewish Response to Hunger, for example, plan to give 3 percent of the total cost as a donation. For other charitable organizations, you may use your discretion.

But in every case, discuss your gift with your youngster and your spouse, if applicable. You should all agree on the amount and the recipient of your giving. And if you can use party favors and centerpieces that can later be donated to a worthy cause, all the better.

Obviously, not everyone includes all of the expenses listed above in their Bnai Mitzvah plans. Furthermore, the cost of each item listed above varies from place to place. In some parts of the country, the custom is to do things simply. In other communities, the celebration becomes quite elaborate. You will have to decide what will work best with your budget and your particular situation. No matter which way you choose to go, keep in mind the significance of the occasion and plan accordingly, so that you mark your child's celebration of reaching Jewish adulthood in a meaningful way.

Keeping expenses down

Even if you decide to have a large party, there are ways to trim expenses. Here are a few suggestions:

∠ Share your day with another family. As mentioned earlier, some congregations are so busy that two or more Bnai Mitzvah are held on the same day. Even though each child is individually honored, you maybe able to share the cost of the flowers, photographer, and videographer with the other family.

∠ Some costs are lower if you can hold the party on a weekday. This is often true for bands, DJs, and hotels.

∠ Ask someone in your family to be the DJ for the celebration. Often there are young people who love to do this, and you can have music at a fraction of the cost. Just be very clear about the kind of music you want played and how you want it performed. You can also ask some of the local Jewish camp staff to lead the youngsters in games and activities during the party instead of hiring an expensive leader of activities for the day.

∠ Instead of purchasing expensive invitations, create your own, either by hand or on a computer. If you keep the invitations to a standard size, with a minimum number of inserts, you can keep postage costs low. To further reduce mailing expenses, and if time and numbers permit, you might opt for a less formal RSVP by asking people to phone you in response, rather than enclosing a stamped response card with the invitation.

∠ Luncheons tend to cost less than formal dinners. You can still wine and dine your guests, but at somewhat less expense.

∠ When planning your reception, keep it simple. Eliminate such unnecessary extras as elaborate centerpieces and floral arrangements, additional musicians, and vocalists. Ice sculptures, an open bar, and lavish entertainment are not necessarily in keeping with the tone of the celebration and can be omitted if you choose.

∠ Kosher food can be expensive, especially with the added expense of the *mashgiach* (*kashrut* inspector) to oversee the kitchen. By serving a cold vegetarian meal or fish as an entree, and using disposable plates and cutlery, you will avoid this expense and still be able to satisfy Jewish kosher dietary requirements. If your synagogue has a kosher kitchen, use their facilities. If numbers permit and if it is possible, prepare a simple luncheon or dinner yourself under the rabbi's supervision.

∠ If you have a sisterhood group at the synagogue or friends who are willing to help, you can save quite a bit of money by enlisting their help in preparing the meal. This is especially true in small communities where outside facilities are not readily available.

∠ You might purchase the beverages yourself. Some hotels are accommodating in this regard, especially if you require just a few bottles of kosher wine, which is not always offered. And when you buy the wine, arrange to return any unopened bottles for credit.

∠ If you are having an informal *oneg Shabbat* on Friday evening, or *kiddush*-luncheon following services on Shabbat morning, use paper goods. This will not only make things less expensive, but will make preparation and clean-up much easier for you.

∠ Bake and freeze! Start to bake cookies, cakes, and other desserts well in advance, and find a place for them in your freezer. Friends are usually only too willing to help with this, and besides keeping costs down, homemade goodies add a special touch to any occasion.

∠ If you are having a large number of youngsters at your celebration, provide some simple items that appeal to children. Finger foods, such as sandwiches, cookies, and simple appetizers, are big hits with small children and are not expensive. Many of these you can prepare yourself and will easily serve large numbers.

∠ For an informal reception, don't order a huge cake. It looks lovely in the pictures, but most of the time, it tends to go to waste. You can still have one, but keep it small.

∠ Instead of buying cut flowers for the *bimah* and as table center-pieces, order potted plants and greens. You can always put these in your garden afterwards. It is also nice to purchase living trees or plants, as they can remain on the *bimah* for other families to enjoy.

∠ If you want to get extra mileage out of the flowers and plants, have them do double-duty by transporting the same arrangements to the reception following the service. Then the next day after the celebration, donate them to a hospital or a home for the elderly.

∠ If you are at all artistic, create your own centerpieces. Don't make them too complicated or fancy. Your child can help with them, and they will have extra meaning because you made them together.

∠ Instead of hiring a professional photographer/videographer, ask a member of your family or a close friend to take care of the photography for you. Because this person knows you and probably most of the other guests, you will have some intimate and memorable photos without a huge expense.

∠ If you hold the reception at the synagogue, check the supplies on hand. Often congregations have tablecloths, cups and saucers, serving platters, napkins, and other items. There may be no fee for these, or if there is a cost, it is usually minimal.

Certain expenses are to be expected

There are still many expenses that may be unavoidable. To be prepared, you should be aware of them. They range from fees for the synagogue and clergy to the full range of activities for the celebration.

Some congregations charge an additional fee for Bnai Mitzvah training and for use of the synagogue. There may be also be additional fees for the rabbi's and/or cantor's time and expertise. You should find all of this out ahead of time and plan accordingly.

You should also be aware that most synagogues do not offer their facilities or clergy to non-members. This is because, in most cases, the synagogue is in use by the congregation for regular services and for *simchas*. Additionally, the rabbi's and/or cantor's schedules are usually filled by celebrations of their congregants. In special situations, a rabbi or cantor may be happy to lead the service for you if he/she is not otherwise obligated to synagogue duties on that date. If you engage a rabbi or cantor to lead the service, you should expect to pay a fee, which is set by the individual member of the clergy. Even if there is no personal fee for their time, you will want to make a donation to their discretionary funds as a token of your appreciation.

Obviously, the more activities you pack into the weekend, the more money you can expect to pay. Even if there is no extra charge for the use of the sanctuary, your synagogue may charge you for the use of the social hall, the kitchen, and the custodian. These costs do add up. If you decide to have a Shabbat dinner at the synagogue on Friday evening, plan to factor into your budget the cost of the food and wine, linens or paper goods, and flowers. If you are hosting an *oneg Shabbat* following Friday evening services, plan to include catering costs, if applicable. In most synagogues when there are Shabbat morning Bnai Mitzvah, the entire congregation is invited to the *kiddush* afterwards. This may take the form of light refreshments—*challah* and wine—or it may be a full luncheon. Either way, these are expenses you should keep in mind.

Some people host the party in the social hall at the synagogue on Saturday evening to keep expenses more modest. But if you are planning an elaborate dinner party at a hotel or country club on Saturday evening, the costs will be greater. Some families like to host a brunch on Sunday morning for the family and out-of-town guests to close out the weekend. Here again, there are expenses. And remember that the more people you invite, the higher the ultimate cost for everything. Most hotels and caterers charge on a per-person basis. While these costs vary, collect information so that you will be prepared in advance.

You can see that it is easy to get carried away, so don't be lured into "keeping up with the Cohens." There are many fanciful stories told about Bar Mitzvah safaris, trips to Aspen for all the classmates, or celebrations held at Disneyland. A bigger and more expensive party is not necessarily more meaningful than a smaller, simpler one. Try to remain realistic, and be sensible as you approach this part of the planning. (After all, you want to have enough money left to make a wedding!)

Making up the guest list

As indicated above, the more people you invite, the more money you will spend—and the more complicated things get. However, most families would prefer to include all the people that are important in their lives—and especially in the life of their son or daughter. So, when you make up your list, start by writing down the names of all the people you would like to invite. Compile the list with your spouse and your child, and plan together.

Remember that this is a celebration for your child. Encourage your child to invite school friends, buddies from religious school and Hebrew school and pals from camp, the youth group and athletic teams. If there are only adults at the party, it is no longer for your child, but for you, and you lose the purpose of the celebration.

Decide if you are going to include younger children in the festivities. If you are having a *kiddush*-luncheon on Saturday afternoon, children are usually invited. But if there is a formal late-night party, you may wish to include some accommodations for babysitting if you have out-of-town guests, or else stipulate teenagers and older when you extend your invitations.

Some families arrange two celebrations: one for everyone following the service, and a kids-only party in the evening. If you decide to have something like this, be sure to consider proper supervision, age-appropriate activities, and suitable entertainment to keep the young guests happy and occupied.

Don't forget to extend a courtesy invitation to the rabbi, cantor, and Bnai Mitzvah educator. Religious school teachers are delighted to be invited. Your child's secular school teachers will also appreciate an invitation, whether or not they are Jewish. And if you have youth group advisors, athletic coaches, or other adults who play an important role in your child's life, it is only natural to include them.

Some families send invitations to the President and Vice President of the United States and their senators, members of congress, governors and mayors. This may seem frivolous, but when a youngster receives a telegram or letter of acknowledgement from the White House, to be read at the celebration, it is something he remembers for years to come.

Establish minimum and maximum numbers of guests. If the numbers get too big, your party will get out of hand. Once you have an overall list, you can begin to refine it. (You'll need to know how many people you are planning for before you decide on a place to hold the reception.)

A computer can be a tremendous help to you in setting up your guest list and keeping the information current. You can keep track of names and addresses, those who can come and those who can't, gifts received, and any special needs of your guests.

Choosing the caterer or hotel

One of the first decisions is whether to hold the party in a hotel or reception hall, or at the synagogue. There are advantages to both. A hotel, club, or hall may be able to accommodate large numbers of people, and you need not bring in an additional caterer. They are set up for social gatherings of all kinds and can make the arrangements easier for you. On the other hand, it may be less expensive to have the celebration at the synagogue. Transportation is easier, as you're not moving people from place to place. And the staff at synagogues are accustomed to working with caterers for Bnai Mitzvah and other Jewish functions. Additionally, it may be necessary for you to consult with the synagogue concerning any security requirements they may have for functions on their premises. While hotels have their own security, you may wish to make special arrangements if you hold the celebration at your synagogue.

Next, you should decide whether you prefer a sit-down meal or a buffet. Your decision may depend on the number of guests, the size of the room, and your budget. Usually, you can expect to pay more for a sit-down meal, but often the food is more plentiful with a buffet and can be adapted more easily to special dietary considerations. If you have many elderly guests, you may choose a sit-down meal, as it is easier to accommodate their needs. Similarly, if you have many children coming, you may find a buffet more suitable because of the variety of food offered.

Don't forget to order meals for your photographer, videographer, and DJ or band members. And be sure to set aside some space so that they can eat in relative peace and quiet. They will bless you for it!

It is also possible to order a separate menu for the children's table. You can decide what is appropriate when you meet with the caterer or hotel banquet manager. (At one Bat Mitzvah, the parents had ordered a fancy dessert for all the adults, with an ice cream bar for the youngsters. As it turned out, the grown-ups all wanted to make their own sundaes, and the fancy desserts went unappreciated!)

When choosing a caterer or hotel, one major consideration is *kashrut* (the Jewish dietary laws). Some synagogues will only allow certain caterers to use their kitchen in order to protect their *kashrut* status. If you need to *kasher* (make kosher) a hotel kitchen, that must be planned for in advance with the hotel and the rabbi/*mashgiach* (one who supervises the *kashering* process). There are additional charges for kosher arrangements, not the least of which is kosher food and wine. If obtaining kosher meat is a problem, consider a dairy, fish, or vegetarian menu. In some communities there are lists of kosher caterers available. In other communities word of mouth and recommendations by friends may be your best guide. Be sure to check your information with your rabbi before choosing a kosher caterer.

Selecting the invitations

The invitation is more than just a folded piece of paper in an envelope. It sets the tone and style for the occasion. It may be elaborate or simple. It may have Hebrew lettering on it or be all in English. It may be a standard size and weight, or you may select one that is on heavy stock with several formal inserts. The choices are endless! To help you get ideas about what you might like for an invitation, start saving Bnai Mitzvah invitations you receive from friends. These will help you decide on the desired wording, colors, type of invitation, and so forth.

Some invitations are printed professionally and are found in stationery stores, Jewish gift shops, your congregation's gift shop, or from catalogues specializing in such items. Others may be originals, handmade and unique. Invitations range in price from modest to expensive, containing messages which may be formal or informal. You will need to look around at different stores to find the style you prefer.

It is helpful to pick a few styles, bring the samples home if possible, and go over your selections with your spouse and child. Another way to proceed is to bring your son or daughter with you to help you pick out the invitation, encouraging your youngster to become actively involved in the process.

Be sure to check for availability of the invitation you choose, and clarify the delivery date. You do not want to be caught at the last minute with an invitation that has been discontinued or that got lost somewhere over the Arctic Circle and couldn't arrive in time. So when you place your order, allow extra time for mishaps. If possible, obtain the envelopes early enough so that you can begin to address them even before the invitations arrive. Order plenty of extra envelopes to allow for mistakes. At the same time, order a plentiful supply of thank-you notes for your child, and arrange for early delivery of these. Some people even have their youngster address the thank-you envelopes ahead of time, and file them in a box alphabetically so that when the gifts come in and things are hectic, there is one less thing to worry about.

You may also want to include in your mailing of the invitation the following items, as needed:

- The RSVP card.

- An additional response card inviting people to the reception if you are not including everyone who is invited to the service.

- Additional response cards if there is a family Shabbat dinner on Friday evening and/or a brunch on Sunday.

- Directions, travel information, and other appropriate materials for out-of-town guests. (Please refer to Chapter 8 for more about this.)

Designing your own invitation

With today's technology, some people prefer to create their own invitations on the computer. The cost is much less, but you must trust your own level of expertise to be sure that you will have a properly finished product.

Here are some ideas for designing your own invitation:

- Using a heavy card stock, imprint your message on the front of the card with the address on a matching envelope. You will also need to print a matching response card (unless you provide a phone number for an RSVP), a map and/or directions, a note letting people know that lodging will be provided for out-of-towners, and perhaps a separate card inviting people to the additional festivities (if you are not including everyone who is invited to the service).

- If you prefer a folded invitation, do a mock-up and bring it to your printer to reproduce. Be sure to have someone else check your spelling and punctuation before submitting it for printing. These invitations can be done on colored stock with contrasting ink, a choice of typefaces, and a wide variety of wording.

- You may choose to put a drawing, a quotation from the Torah, a saying from one of the rabbinic commentaries, or some other appropriate passage on the front of the invitation. You may put the details of the occasion on the inside page.

- Some parents encourage their child to design the front cover of the invitation and sign the illustration. This makes it very personal, and can be quite charming and unique.

Once you have chosen an invitation you like, you must decide on the proper wording. Again, there are many variations. Here are a few examples:

Please join us on Saturday morning,
August 2nd,
when our son,
Maxwell James Shapiro,
is called to the Torah as a Bar Mitzvah
at
Congregation Beth Israel
[address]
at
10:00 a.m.

Ruth and Harold Shapiro

———

We invite you to share our joy as our daughter,
Anna Rose Jacobs,
Chana Rivka bat Shmuel v' Leah
becomes a Bat Mitzvah.
Services will take place on
Saturday, February 13, 1999
corresponding to the Hebrew date of 27 Shevat, 5759
at 9:30 a.m.
at
Congregation Shir Ami
[address]
Please respond by January 15.
Linda and Stanley Jacobs

George and Audrey Greenberg
invite you to join us in celebration
as our daughter,
Melinda Ann,
is called to the Torah as a Bat Mitzvah,
Saturday, June 12, 1999
at ten in the morning
Temple Judea
[address].
Luncheon to follow
at the synagogue.

If you are divorced or separated, you may wish to list your names on two separate lines on the invitation. Or, if appropriate, you may write both names along with the stepparents:

Barbara and Mark Davis
and
John and Delores Kaufman

Your printer, stationer, or invitation supplier can assist you with proper wording. It is often helpful to work with someone who has had some experience with Bnai Mitzvah or other Jewish celebrations.

Here are some other considerations:

∠ When choosing a printer or lithographer, be clear about the technical requirements or recommendations he or she gives you. Consider the size of the invitation and the size of the envelope. If the invitation is oversized, it will cost more to mail. The same pertains to the weight of the stock used. Remember, with all the necessary inserts you may end up with extra postage.

∠ Be careful with colors. Some people like to coordinate the entire celebration, using the same color scheme or theme for everything from invitations, to centerpieces to party favors, to thank-you notes, to you name it! So be sure that this is a combination you and your child really like.

∠ If you are doing hand-lettering, calligraphy, or other special touches, be sure you are accurate and that the copy is clean and easy to reproduce. Your printer may stipulate that artwork be camera-ready. Or you may be asked to make an enlarged original, which can then be reduced to the appropriate size, rendering a clear and sharp copy.

∠ If you are including Hebrew lettering on the invitation, be sure to have a knowledgeable person double check your work for accuracy. Once an invitation is printed, it is often too late to do it all over again if there is an error. You may want to engage a professional calligrapher to do specialty writing. You can find names of such people through your synagogue or in the Jewish community newspaper. Your local Jewish gift store will also be a good resource for you.

∠ To keep track of gifts, RSVPs and thank you's, one method is to put a little number on the back of each response card to match a corresponding index card kept in a file. This card will contain the complete name, address and phone number of each guest. As each gift and response comes in, and as each thank you for each gift is written, note the information on the card. This will also help you when giving an accurate count of guests to the caterer or hotel and when planning your seating arrangements. Another way of keeping track is to log everything into your computer as responses and gifts come in.

Selecting music

Invitations, guest lists, location of the celebration—all of these are important, but it is the music that can often make or break the party. If the musical accompaniment to the festivities is lively and engaging, you'll have a grand time. If it is inappropriate, your guests may be ready to leave before the main course is served. And if the music is too loud while people are eating, it can destroy your guests' eardrums! So choose wisely. You have a number of options. Do you want a DJ, a band, or both? A Klezmer band, Israeli folk dancing, ballroom dancing, or the "funky chicken?" Or maybe karaoke or other entertainment for the kids?

A lot depends upon your budget, the ages of your guests, the space you have available, the time of day, and the atmosphere you want to create. Not only is this is one of the bigger decisions you will make, it can be one of the more expensive. And you must decide very early in your planning, as entertainers tend to get booked as much as two years ahead of time, in some cases. The more popular the DJs or bands, the more difficult they may be to reserve.

If they are well-prepared, they will give you references of other Bnai Mitzvah where they played. They may also have a sample of their format, as well as a demo tape or video. Some musical groups can take care of all the entertainment on the schedule. They will also run the whole party for you, if you would like them to. Bands usually have vocalists and ensembles of different numbers of musicians, depending upon the size of your party and your budget. Some Bar Mitzvah DJs include a whole package of programming for the youngsters during the party. They will provide games, prizes, suitable music, and other activities to make the party appropriate for your child and his/her friends. When you and your child decide what you would like for this part of the entertainment, clarify these details with the person you hire.

Picking flowers and other decorations

Floral arrangements play an important part in enhancing the beauty of the day, for both the service and for all the festivities surrounding it. You will want flowers or greenery for the *bimah*. You might also consider corsages for the mother and grandmothers, and boutonnieres for ushers and the father and grandfathers. Table centerpieces and other floral decorations for the party add color and complete the look of the day. These may all be coordinated with the color scheme and/or theme you choose.

To do all of this with a minimum of fuss and expense, do your homework by talking to friends who have hired florists for their own children's Bnai Mitzvah. Get recommendations from your synagogue and others in your area.

You may want to keep things simple, or you may desire more elaborate flowers. Either way, you will want to be provided with the freshest flowers and foliage, and you will want the arrangements delivered to the site in plenty of time. Be sure to specify the exact time of delivery and setup for the flowers, for both the synagogue and the celebrations to follow.

When you meet with florists, ask to be shown photos of other similar events they have done. Also request information about any special effects they might do, such as special lighting with the flowers, balloons, unusual ribbons or containers, and floral arrangements on the *bimah* and at the reception.

One more tip: Be careful when you order flowers to use varieties that will not set off allergies in your guests. Those with a lot of pollen can leave people sneezing and coughing; discuss this with your florist. Another way to deal with this is to use silk or artificial arrangements, dried flowers, or some other kind of centerpiece.

The biggest drawback with floral arrangements is that they wither and die in just a few days. So, following the celebration, you may choose to give the centerpieces to honored guests to take home, or you can donate them to a children's center, hospital, or home for the elderly. Such a gift is always appreciated. If you involve your son or daughter in such a donation, the act becomes that much more meaningful.

Considering photography and videography

The photographer and videographer are important components of Bnai Mitzvah. The pictures taken will stay in your family for many years to come and will provide you with precious reminders of the service and celebration.

When you engage one of these professionals, ask to see some other events they have photographed. This way, you will have a better idea of their style. Find out if they are familiar with other Jewish celebrations and if they have taken pictures at other Bnai Mitzvah. You might also speak to your friends and others who have had Bnai Mitzvah recently. They will be good advisors for you when you make your selection. Your synagogue may also have a list of people for you to call.

You should be able to obtain quite a large number of photos to choose from after the party, including a large set of proofs, which often can be purchased as well.

Once you hire someone, be clear with them about what you want. If you have specific people you want photographed, make a list to give to the photographer and/or videographer. You may also wish to have the videographer go table by table at the party to interview friends and family. These short little testimonials make lovely keepsakes for your family later on.

Find out if the person you engage enjoys working with youngsters and has had experience with other Bnai Mitzvah. If a photographer is gifted at taking pictures of scenery but not very familiar with getting teenagers to loosen up for the camera, you may have a problem.

We have already considered some of the policies of the synagogue and practices of photography/videography during the service. In most cases, in keeping with the religious aspect of the moment, flash photography is not allowed. In many congregations videography is permitted if it is done in an unobtrusive manner. You should double-check with your synagogue to be sure of the requirements, and make sure that the people you hire are well aware of the restrictions. If you are more liberal in observance, and if your synagogue permits, you may wish to have photos taken at the Shabbat dinner on Friday evening. However, in Conservative and Orthodox congregations this is generally not acceptable.

If you want formal photographs for an album, it is best to allow time before or after the service for these. There should be pictures taken of the family, the rabbi and cantor, visiting family members, and friends. And if you are having a Sunday brunch to cap off the weekend, then by all means have your photographer take some more formal poses as well as many candid shots of you and your family.

During the party following the service, especially if it is a formal dinner on Saturday night, you will want many formal and informal photographs. A good photographer will know how to capture the moment without being in everybody's way.

In addition to the professional photographer, friends or family members can take photos for you. These will often be candid shots of your family and friends and will capture special moments in a spontaneous way. And still one more way to get some great candid photos, is to place disposable cameras on each table for your guests to use throughout the party.

The success of your party will depend in large part upon your preparation. Knowing ahead of time what to expect and how to proceed will go a long way in allowing you and your family to enjoy every moment of this once-in-a-lifetime experience.

Chapter 8

A

Party-Planning

Timeline

As you can see, Bnai Mitzvah parties don't just "happen." They take thoughtful consideration and careful organization. Whether the Bat Mitzvah celebration is a simple affair or a more complicated one, the secret to success is planning. Keeping this in mind, your preparation begins far in advance. In this chapter we present an overall timeline for making the party wonderful from start to finish. The framework given here is for a rather elaborate celebration, beginning on Friday evening and lasting throughout the weekend. You may utilize every part of the plan, or pick and choose just those segments that suit your situation and/or your budget.

(For much of the information included in this chapter, I am indebted to Leslie Reisfeld, who graciously shared her planning strategies with me, and who is probably the most organized Bat Mitzvah parent on this planet!)

So, hold onto your *kippah*, be brave, and here we go!

Two to three years ahead

∠ Discuss with your spouse and child how each of you feels about this life-cycle event. Explore your expectations and responsibilities. Be sure to consider ways to enhance the moment—through *tzedakah*, opportunities for extended study, and meaningful contributions to your synagogue and/or larger Jewish community.

∠ Reserve the date at the synagogue. (For detailed information about choosing a date, please refer to Chapter 2.) If you are not holding the service in a synagogue, decide exactly where you would like it to be, and reserve that date and place.

∠ Research photographers and, if possible, decide on one.

∠ Choose your videographer, if possible.

∠ Begin researching entertainment for the party. Select and possibly book the DJ or band, if you are going to hire one. Do not wait too long on this, as these people get booked up early.

One to two years ahead

∠ Now that your child is actively preparing, have another serious conversation with him or her and with your spouse concerning the importance of this event in your lives. Discuss its religious significance and decide on specific avenues of *mitzvot* observance and acts of *tikkun olam* (repairing the world) for each of you. Then clarify what each of you wants for the reception.

∠ Talk to each other about finances. Be realistic.

∠ Draw up a guest list.

∠ With the above in mind, research the different places in your area to hold the reception: a hotel, a private club, the social hall at the synagogue, or a less formal setting. If you prefer and the numbers permit, consider holding the party at home or in your garden.

∠ Start to collect names from friends about the following: caterers, balloon providers, florists, entertainment, ideas for favors, rental companies for linens and party supplies, party planners, party decor, and places to purchase invitations and paper goods. Decide if you will need or want any of these.

∠ If you have not already done so, and if appropriate, book your DJ and/or band, Karaoke equipment, magician, or other children's entertainment.

∠ Inform your out-of-town family and close friends of the date, and ask them to reserve it.

Nine to 12 months ahead

∠ Reserve the place where you want to hold the party. (If the place you choose is a very popular one, you may need to do this even earlier.) If it is to be at a hotel, you may want a separate area for cocktails and hors d'oeuvres before sitting down to luncheon or dinner in the main dining room or ballroom. Some parents arrange an adjacent room for the youngsters during the cocktail hour so they can have their own refreshments in an appropriate atmosphere. (A suggestion: If you are having a cocktail hour, keep it short. The emphasis should not be on the drinks, but on the opportunity to gather together and share the festivities. Consider the message you are giving the youngsters in attendance, and remember that this is in celebration of your child.)

∠ Reserve a block of rooms at a hotel for out-of-town guests. This may be at the same hotel where you are holding the party, or nearby. Be sure to take into account those guests who may be *shomrei Shabbat* (strictly observant of the Sabbath). These guests will not drive on the Sabbath, and you may have to be creative about accommodations for them if your community does not lend itself to such Shabbat observance. If a hotel is not within walking distance of the synagogue, you may wish to arrange to put them up as house guests of friends or family who do live nearby.

∠ If you decide to hold events at the synagogue, reserve the necessary space for the following: a Friday night dinner; the *oneg Shabbat* on Friday evening after services; the *kiddush*-luncheon following services on Saturday morning; dinner and festivities on Saturday evening. You may also want to set aside a room for formal photographs of the family prior to the service. All of this should be arranged with the administrator or other responsible person at your congregation well in advance.

If your congregation is small, things become a little more time-consuming because you may have to do much of the actual setup and take-down yourself, or with help from family and friends.

∠ Begin to finalize your guest list.

∠ Finalize ideas with your child about the type of party, theme (if you wish to have one), decor, party favors, and so forth.

∠ Interview and select a party-planner (if you wish to engage one). Party planners take the hassle out of preparations by doing all the leg-work for you. They find out what you would like and get it for you. They also do the follow-up and take care of all the details. They charge a fee, but many busy people find them indispensable.

∠ Find a place to rent decorations.

∠ Interview and select a florist. When you are planning floral decorations for the synagogue service, don't forget to order flowers for the *bimah*. You may also wish to have corsages for grandmothers and other specially honored family members. If your florist is to handle other decorations for the party—such as balloons, party favors, and centerpieces—be sure to go over these details together so you are both clear about what you have in mind.

∠ Begin to shop for invitations and such paper goods as thank-you notes and place cards. Inquire about delivery dates for these items, availability, calligraphy, and so on. (For more information about invitations, please see Chapter 7.)

∠ Interview and select the caterer for the Friday night Shabbat dinner, the Saturday *kiddush*-luncheon, and Sunday brunch or luncheon. (For specifics about caterers, please refer to Chapter 7.)

Six to nine months ahead

∠ Communicate consistently with the rabbi/cantor or Bnai Mitzvah specialist to be sure your child is progressing properly in order to avoid any undue stress as the time draws near.

∠ Order the invitations. Be sure you order extra invitations and plenty of extra envelopes in case you make mistakes in addressing them.

∠ When you include the RSVP card for the party, you may have the guests indicate their food preferences by checking one of the choices available. Stipulate if the food will be kosher, and arrange a vegetarian option, if possible. (Enter this information on your index cards or in your computer, as well.)

∠ Order the rest of the paper goods and stationery items. This includes thank-you notes (if not already purchased) and imprinted items such as napkins, ribbons, *kippot*, party favors, and so on.

∠ Go over the details with the catering service at the hotel or other party hall. Be sure to consider layout of the room, number of tables, place for the band or DJ, head table, and color of tablecloths and napkins. It is also a good idea to have a separate table in a corner of the room for people to leave their gifts. If you are having guests bring canned food or other donations for charitable causes as part of the celebration, be sure to have a few large containers, clearly labeled, for such items in one corner of the room.

∠ Speak with your caterer about your menu selection for the Shabbat dinner, *oneg Shabbat*, *kiddush*-luncheon, and Sunday brunch. If you have an opportunity to taste some of the menu selections, do so. (Your child will love participating in this part of the planning!)
At this time, also finalize whether you are going to have a separate kids' menu at the party. If the group of teenagers you invite would prefer pizza or hamburgers and fries to fancy fare, you may wish to accommodate them.

∠ Send out save-the-date postcards to out-of-town friends and family. If you are inviting many people coming from across the country, it is helpful to get an idea of just how many will actually attend. This is especially important if you are setting aside a block of hotel rooms for your guests.

∠ Refine your guest list.

∠ Order the party favors. These may coordinate with the party theme, reflect a special hobby or interest of your child, or be personalized for the guests. One family had a son who was a baseball fan. Their favors were baseballs signed by some players on the local team. Another couple whose daughter was a budding pianist gave out rolled up sheet music of favorite Jewish tunes, tied with imprinted ribbon and flowers. Miniature boxes of Elite chocolate from Israel or other sweets imprinted with your child's name are always big hits. The possibilities are endless and may be adjusted to every budget. Use your imagination to select just the right little memento.

∠ If you can include party favors or centerpieces that can be recycled for worthy causes, do so. One family had small stacks of children's books tied with decorative ribbons and topped with balloons and lollipops in the middle of each table. After the party, the centerpieces were taken to a nearby children's hospital.

∠ Select a *tallit* and *kippah* for your child, as appropriate. Also, if your youngster is going to lay *tefillin*, get them now. In some observant communities, the *tefillin* are presented three months before Bnai Mitzvah so the student can begin to practice fulfilling this commandment and grow accustomed to using them. However, it is a good idea to purchase a set early to keep them ready. In traditional Jewish families, it is customary for the father to teach the child how to lay *tefillin* before the coming of age. If you are not comfortable doing this and your child will be laying *tefillin*, ask your rabbi or cantor to teach your child how to do it properly. You may also consider asking someone in your family who is knowledgeable about the procedure. If you have a grandparent who lays *tefillin*, it is a special tribute and very meaningful to pass the *mitzvah* along in this way.

∠ Consider the needs of your out-of-town guests: Begin to create printed sets of directions or maps from the airport and/or hotel to the synagogue, including travel time from the hotel to the synagogue and then to the reception. Have extra copies of the itinerary of the weekend on hand. Discuss transportation. Will guests use taxis? A shuttle bus? Private cars? Limousines? The choice will depend upon the number of people, the distance between the hotel and the synagogue, and your budget. It is even possible to rent a small bus to transport people from one point to another, eliminating worries about parking and getting lost in traffic. Begin to think about welcome baskets for the people who will be staying at a hotel. Will you have anyone staying at your house? If so, be sure you have enough linens, toiletries and other personal items for their use.

∠ Talk with your child about a candle-lighting ceremony. This is a popular ritual at Bnai Mitzvah parties, paying tribute to those who are important in the child's life by having them come up and light one of thirteen candles in honor of the child. Consider the following: Who would they like to honor? In what order would you prefer to call them up for the ceremony? Which friends or relatives will be honored at the service, and which at the party? What songs would you like the band or DJ to play as each person (or group of people) comes up to light a candle? What are some creative tributes your son or daughter can compose to honor these special people? (For more about the candle-lighting ceremony, please refer to Chapter 9.)

∠ If you choose not to have a candle-lighting ceremony, in what other ways might you honor special people? Some suggestions: a photo display, flowers for special guests, balloons with their names on them, or little tribute booklets put at each person's place.

∠ It is also a popular idea to have a large photo or poster of your child set up on an easel at the entrance to the party. A felt-tip pen is attached to the easel with a long ribbon so that people can write messages of congratulations as they enter the party. If you decide to do this, you should arrange a photography session early to take the picture. Or you may prefer to use an old baby picture, blown up to poster size. Allow plenty of time to obtain the poster or enlarged photo.

Four to six months ahead

∠ Review your six-to-nine-month list and complete anything still to be done.

∠ If you have not yet done so, speak to the rabbi, cantor, or Hebrew tutor to be certain that your child is on track in her studies. If it's necessary, don't wait too long to get extra help.

∠ Finalize your guest list. Speak to your calligrapher, if you have one, to find out if the names must be in any particular order for inscription. Check all the addresses and zip codes to be sure they are current and correct.

∠ Begin a preliminary draft of your speech to your child at the service.

∠ Select extra songs or meditations to be included in the service.

∠ Make your final selection of family members for *aliyot* and other pulpit honors. Either you or your child should write or phone each person to request their participation. Once they let you know that they will take part, find out each one's Hebrew name. Keep these on a list in the proper order so that you can give it to the rabbi or cantor several days before the service.

∠ Finalize the candle-lighting ceremony.

∠ If you have not already done so, send out-of-town family and friends information on the hotel and the agenda for the weekend. (This is especially important so that people can book flights early and arrange other transportation as needed.)

∠ Have your son or daughter start a list of their favorite songs for the DJ or band.

∠ Take the invitations to the calligrapher, or begin to address them yourself. Calligraphers usually require one to three weeks, but it could take longer, depending upon the number of invitations. Be sure to allow time for mistakes. If you are writing them, don't leave this for the last minute, as this task is time-consuming.

Two to three months ahead

∠ Meet with the temple administrator to discuss the details of arrangements at the synagogue: the reserved rooms, the provisions for videography and photography, the sound system for tape-recording the service, and the flower delivery. Also clarify what the kitchen provides at the synagogue and what your caterer should bring. Complete any financial matters and deposits with the synagogue. Finalize the details for the *oneg Shabbat* on Friday night following the service, if that is applicable. Double-check the calendar at the synagogue to be sure there are no conflicts.

∠ Finalize flowers for the synagogue—both for the service and for the *oneg Shabbat* and/or the *kiddush*-luncheon.

∠ Finalize the flowers, balloons, decorations, party favors, setup, and so forth for all events and for the main party.

∠ Make preliminary arrangements to donate the flowers, balloons, decorations, and centerpieces/party favors to charitable organizations following the celebration. You may wish to contact these organizations ahead of time to alert them as to the date and to make sure they will accept your gifts.

∠ Finalize the guest list. Add any last-minute names to give to the calligrapher, if necessary.

∠ Go shopping! Treat your child and yourself to some new clothes to celebrate the occasion. Attire should be rather formal.

∠ Stuff, seal, and stamp the invitations when they come back from the calligrapher. Take one to the post office to check the amount of postage required. After all your hard work, you don't want the invitations to come back to you because you didn't put enough stamps on them.

∠ Meet with your photographer and videographer, giving them a list of who you want photographed. Do not leave this to chance. (You might feel quite upset if someone you love is not included in any of the pictures, especially someone who is elderly or who lives far away.) Update this list as the RSVPs come in.

∠ Arrange for the Friday night *oneg Shabbat,* and check the details with the synagogue staff. Are you having this catered? Will you have friends bake? Will you be baking the goodies? It helps to ask one or two friends to coordinate the baking and bringing of food and beverages for the *oneg* and/or the *kiddush*-luncheon. If applicable, make sure you order enough *challah* for both Shabbat dinner and the *oneg.* Be sure there is kosher wine for Shabbat dinner and *Kiddush* on Friday evening.

Six to eight weeks ahead

∠ Mail the invitations. It's a good idea to take them to the post office and hand-cancel them. (This will prevent your beautiful invitations from getting ripped or crumpled by the postal machines!)

∠ Go over your earlier lists and make sure everything is done.

∠ Meet with the DJ or band leader and discuss the schedule of the party: Israeli folk dancing, chair games, when to eat, adults' dance time, kids' dance time, candle-lighting time, other special moments, specific songs your child has requested, and the general tone of the celebration. You may want to request that the DJ or band take a break during the meal, or play quietly, so that people can talk. Many a party has turned into a disaster because the music was continually too loud.

∠ Finalize the candle-lighting ceremony and other special tributes during the celebration. Are there going to be telegrams read? Poems or songs offered in honor of the child? Video montages of the her growing-up years? Family scrapbooks on display? Other entertainment by members of the family or close friends? (See Chapter 9.)

∠ If you have not yet done so, arrange a food-tasting with the caterer and/or hotel, and finalize the menu selections. Order a few extra plates, in case people show up at the party unexpectedly. (Usually, the caterer and the hotel will provide you with extra servings to allow for this.) Also, remember to order meals for the DJ and/or band, the videographer, and the photographer. You should have a quiet place for them to enjoy their meals during their intermission.

∠ Buy anything you are personally providing, such as wine or soft drinks.

∠ If you are having a *Havdalah* service for the close of Shabbat, either write an original one with the help of your child or use one from the prayer book. Get a braided *Havdalah* candle; a spice box filled with fresh whole cinnamon, whole cloves, and allspice; and a *Kiddush* cup with kosher wine. And don't forget to bring some matches! (For more about the *Havdalah* service, see Chapter 9.)

∠ Write a letter to your out-of-towners with the schedule for the weekend and directions (if not included in the invitation). Tell them how happy and honored you are that they will be sharing this *simcha* with you and your family. This is also something your child can do. It is especially touching to elderly relatives and friends if they receive such a note from your daughter, and it brings the child into the process in an important way.

∠ Keep track of the RSVPs as they come in. Keep a record of the gifts sent, and encourage your child to acknowledge any gifts upon receiving them.

∠ Write a note to your child's teachers explaining the significance of this event in your youngster's life, and apologizing for possible absence from school. You may want to send a similar note to athletic coaches, music teachers, and the like. If you know the dates and times of last-minute rehearsals, include this information in the letter. Also request any make-up assignments so your child can plan ahead. This may relieve some last-minute pressure on everyone.

Four weeks ahead

∠ By now you should have a pretty good idea of who is coming to each part of the celebration, so you can begin preliminary seating arrangements and other special details.

∠ Meet again with the hotel, caterer, DJ or band, party-planner, balloon provider, and florist.

∠ Purchase items for welcome baskets for out-of-town guests to be placed in their hotel rooms.

∠ Keep track of RSVPs and gifts. Encourage your child to keep up with the thank-you notes.

∠ Finalize and print up the service booklet, if you are having one. If you have created your own prayer book, do a final proof and have it printed. If you are having any other special mementos printed, have them completed at this time.

∠ Finish writing the parents' remarks in the service.

∠ You may wish to send an information letter to your child's friends who will be attending, explaining the significance and time frame of the service and reception and advising them of the proper attire and etiquette. (For a sample letter, see Appendix I.)

∠ Some families send out a follow-up note to guests who have indicated they will be attending. This letter thanks people for coming and serves as an opportunity to give them more information and to advise them of any special circumstances. For example, if your synagogue has restrictions about Shabbat observance, this is a good time to inform people who may be unfamiliar with such rules. (These might include required attire and the prohibition of smoking in or around the building, handling money, or using a telephone, camera, or tape recorder.) Anything that you can do to make people feel comfortable will be appreciated. If you are making any special requests of your guests to bring canned goods or other *tzedakah* items, you may include a little card indicating this when you mail your follow-up notes.

Ideally, you included transportation information with your invitations, as mentioned earlier. But if you did not, then you may do so in the same letter. You should include details about car rentals, transportation to and from the airport or train station, and other specifics. If you did not include a map and sets of directions when you sent out the invitations, you may do so now. You should clearly indicate how to reach the hotel or other place where they will be staying, the synagogue or other location for the service, and the place of the celebration. You might also wish to include directions to your home. List phone numbers for all the destinations. Some people also indicate how long the travel time will be from one point to another.

If you have people coming from out of town who have never been to your community before, you may wish to include in this letter a brochure of local attractions and points of interest. This may be their one chance to see the Golden Gate Bridge, the Statue of Liberty, or the Grand Canyon. If they know what is available to them, they may want to arrange their visit to include such places.

∠ Double-check to make sure you have not left anyone off the guest list. Also, if you have mailed invitations to people who have not responded, you may wish to call them to be sure they received them. Things do get lost in the mail, and it is easier to correct it with one phone call than try to explain later. If you prefer, you might ask a close friend or someone in the family to follow up for you.

∠ Write the place cards. Be sure you have extras, just in case.

Two weeks ahead

∠ Finalize your seating arrangements. One easy way to do this is to make a mock-up of a round table by using sticky notes on a paper plate. Another solution is to use a large poster board and draw circles on it to diagram the tables, then label the place-settings with small sticky notes or writing in light pencil. Some people prefer to do this on the computer.

∠ Hold a final meeting with the caterer, hotel, and other providers.

∠ Give the final list of "who's who" to your photographer and videographer. Remind them of any restrictions set by the synagogue during the service.

∠ Finalize the candle-lighting with your child. Give the list of honorees to the DJ, band leader, or master of ceremonies.

∠ Finalize the schedule of the celebration with the DJ/band. Give copies of this to the photographer, videographer, catering manager, and head waiter.

∠ Get your house really clean. (You may want to repeat this just before the big day.)

One week ahead

∠ Stay calm.

∠ Be sure your child attends the last-minute rehearsals and/or run-throughs with the rabbi and cantor.

∠ Keep track of last-minute RSVPs, and adjust the seating arrangements accordingly.

∠ Assemble the welcome baskets for out-of-towners, and drop them off at the hotel one or two days before guests arrive.

∠ Order some fresh flowers for your clean house.

On the big day

∠ Try to spend some quiet time with your child, alone. Take precious moments to talk about how special this time is in your lives, and how proud you are of the effort put into this moment. Express your love for your youngster and your joy in having this opportunity to celebrate this milestone together.

∠ Get to bed early the night before, if possible, setting aside all items needed for the service: *tallitot, kippot, siddurim,* a copy of your child's *d'var Torah,* and a copy of your speech to your child.

∠ Be sure you and your youngster eat a good breakfast. It will be a long time between meals.

∠ Get to the synagogue on time or early and advise other family members to do the same.

∠ Allow time to touch base with the rabbi and/or cantor.

∠ Try to relax and enjoy!

Afterwards

∠ Take time to talk about the good feelings and magic moments you have enjoyed together as a family.

∠ Remember to praise your child for this accomplishment. Speak with each other about what this life passage has meant to each of you. (This is often an opportunity for young people to express appreciation to their parents for all the love and support given to prepare for this occasion. Some youngsters write notes to their mothers and fathers, saying the words that are difficult for them to articulate in person. Cherish such heartfelt sentiments; they are precious indeed.)

∠ Arrange to take any donated items (such as canned food, books, or other materials for the needy) to the designated *tzedakah* organizations. Be sure your child does this with you in order to more fully appreciate the act of giving connected with the Bat Mitzvah.

∠ Send thank-you letters and gifts to friends who helped in special ways.

∠ Write thank you notes and make a contribution to the synagogue in appreciation of your rabbi, cantor, Bnai Mitzvah specialist, and other staff.

∠ Help your child complete the remaining thank-you notes.

∠ Update any record keeping you have done. Make notes on what worked and what didn't.

∠ Pay any outstanding bills.

∠ Write thank-you notes to your vendor/providers. Consider small gifts to show your appreciation for outstanding service.

∠ Order pictures, video, etc.

∠ If possible, get away for a weekend of rest and relaxation. You've earned it!

Chapter 9

Making Special Memories

So much happens during Bnai Mitzvah! There are so many elements, all coming one right after another, that afterwards it is hard to remember anything. For your child, once it is over it will all be like a pretty dream. After all the months or years of preparation, the actual service seems to go by in a flash, and the party is one big blur. For you, the parent, there should be great satisfaction in seeing things come to fruition, but looking back you may find big gaps in what you can recall. You may not have been able to see everything, and the things you did see were a jumble of noise, music, smiles and tears.

If it is difficult for the parent and child to remember, think how hard it must be for a grandparent or close friend. And even more so for guests who may not know your family all that well. They may go home having had a lovely time, but unable to articulate what was so special about the experience.

Bnai Mitzvah are more than just collections of unrelated moments and more than the sum total of the preparation, service, and celebration. When each of these components is invested with meaning, the impact is far greater than the actual event, itself. And just as the significance of Bnai Mitzvah can be heightened by special moments in the service, so too, the party can be elevated by creating opportunities for unique moments to be remembered for a lifetime.

Chapter 6 offered suggestions about creating memorable moments during the prayer service. This chapter offers ideas for making beautiful memories throughout the rest of the weekend. You may incorporate all of them as they are, or they may be tailored to your tastes and needs.

At the Friday evening Shabbat dinner

From the very beginning when family and friends come together for the Shabbat evening meal, you have opportunities for making memories. Here are some suggestions:

∠ Sometime before the date of the Shabbat dinner, ask that people write short poems in honor of your child. These can be read at the dinner and then placed in an album to be presented to the child during the meal.

∠ Another variation of this is to ask people to sign a "wish book" for the child. This can be done at the very beginning of the evening, before Shabbat actually begins. These messages make wonderful keepsakes that you and your family will treasure long after the weekend is over.

∠ If your child has a favorite Shabbat food, incorporate that into the menu. For example, one boy grew up loving his grandmother's noodle *kugel*. It was served every Friday night and on every Jewish holiday, with the exception of Passover. When it came time for the family to gather for the Shabbat dinner the night before the Bar Mitzvah, his grandmother's noodle *kugel* was right at the top of the menu, making the evening very special for him.

∠ If you are inviting a large crowd to the Shabbat dinner, find ways to help them get acquainted with each other. Print up some name tags and allow time for pre-dinner socializing. You might even plan time for a short ice-breaker game if people are coming from various parts of the country and might not know one another.

One easy ice-breaker is to ask that people get acquainted with two new individuals at the dinner, and then ask them to introduce these two people to the rest of the group. Another idea is to print up individual tidbits of information about each guest, distribute them at the beginning of the evening, and have everyone try to match up the information with a person who is there. Then share the information with the rest of the guests at the start of the meal. For example: "A woman who knew the Bar Mitzvah from birth" (Mom); or "A man who taught the Bar Mitzvah to ride horseback during last year's summer vacation" (Uncle Harry); or "Someone who made the *kippah* the Bar Mitzvah is wearing this evening" (Grandma).

∠ If you have quite a few out of town guests, do a little "Jewish geography" to help people get acquainted. Put a large map on one wall and ask people to place colored push-pins in it to show where they are from. Then ask them to find others at the dinner who came from the same area. It is another great ice-breaker.

∠ If you would like people to mix and mingle, have place cards printed up for each person, seating them with others they may not know very well. Since everyone will be together for the whole weekend, this is a perfect opportunity to initiate new friendships or renew old acquaintances.

∠ At the beginning of the Shabbat meal, you and your spouse can introduce yourselves, your child, and your immediate family. It is most appropriate to ask your child to open the evening with a few words of welcome. Then you might go around the table and request that people share something about themselves in relation to the child who is being feted.

∠ Ask one or both of the grandmothers to light the Shabbat candles at the start of the dinner, and accord the honor of reciting the *Kiddush* to the grandfathers. (These blessings are found in Chapter 4.)

∠ Make arrangements for the traditional washing of the hands before reciting *Ha-Motzi.* If there are too many people and not enough time for each person to wash his/her hands, sometimes one person symbolically washes for everyone at the table. You will need tables in the corners of the room. Under the tables are small wastebaskets, and on top are placed some large bowls, disposable hand towels, and cold water in containers that do not have pouring spouts. Remind people not to talk from the time they wash their hands until they join together in chanting the blessing over the bread. (The procedure for ritually washing the hands and the blessing to be recited may be found in Chapter 4.)

∠ Have *challot* on the table, and encourage everyone to join in *Ha-Motzi*. (You may also find this blessing in Chapter 4.)

∠ Make time for the traditional Shabbat blessings for all the children present. On Shabbat evening it is customary for parents to place their hands on their children's heads and recite the following words, included here for your reference:

Parents' Blessing for the Children

* For sons:

  Y'sim-cha Eh-lo-him k'Efraim v'ki Menasheh.

  May God make you as Efraim and Menashe.

* For daughters:

  Y'sim-ech Eh-lo-him k'Sarah, Rivka, Rachel v'Leah.

  May God make you as Sarah, Rebecca, Rachel and Leah.

* Concluding blessing for boys and girls:

  Y'va-reh-che-cha Adonai V'yish-mi-rech-a. Ya'er Adonai pa-nav eh-le-cha v'chu-neh-kah. Yi-sa Adonai pa-nav eh-lech-ah v'ya-sem l'cha sha-lom.

  May the Lord bless you and protect you. May the Lord watch over you and be gracious to you. May the Lord favor you and grant you peace.

∠ Print copies of *zemirot* (songs) to be sung at the dinner. This helps people participate, especially if they are unfamiliar with Hebrew. When you sing these songs between courses at the dinner, have someone in the family lead the singing to make things more personal and lively. To make it easier to follow along and get in the spirit of *Shabbat*, include some old favorites when you choose the melodies.

Some of the most popular Shabbat *zemirot* are *"Shalom Aleichem," "Bim Bom,"* and *"Oseh Shalom."* Here are the words:

* Shalom Aleichem

  Sha-lom a-lei-chem, mal-a-chei ha-sha-reit, mal-a-chei El-yon,
  Mi-meh-lech ma-l'chei ha-m'la-chim, ha-ka-dosh ba-ruch hu.

  Bo-a-chem l'sha-lom, mal-a-chei ha-sha-lom, mal-a-chei El-yon,
  Mi-meh-lech mal-a-chei ha-m'la-chim, ha-ka-dosh ba-ruch hu.

*Ba-r'chu-ni l'sha-lom, mal-a-chei ha-sha-lom, mal-a-chei El-yon,
Mi-meh-lech mal-a-chei ha-m'la-chim, ha-ka-dosh ba-ruch hu.
Tzei-t'chem l'sha-lom, mal-a-chei ha-sha-lom, mal-a-chei El-yon,
Mi-meh-lech mal-a-chei ha-m'la-chim, ha-ka-dosh ba-ruch hu.*

Peace be to you, O ministering angels, messengers of the Most High, the supreme King of kings, the Holy One, blessed is He.

Enter in peace, O messengers of peace, messengers of the Most High, the supreme King of kings, the Holy One, blessed is He.

Bless me with peace, O messengers of peace, messengers of the Most High, the supreme King of kings, the Holy One, blessed is He.

Depart in peace, O messengers of peace, messengers of the Most High, the supreme King of kings, the Holy One, blessed is He.

* Bim Bom

*Bim bom, bim bim bim bom, bim bim bim bim bim bom. (Repeat)
Shabbat Shalom! Hey! Shabbat Shalom Hey! Shabbat, Shabbat, Shabbat, Shabbat Shalom. (Repeat)*

* Oseh Shalom

O-seh sha-lom, bi-m'ro-mav, hu ya-a-seh sha-lom a-lei-nu, v'al kol Yis-ra-el, v'i-m'ru: A-mein.

May the One who causes peace to reign in the high heavens let peace descend on us, on all Israel, and all the world. Amen.

∠ During the meal, ask someone from the family to give a short *d'rash* (homily) or tell a moving Jewish story. This is a time-honored Jewish custom, following the Talmudic teaching that a meal with words of Torah allows God to become part of the gathering.

∠ At the close of the Shabbat dinner, ask everyone to join in for *Birkat Ha' Mazon* (Grace after meals). The directive for the Grace is found in the Torah. It is written: "When you have eaten your fill, give thanks to God for the good land which God has given you" (*Deuteronomy* 8:10). It is recited after any meal that began with *Ha-Motzi* (the blessing over bread). It is customary to give the honor of leading *Birkat Ha-Mazon* to a guest. If you ask guests to lead the Grace, be sure to give them plenty of notice. Here again, make the words available so that everyone can take part. An abridged version follows for your reference:

A short version of the
Birkat Ha-Mazon

(This version of the *Birkat Ha-Mazon* is from the Reform *siddur*, *Gates of Prayer for Shabbat and Weekdays*, published by the Central Conference of American Rabbis and printed here with permission.)

(*Shir Ha-ma-a-lot* is sung before the Grace on Sabbath, holidays, and other festive occasions.)

Shir ha-ma-a-lot.
B'shuv Adonai
Et shi-vat Tzi-yon
Ha-yi-nu k'chol-mim.
Az yi-ma-lei s'chok pi-nu
U-l'sho-nei-nu ri-na,
Az yo-m'ru va-go-yim:
Hig-dil Adonai la-a-sot im ei-leh
Hig-dil Adonai la-a-sot i-ma-nu
Ha-yi-nu s'mei-chim!
Shu-vah Adonai et Sh'vi-tei-nu
Ka-a-fi-kim ba-neh-gev.
Ha-zo-r'im b'dim-a, b'ri-na yik-tzo-ru.
Ha-loch yei-lech u-va-cho,
No-sei meh-shech ha-za-ra,
Bo ya-vo v'ri-na no-sei a-lu-mo-tav.

A Pilgrim Song.
When God restored the exiles to Zion, it seemed like a dream. Our mouths were filled with laughter, our tongues with joyful song. Then they said among the nations: God has done great things for them. Yes, God is doing great things for us, and we are joyful. Restore our fortunes, O God, as streams revive the desert. Then those who have sown in tears shall reap in joy. Those who go forth weeping, carrying bags of seeds, shall come home with shouts of joy, bearing their sheaves. (Psalm 126)

* On weekdays begin here:
Leader:
Cha-vei-rim, va-cha-vei-rot, n'va-reich.

Friends, let us give thanks.

Group:
Y'hi-sheim Adonai m'vo-rach mei-a-ta v'ad o-lam!

Praised be the name of God, now and forever.

Leader: (The others respond, and the leader repeats:)
Y'hi sheim Adonai m'vorach mei-a-ta v'ad o-lam!

Praised be the name of God, now and forever.

Bi-r'shut ha-chevrah, n'vareich Eloheinu sheh-a-chal-nu mi-shelo.

Praised be our God, of whose abundance we have eaten.

Group:
Ba-ruch Eh-lo-hei-nu sheh-a-chal-nu mi-sheh-lo u-v'tu-vo cha-yi-nu.

Praised be our God, of whose abundance we have eaten, and by
whose goodness we live.

Leader and others:
Ba-ruch hu u'va-ruch sh'mo.

Praised be the Eternal God!

Ba-ruch a-ta Adonai Eh-lo-hei-nu meh-lech ha-o-lam,
ha-zan et ha-o-lam ku-lo b'tu-vo b'chein b'cheh-sed
u-v'ra-cha-mim. Hu no-tein leh-chem l'chol ba-sar, ki l'o-lam chas-do.
U-v'tu-vo ha-ga-dol ta-mid lo cha-sar-la-nu v'al yech-sar la-nu
ma-zon l'ol-am va-ed, ba-a-vur sh'mo ha-ga-dol. Ki hu Eil zan
u-m'far-neis la-kol
u-mei-tiv la-kol u-mei-chin ma-zon l'chol b'ri-yo-tav a-sher ba-ra.
Ba-ruch a-ta Adonai, ha-zan et ha-kol.

Sovereign God of the Universe, we praise You. Your goodness
sustains the world. You are the God of grace, love, and compassion,
the source of bread for all who live—for your love is everlasting.
Through Your great goodness we never lack for food; You provide
food enough for all.
For all this we thank You. Let Your praise ever be on the lips of all
who live, as it is written: "When you have eaten and are satisfied,
give praise to your God who has given you this good earth."

Ka-ka-tuv V'a-chal-ta v'sa-va-ta, u-vei-rach-ta et Adonai Eh-lo-heh-
cha al ha-a-retz ha-to-vah a-sher na-tan lach.

As it is written: When you have eaten and are satisfied, give praise
to your God who has given you this good earth.

U-v'nei Y'ru-sha-la-yim ir ha-ko-desh bi-m'hei-ra b'ya-mei-nu. Ba-
ruch a-ta Adonai, bo-neh b'ra-cha-mav Y'ru-sha-layim. A-mein.

Let Jerusalem, the holy city, be renewed in our time.
We praise You: in compassion You will rebuild Jerusalem. Amen.

* On Shabbat:

Ha-ra-cha-man, hu yan-chi-lei-nu yom sheh-ku-lo Sha-bat.

Merciful One, help us to see the coming of a time that is all Shabbat.

*O-seh sha-lom bi-m'ro-mav, hu ya-a-seh sha-lom a-lei-nu v'al kol
Yis-ra-el, v'i-m'ru: A-mein.*

May the Source of perfect peace grant peace to us, to all Israel, and
to all the world.

Adonai oz l'a-mo yi-tein, Adonai y'va-reich et a-mo va-sha-lom.

Eternal God: give strength to Your people. Eternal God: bless Your
people with peace.

∠ If your Shabbat dinner is being held in the social hall of the synagogue before *Kabbalat Shabbat* services, ask that everyone walk into
the sanctuary as a group and sit together during services.

∠ During services on Friday evening, acknowledge the special people
in attendance by giving them honors—such as distributing the
prayer books, reading various parts of the service, or opening and
closing the Ark doors, according to the custom of your congregation. In some synagogues the mother and/or grandmothers
recite the blessing over the Shabbat candles at the beginning of
the service and the father and/or grandfathers recite the *Kiddush*.
Find out from your rabbi or cantor what the possibilities are in
your congregation.

Making special memories
at the party and/or the Sunday brunch

Whether your party is an *oneg Shabbat* following a Friday night
service, a *kiddush*-luncheon after a Shabbat morning service, or a more
elaborate dinner–dance in the evening, there are several things you can
do to make it special. Here are a few suggestions, some of which will
also work well at a farewell Sunday brunch.

Involve your child in important ways

It is important to include your child in the planning for the celebration. It will give you all great pleasure to feel the joy of the occasion
together. Your youngster will have a wonderful time helping to choose

the invitations, the party favors, the theme, the color scheme, the menu, and all the extra touches that will make the celebration something never to be forgotten.

Even more important, your son or daughter will learn about hospitality and sharing the joy of the day with others. The celebration is a natural expression of the Jewish emphasis on *hachnasat orchim* (hospitality to guests), which is stressed in the Torah and in rabbinic writings. Ever since the biblical story when Abraham offered food to the three strangers who came to his tent after his circumcision, such hospitality has been a hallmark of Jewish life. It is integral to any Jewish gathering throughout the life cycle, from *brit milah* to burial. And it is especially appropriate in conjunction with celebrating the performance of a *mitzvah*.

On an even broader scale, it is hoped that as part of your preparation, you and your child will have many opportunities to consider what might be some ways to give to others. You should have some time to look into the organizations in your community and to pick one or two that are especially meaningful to you.

Before the big day, in order to extend the concept of caring for others, you may ask your child to give to Mazon—A Jewish Response to Hunger, donate some food to the local food bank, or send some money to an agency in your community to help feed the homeless.

✡ ✡ ✡

Cantor Ellen Schwab: *"Rabbis and cantors encourage families to 'keep the mitzvah in Bnai Mitzvah.' We teach and plead, we write parents' handbooks. Every movement publishes books, and parent meetings are held. I wonder if it is possible to change the tide, to reverse the trend. Do we even have a right to comment? I think we must comment. While the days of a bit of cake and a few coins may be long gone, balance, moderation, and mitzvot must be the key. Young people learn the joy of giving and the satisfaction that comes of making a difference in the world. Non-Jewish visitors glimpse a bit of what makes us unique. One of my proudest moments came when I asked a student about her upcoming celebration. She said, 'I'm just looking forward to the service, and giving my gift money to the animal shelter. I really have everything I need.' This was truly music to a cantor's ears."*

✡ ✡ ✡

If you would prefer guests to give other donations, you might include such a request in your party invitation. This way, people can plan ahead. If they do not wish to handle money on Shabbat, they can send their gifts directly to the organizations well in advance. Some families even stipulate some of the child's favorite charities so that people have a clear idea of what is important to the youngster.

Many families ask people to bring canned food to the party. Such donations are given to the needy, and if your child can be an active part of this endeavor, it will be very meaningful to him or her.

However you decide to do this, the important thing is to put the emphasis on the giving, rather than on the receiving. You will be sending a clear message to your child, your family, and your guests about your values. Judaism stands solidly upon the foundation of caring for others. Bnai Mitzvah are wonderful opportunities to build upon that foundation in a significant way.

Making *Havdalah* at the close of Shabbat

If you are holding the celebration on a Saturday night, it is most appropriate to include a *Havdalah* ceremony preceding the festivities. *Havdalah* marks the separation of Shabbat from the beginning of the week. On this special occasion, you will be bringing to a close this very special Shabbat when your son or daughter becomes an adult in the eyes of the Jewish community, so it is fitting to mark the occasion in this way. The service for *Havdalah* is short and simple, so everyone can participate. And it is a beautiful ritual that everyone will remember as a highlight of the day.

What you will need to make *Havdalah*

- Braided *Havdalah* candle. This symbolizes that everything in life is paired. Man and woman, work and rest, life and death—all are intertwined.

- *Besamim* container (a spice box). The spices remind us of the sweetness of Shabbat, and we inhale their scent to take some of that sweetness with us throughout the rest of the week.

- Cup of kosher wine for making *Kiddush*. Wine is always a symbol of joy in Judaism. We use a sweet kosher wine, carrying with us into the new week some of the Shabbat joy we have experienced.

● In addition to a spice box and *Kiddush* cup, you will need a holder for the *Havdalah* candle, perhaps with some aluminum foil or other shield around the bottom so that the hot wax does not drip onto the one holding it. (Once again, don't forget the matches!)

The *Havdalah* service

Havdalah was established by the rabbis of the Great Assembly (500–300 B.C.E.) and takes place at least one hour after sunset on Saturday night, or when three stars appear in the night sky. A rabbi, cantor, or layperson may lead it. If you have guests who are knowledgeable and feel comfortable leading the ceremony, enlist their participation ahead of time. Ask everyone to join in a large circle, joining arms together. (In Orthodox gatherings, women and men stand separately.) With the room in semi–darkness, have the Bar Mitzvah stand in the center of the circle, holding the braided candle while everyone hums a *niggun* (any Jewish melody sung without words) to begin the service.

The *Havdalah* ritual is as follows: The wine cup is held as the blessing over the wine is chanted. Then the blessing is recited over the spices. Passing the spice box around, the blessing is recited for fire, represented by the *Havdalah* candle. Following this blessing, all the participants hold up their hands and see the light of the candles reflected in their fingernails, making shadows on their palms to distinguish between light and darkness. The final blessings are chanted and the *Havdalah* service is completed.

Havdalah

(The version below is from the Reform *Gates of Prayer for Shabbat and Weekdays*, published by the Central Conference of American Rabbis, New York, 1994.)

Hi-nei Eil y'shu-ati, ev-tach v'lo ef-chad.
Ki o-zi v'zim-rat Ya Adonai, va-y'hi li li-shu-a.
U-sh'av-tem ma-yim b'sa-son mi-ma-a-y'nei ha-y'shu-a.
La-a-do-nai ha'y'shu-ah, al a-m'cha bir-cha-teh-cha, seh-la.
Adonai tz'va-ot i-ma-nu, mis-gav la-nu Eh-lo-hei Ya-a-kov, seh-la.
Adonai Tz'va-ot, ash-rei a-dam bo-tei-ach bach!
Adonai ho-shi-a; ha-meh-lech ya-a-nei-nu v'yom kor-ei-nu.
La-y'hu-dim ha-y'ta ora v'sim-cha v'sa-son vi-kar; kein ti-h'yeh la-nu
Kos y'shu-ot e-hsa, u-v'sheim Adonai ek-ra.

Behold, God is my Help, trusting in the Eternal One, I am not afraid.
For the Eternal One is my strength and my song, and has become my
salvation. With joy we draw water from the wells of salvation. The
Eternal One brings deliverance, and blessing to the people. The God of
the hosts of heaven is with us; the God of Jacob is our stronghold. God
of the hosts of heaven, happy is the one who trusts in You! Save us,
Eternal One; answer us, when we call upon You. Give us light and joy,
gladness and honor, as in the happiest days of our people's past. Then
shall we lift up the cup to rejoice in Your saving power, and call out
Your name in praise.

All join in the blessing over the wine:
Ba-ruch a-ta Adonai, Eh-lo-hei-nu meh-lech ha-o-lam bo-rei p'ri ha-ga-fen.
We praise you, Eternal God, Sovereign of the Universe, Creator of the
fruit of the vine.

(The leader does not drink the wine until after the final blessing
when *Havdalah* has been completed.)

All join in the blessing over the spices:
*Ba-ruch a-ta Adonai, Eh-lo-hei-nu meh-lech ha-o-lam, bo-rei mi-nei
v'sa-mim.*
We praise you, Eternal God, Sovereign of the Universe, Creator of the
world's spices.

The spice box, symbol of the "additional soul" that makes Shabbat
sweeter than the weekdays, is now circulated for all to smell.

All join in the blessing over the flames of the braided *Havdalah*
candle as it is raised:
*Ba-ruch a-ta Adonai, Eh-lo-hei-nu meh-lech ha-o-lam bo-rei m'o-rei
ha-eish.*
We praise You, Eternal God, Sovereign of the Universe, Creator of fire.

(Note: Words in brackets are omitted in Reconstructionist services.)
*Ba-ruch a-ta Adonai, Eh-lo-hei-nu meh-lech ha-o-lam, ha-mav-dil bein
ko-desh l'chol bein or l'cho-shech [bein Yis-ra-eil la-a-mim] bein yom
ha-sh'vi-i l'shei-shet y'mei ha-ma-a-seh. Ba-ruch a-ta Adonai ha-mav-dil
bein ko-desh l'chol.*
We praise You, Eternal God, Sovereign of the Universe: You make
distinctions, teaching us to distinguish the commonplace from the holy;
You create light and darkness, Israel and the nations, the seventh day
of rest and the six days of labor.
We praise you, O God: You call us to distinguish the commonplace from
the holy.

(Sip the wine or grape juice.)

At the conclusion of the *Havdalah* ceremony, the candle is extinguished, either in a little dish of the remaining wine, or by pouring some of the wine over the candle. The following passages are sung or said, and everyone proclaims *"Shavua tov!"* ("A good week!")

Ha-mav-dil bein ko-desh l'chol, cha-to-tei-nu hu yim-chol, Zar-ei-nu v'chas-pei-nu yar-beh ka-chol, v'cha-ko-cha-vim ba-lai-la.

May He who separates holy from mundane, pardon our sins, may He increase our offspring and our wealth like the grains of sand and like the stars at night.

Sha-vu-a tov...

A good week, a week of peace, may gladness reign, and joy increase.

Ei-li-ya-hu ha-na-vi. Ei-li-ya-hu ha-tish-bi.
Ei-li-ya-hu, Ei-li-ya-hu, Ei-li-ya-hu ha-gil-a-di.
Bi-m-hei-ra v'ya-mei-nu, ya-vo ei-lei-nu,
im Ma-shi-ach ben Da-vid, im Ma-shi-ach ben Da-vid.

Elijah the Prophet, the Tishbite, the Gileadite:
Come to us soon, to herald our redemption.

What about a theme for the party?

In earlier times, the theme for the day was the Bar Mitzvah itself. Nowadays, it has become common in some communities to have an additional theme for the celebration, coordinating all the elements of the party. It can be expressed in everything from the invitations, centerpieces, and party favors to the music, menu, and decorations.

The most appropriate themes are those that reflect Jewish content. They might include biblical heroes and heroines, modern Jewish stars, Israel old and new, Jewish holidays and festivals, famous Jewish communities of the world, and favorite Jewish music.

Another option is a theme based upon the child's interests. Almost any hobby or talent your youngster enjoys will make a suitable theme for the party. Music, sports, art, drama, science—all are adaptable for a theme.

It is important to involve your child in choosing and executing the theme for the party. After all, this is your child's celebration, and it can be a wonderful opportunity to create something together. The key here is to keep it in good taste and not allow it to overwhelm your child's place as the center of the day. The theme is meant to be a backdrop for the festivities, not the focal point of the party. So, be creative in coming up with some appropriate ways to express yourselves.

Other ways to make the celebration memorable

∠ Purchase several disposable cameras. Place one on each table, and ask that your guests be responsible for capturing everyone at their table on film. (Number each camera to correspond to the numbered tables, and when you have them turned in to you at the end of the party and later have them developed, you will be able to organize the photos easily.)

∠ If people have sent messages to the child, these can be read during the party. This is especially meaningful if family and/or friends live far away and are not be able to join you in person.

∠ Create a family album, filling it with your child's baby pictures, elementary school and religious school report cards, and other mementos. Put it on a table in a place of honor, perhaps surrounded by flowers. Invite your guests to take turns looking through it. Add to it any messages written to your child for people to enjoy throughout the celebration.

The candle-lighting ceremony

It has become a popular custom to hold a candle-lighting ceremony, honoring those who have played an important part in the life of your child. Many people make an elaborate presentation of this, and it can be quite meaningful. You will need 13 large tapers. (You can color coordinate the colors with your theme, or you can use the Jewish colors of blue and white.) Place the unlit candles in candle-holders arranged on a specially decorated table, perhaps edged with flowers. Have this table placed in the front of the room, and call upon the Bar or Bat Mitzvah to come up and lead the ceremony. In a large gathering, be sure to have a microphone for this, so your child can be heard easily. For safety, have a little shield or extra piece of aluminum foil placed at the base of each candle.

As indicated earlier, decide before the celebration who will be called up and in what order, what music you play as they are called up to light their candle, and what your child will say in tribute to them. All of this must be coordinated with the DJ or band leader so that it flows smoothly. You may choose to have original short poems written in each person's honor, or simply a short statement of why they are important in your child's life. You may have people come up individually or in groups to light a taper from the lit candle held by your child.

Usually, you call up people in the following order, but there is no hard-and-fast rule and you may choose to include others instead:

1. Grandparents.

2. Aunts and uncles.

3. Cousins.

4. Closest friends and/or classmates.

5. Rabbi, cantor, and/or Bnai Mitzvah specialist.

6. Religious school and Hebrew school teachers.

7. Regular school teachers.

8. People who are important in your child's extracurricular activities (such as coaches, scout masters, Jewish youth group advisors).

9. Friends of the family who have come from far away.

10. Family members who have come from far away.

11. Brothers and sisters.

12. Parents.

13. The Bar or Bat Mitzvah, who places the 13th candle in its holder.

Following the ceremony, the child may blow out all the candles.

The Sunday brunch or luncheon

As the celebration winds down, the people who are included in the closing parts of the occasion are often those who are the closest family and friends, and also those who have come from far away to share in your joy. Here are a few suggestions for making these final hours even more special:

- Print up a small keepsake booklet for each guest. This booklet may have a list of the names and addresses of all who are at the closing brunch or luncheon so that people can stay in touch afterwards. It might also contain a short message from the parents and Bar Mitzvah expressing appreciation that everyone could be together. It should also contain the words to *Ha-Motzi* and *Birkat Ha-Mazon* so that people can follow along.

- Have an open microphone during the meal, and ask everyone to take turns briefly sharing their thoughts about the weekend and their wishes for the future.

- If someone at the earlier events of the weekend took candid photos, have these mounted on one wall so people can enjoy them during the luncheon and take them home as mementos.

- If you took a short amateur video of the weekend, show this during the luncheon.

- Make a donation in honor of all your guests to a favorite Jewish charity, and during the brunch inform them of this gift in their honor.

- Take time during the brunch or luncheon to speak with each of your special guests and thank them for coming. Encourage your son or daughter to do the same.

- Remember to start your meal with *Ha-Motzi* and conclude it with *Birkat Ha-Mazon*.

- Close the celebration with a few favorite Jewish songs.

The moments we share with loved ones during our lifetimes seem never to be enough, and are therefore precious to us. Our family celebrations are opportunities to express the love we feel for those who are dear to us. And whatever we can do to invest our celebrations with meaning helps us to heighten the significance of those moments. The memories you create during your children's Bnai Mitzvah will elevate the experience in ways that you will always remember.

Part Four:

Other Possibilities

Chapter 10

Alternatives to The Traditional Synagogue Service

If not in a synagogue, then where?

While Bnai Mitzvah traditionally take place in a synagogue, some families hold services elsewhere. A family may choose a natural setting, such as a redwood grove or a favorite spot by the beach. Others prefer to make arrangements for the ceremony at home. Still others celebrate Bnai Mitzvah in Israel. There are several alternatives to a traditional synagogue service. Here are some possibilities:

- A celebration in your home.
- A weekend retreat.
- A celebration in Israel.

A celebration in your home

If you have a small extended family, if you live in an area without a synagogue, or if you are not able to affiliate with a congregation, it is possible to hold the service and celebration in your own home. It need not be lavish, but it can be meaningful and *haimish* (less formal and more comfortable). We discussed the celebration in Part 3, but for the service, here is what you will need:

- A Torah scroll. This may be obtained from a local college or university's Jewish Studies department or Jewish student organization. Many are willing to lend them with a deposit and reasonable rental fee. You might also contact your local board of Jewish education. Some synagogues may be able to lend you a Torah scroll for a short period of time. Look into this early on.

- A reading table or broad lectern on which to rest the Torah scroll and from which to lead the service. If you do not have a portable Ark in which to keep the Torah, you may want to cover the table with a cloth of lace or other suitable fabric, and have a piece of velvet or other fabric to lay over the scroll before you remove the mantle to read from it.

- *Siddurim.* You may wish to put together your own, using the guidelines for the service in this book or copying the service from an existing prayer book. If you are planning a standard service, you may be able to borrow *siddurim* from your local synagogue, providing you leave a small deposit and return them as soon as you are finished using them. If your group is particularly small, you may wish to purchase prayer books for everyone to keep as a memento of the day.

- Ritual items for a Friday night *Kabbalat Shabbat* service and an *oneg Shabbat* if these are included in your plans: Shabbat candlesticks and candles, a cup of kosher wine for *Kiddush* (the blessing over the fruit of the vine), a large *challah* (the braided sweet bread eaten on the Sabbath), kosher candles, matches, a platter for the bread, a *challah* cover, and a small bowl of kosher salt to ceremonially dip the bread in. Although many people prefer to tear the *challah*, you might like to have a special knife on hand to cut it for the guests. With the exception of the candles and candlesticks, you will need the same items for a Saturday morning *kiddush*-luncheon following the service. You may also want to provide *kippot* for each of your male guests. You can buy these at Jewish gift stores and have them inscribed with your child's name and date if you like.

- Adequate seating for your guests. If you have a fairly large crowd, it may be necessary to rent folding chairs, so plan ahead.

- Space for an *oneg Shabbat* or a *kiddush*-luncheon afterwards. It need not be elaborate, but you'll want to make adequate arrangements. Here again, take into consideration the dietary requirements of your guests. If people keep kosher, your refreshments should reflect that level of observance. The general rule is to serve what the most stringent person at the gathering is able to eat. This means that you should prepare foods that are either *milchik* (dairy) or *pareve* (neutral). Kosher wine, kosher cakes and cookies, and any fruit are all suitable for a light reception. These may be served on paper plates, or provided by a kosher caterer.

The weekend retreat

Sometimes, a family wants to hold an entire weekend of celebration at a campsite, hotel, or resort. If you live in an area with such facilities, and your guest list lends itself to this arrangement, you might want to consider this. If you have the time, means, and imagination to make this a reality, it can be a wonderful way to bring loved ones together for a meaningful and memorable experience.

It may be arranged as follows: You can host a Shabbat dinner on Friday night, followed or preceded by a *Kabbalat Shabbat* service. If the dinner is before *Kabbalat Shabbat*, dessert can be served after the service at an *oneg Shabbat*. In the morning after breakfast, the entire group can easily come together for the service, followed by a *kiddush*-luncheon. There can be entertainment, Israeli folk dancing, singing, and other festive moments to mark the occasion. After a relaxing afternoon and a little rest, the group may come together again for a formal dinner and further celebration in the evening, following *Havdalah*. To close out the weekend, the family might have a brunch or lunch on Sunday.

If you want to have a rabbi or cantor there for the entire weekend, you will have to make special arrangements, as most congregational leaders have full weekend schedules.

It is customary to have a rabbi for Bnai Mitzvah, but it is not necessary, provided someone experienced in leading a prayer service is available. It may be a little more difficult and time-consuming in preparation, but it can be a powerful learning experience for you and your child, and it can involve the entire family in a very meaningful way.

In addition, if *kashrut* is a concern, discuss it with the hotel staff. They may need to have their kitchen *kashered* (made kosher), or to change the menu to accommodate your guests. If you decide to take care of the catering yourself, it is best to work with a caterer who knows about *kashrut*. It will be helpful if you also discuss your plans with a local rabbi. He or she will be able to explain the best way to proceed.

You will probably need to obtain the same ritual objects indicated for a Friday night home service. It is also necessary to obtain a Torah scroll and prayer books. Some Jewish retreat facilities and camps have these on-site. Some people write their own services and invite family and friends to participate. This can be a wonderful way to involve those you love in this important rite of passage.

A celebration in Israel

By far one of the most memorable experiences is holding the celebration in Israel. (As an alternative, some people hold the service at the synagogue in their hometown and, instead of hosting an elaborate party afterwards, take the family to Israel.) For many Jews all over the world, a trip to Israel is a dream come true, and making the journey for such a happy occasion is a once-in-a-lifetime experience. Many families travel to Israel for Bnai Mitzvah to be with family members living there. Other people do not have relatives living in Israel but feel a strong connection to the country and wish to celebrate their children's Bnai Mitzvah there in order to transmit their love of the Holy Land. There are any number of tour companies and programs that will be glad to arrange such a celebration. You can go as part of a larger tour, holding the service at the *Kotel* (the Western Wall) in Jerusalem, or on top of Masada, near the Dead Sea. Or you can make it your own family pilgrimage and arrange a trip specifically to your own needs. If you do have family in Israel, they will be thrilled to help you find just the right place.

✡ ✡ ✡

Dahlia: *"I will always remember my Bat Mitzvah because it was so special. My cousins live on a kibbutz in Israel, and we had not seen them for several years. My mother and father took my grandparents, my brother and sister, and me. We spent a week on the kibbutz, and held the service in the orchard on a beautiful Shabbat morning in April. We got reacquainted with our family and toured the country. I can't wait to return one day soon!"*

✡ ✡ ✡

Even if you do not have relatives living there, Israel beckons to you as the homeland of the Jewish people. In a sense, everyone there is your extended family and takes pride and joy in your *simcha*. Whether it is at the Western Wall or on a mountaintop, everyone will make you feel at home.

Such a trip is not inexpensive, but it is worth more than the money you spend. You will be instilling and strengthening Jewish identity, creating Jewish memories, and forming bonds with Israel so that you and your child will want to return in the future.

Planning for Bnai Mitzvah in Israel takes time and organization. You should reserve a synagogue there at least a year in advance, especially if you want a particular place, date, and time. If you are going with a large group, you will need to book your hotels and flights well in advance. If you are a member of a synagogue, you might start by discussing your plans with your rabbi, cantor, and/or educational director. They will be of help to you and can arrange appropriate contacts for you in Israel. They can also assess your youngster's level of competence in Hebrew. You will want to be sure that your child has all the necessary Hebrew and prayer skills to feel comfortable leading a service and reading from the Torah in a environment different than what he or she is used to.

Your rabbi may be able to put you in touch with the proper rabbinic liaison in Israel to assist you. Also, each of the movements has an office in Israel. You may contact them directly, or through the movements' national offices outside of Israel. Their Israeli counterparts will be happy to help you.

Some considerations for Bnai Mitzvah in Israel

There are several things to include in your planning when you decide to hold Bnai Mitzvah in Israel, including the site, season of the year, and time of day for the ceremony, and organizations, congregations, and tour companies that can help you plan.

The site, season of the year, and time of day for the ceremony

There are many choices for Bnai Mitzvah sites in Israel. When you make your decision, take into account the Jewish movement you are most comfortable with. The rules and regulations will vary accordingly. Here are a few possible locations:

∠ The Kotel: The *minhag* (custom) operating here at the Western Wall is an Orthodox one. This means that men and women pray in separate sections and that there is a *mechitzah* (divider) between the sections. So, be aware that your family will not be all together in a mixed assembly at the Wall. However, if you have a son who is going to have his Bar Mitzvah in Israel, the Wall is a perfect place to hold the religious ceremony.

Because girls are not allowed to lead a public service at the Wall, you may have to move to the rear of the plaza or find another location for a Bat Mitzvah service. This is a sensitive issue in Israel, due to conflicts between the movements. Be sure to consider this when you make your plans.

Modest clothing, especially for women, is required. Hats and/or head scarves for married women, sleeves covering the elbows, and dresses covering the knees are *de rigueur*. Men should wear *kippot*. If the service is on Shabbat morning, men should wear *tallitot*. Shorts are not acceptable, and men traditionally wear white shirts, with sleeves at least to the elbow. Some prefer long sleeves, just to be proper.

You will need to bring your own Torah and rabbi for services here. Arrangements should be made ahead of time by contacting one of the movements in Israel.

∠ Synagogues in Israel: There are several possibilities under the auspices of the various movements in Israel, from Orthodox and Conservative to Reform and Reconstructionist. Most of these will allow you to join their regularly scheduled Shabbat services. If you wish to hold your service on a Monday or Thursday, the details must be arranged. Many of these synagogues have standards of student competence. Contact the synagogue directly to find out the specifics.

You may also hold services in some of the ancient synagogues in Jerusalem and Safed, or in more rural environs. For information, contact the Israel Ministry of Tourism or your local Israeli consulate. The Ministry of Tourism and the consulate can also give you suggestions for other locales, such as those indicated below.

∠ Non-synagogue sites: These may range from a *kibbutz* or a *moshav* (collective farm community) to public parks and government field schools.

∠ On Masada: Another viable alternative for both boys and girls is in the ancient synagogue on top of this mountain, where Jews made their last stand against Rome in 70-73 C.E.

If you are going to hold the service on Masada, be sure to take the time of year and the time of day into account when you do your planning. It can be very, very hot there. Masada is adjacent to the Dead Sea, and the temperature often climbs to more than 100 degrees by 10 a.m., especially in the summer. Athletic types may want to arrive before dawn and hike the snake path to the top. Another alternative is to hike the Roman ramp; this should also be planned before sunrise, so as to see the sun come up from the top of the mountain. It is breathtaking and truly unforgettable. For those who are less athletically inclined, there is a cable car. A new one opened in April of 1999. It is larger and stops right at the top of the mountain, so there are no additional steps to climb. If you have elderly people traveling with you, this is an important plus.

Plan to arrive at Masada very early, dress in cool clothes, and bring hats, water, juice, and good hiking shoes. The ceremonies are on a first-come, first-served basis. If you are not the first one on top, you may have to wait while someone else has a service before you. The services are held on Monday and Thursday mornings. If you are going as part of a larger group or have made arrangements with one of the movements or organizations, a Torah scroll will be made available to you.

✡ ✡ ✡

Kim: *"My Bat Mitzvah was unforgettable! It was held on top of Masada. It was the first "twinning" ceremony from our community, in which I celebrated my Bat Mitzvah with a girl who was living at that time in the Soviet Union. She is now in Israel with her whole family. My parents arranged to have us fly to Israel, along with some members of my immediate family. Following the service, we spent extra time in Israel, seeing everything. It was my first trip there, and I couldn't wait to go back!"*

✡ ✡ ✡

You will be able to find specific information about many aspects of Bnai Mitzvah in Israel in Judith Isaacson and Deborah Rosenbloom's

Bar and Bat Mitzvah in Israel: the Ultimate Family Sourcebook. Published by Israel Info. Access in 1998, the book has lists of locations, contacts, and other details.

Organizations, congregations, and tour companies

There are a variety of Jewish communal organizations that arrange family trips and Bnai Mitzvah tours in Israel, and several travel companies have experience in this area as well. There are also some liberal Israeli congregations that will welcome you if you want to hold your service there. (For detailed information about these and other resources, please refer to Appendix A.)

Chapter 11

Choosing to Become an Adult Bar/Bat Mitzvah

It is never too late to become a Bar or Bat Mitzvah. Many Jewish adults did not have the pleasure and privilege of a public Bar or Bat Mitzvah ceremony and celebration earlier in their lives and seize the opportunity later on in life.

If you do decide to become a Bar or Bat Mitzvah in your adult years, be certain it is something you really want to do, and that you are ready to make the commitment to give time and effort to achieving your goal. Don't be dissuaded by friends or family who might not understand your desire, and don't be discouraged if the task seems a bit overwhelming. If you know in your heart that this is something you truly want to undertake, give it your best effort.

One caution: If you are the parent of a child who is becoming a Bar or Bat Mitzvah, you may not want to hold your adult ceremony at the same time as your child. It is a wonderful experience to share the preparation together, and you will both gain greatly from it, but you might want to think twice about stealing the attention away from your son or daughter by scheduling a double-header on the same day. You may want to complete your preparation before your child's date, or you may schedule your own celebration after your child's moment on the *bimah* has passed.

✡ ✡ ✡

Bob: *"After my conversion to Judaism in 1997 Bar Mitzvah was the next step I chose on the road to adult Jewish literacy. After converting, I was eager to do more, for many reasons: I yearned for a spiritual connection, wanted to enhance my participation in services by being able to read Hebrew, and needed to find my place within the structure of community worship.*

I was surprised to find how easy it was to do so. The B'nai Mitzvah class was organized each year by our cantor and was attended by born-Jews who had missed the opportunity during adolescence and by adult converts like me. We were all enthusiastic, willing to work hard, and thick-skinned enough not to be too embarrassed at our mistakes. Studying with others got me involved in synagogue life, and I made new friendships in the process.

The ceremony was a very happy and memorable occasion. Many of my relatives (Jewish and non-Jewish) traveled thousands of miles to be there. My anticipation and fear of making a public mistake were overshadowed by the transcendent spirit of the occasion. Reading my Torah portion was a timeless, perfectly peaceful moment. I will never forget it."

✡ ✡ ✡

No matter how carefully you plan, there may never be a perfect time for you to prepare for an adult Bar or Bat Mitzvah. In the real world, life often gets in the way of our plans. But you can *make* the time right— for you. Here are some examples of people who did just that: One woman, who was raised in an Orthodox home and who is today the wife of a Reform rabbi, decided to celebrate her Bat Mitzvah when she turned 60, as a birthday present to herself. A man whose parents were Holocaust survivors and who had not had any formal Jewish education as a child decided to hold his Bar Mitzvah on his father's 80th birthday. A 50-year-old Jew-by-choice celebrated her 13th year as a Jew by becoming a Bat Mitzvah.

There is a story in the Talmud about Rabbi Akiba (c. 135), who did not start his Hebrew studies until he was 40 years old. If it was not too late for him, then it is not too late for you.

The preparation

Just as with any child's Bar Mitzvah, preparation is necessary. Nowadays, most liberal synagogues have programs to prepare adults for this important endeavor. Although the requirements may differ from congregation to congregation, the fundamentals are the same: As a general rule, there is study of both Hebrew and Judaism, attendance at services throughout the process, a commitment to participation in Jewish communal life, and in-depth instruction in Torah and *Haftarah* reading or chanting.

Leslie: *"I became a Bat Mitzvah at age 55. It was a year-long process of study. As I was preparing for this life-affirming event, I found myself looking inward more and more. I was reaching deep inside myself for the spiritual core of Judaism, which had been dormant inside me for a long time. As I wrote my* d'var Torah, *I found the connections in my life between my growth as a person and my spiritual growth as a Jew. I learned about the meaning of Torah and where my more treasured and deeply-felt values came from. I was actually surprised to discover that my need to help people, my concern for those less fortunate than myself, my embracing of diversity and differences, were all values taught to Jews by God and found in the Torah. I intend to continue Torah study, as I found this to be extremely satisfying, rewarding and healing."*

The course of study

- There is an extended period of study, which requires a personal commitment on the part of the student.

- Sometimes, the synagogue has an adult B'nai Mitzvah class that will accommodate anywhere from three or four students to 15 or 20, depending upon the size of the congregation and the number of people interested in participating.

- Usually, the rabbi and/or cantor teaches the classes, which meet weekly. As the date of the service approaches, the sessions may increase in length and in frequency.

- The course of study may take one year, and often takes longer. It may include a Hebrew component that begins with an introduction to reading Hebrew, with emphasis on the prayer book, progresses to reading Torah and *Haftarah*, and concludes with chanting these with the appropriate *trope*. There may also be a component of Judaic content, including an overview of Jewish history, an examination of the meaning and observance of the Jewish holidays and festivals, a discussion of the *mitzvot* and their place in modern Jewish life, an in-depth study of the Torah, and consideration of other important Jewish texts. Additional topics may be covered, depending upon the wishes of the rabbi and the requirements of the synagogue. Many congregations also have a *mitzvah* component, in which the students commit to the ongoing observance of various *mitzvot*. These may include Shabbat observance, *kashrut*, and engaging in acts of *chesed* (kindness) for others in the larger community as part of *tikkun olam* (repairing the world).

- To help with individual preparation, the instructor may prepare audiotapes of each Torah portion and *Haftarah*.

- As the date of the celebration nears, there are usually several rehearsals privately and with the group. These sessions include full readings of the entire service, practice in reading from the *siddur* in front of the group, and chanting from the Torah and the *Haftarah*.

- Each participant is usually asked to prepare a *d'var Torah* and to include some observations in a personal statement about the adult Bar or Bat Mitzvah experience.

- There is often an expectation of involvement in Jewish life and extended Jewish study, continuing beyond the Bar or Bat Mitzvah.

If you are considering preparing for an adult Bar or Bat Mitzvah, allow yourself plenty of time. Aside from the fact that adult lives are often extremely busy anyway, it may seem more difficult to you to learn the intricacies of Hebrew if you have not done any formal studying in many years. Don't be discouraged! Although it may take you a little longer than you might like, you will discover a wealth of meaning in the learning you undertake.

Include your family in your decision, for your experience will have a powerful impact upon them too. Share with them your reasons for wanting to do this and tell them how important it is to you. Let them know that it will not always be easy. There may be times when dinner might not be on the table at the usual hour because you will be in a meeting with the rabbi. There may be other times when you might be late driving carpools or picking up the laundry because you were practicing with your classmates. And if you work outside the home (as most people do these days), your workload will increase with the additional responsibility of your studies.

Furthermore, don't be surprised if your spouse and children are skeptical at first, because you are attempting something they may take for granted. After the novelty wears off, however, they will usually become interested and supportive of your efforts. Once you are in your routine of study, you can often count on your family to offer helpful advice, help you practice your Hebrew, and listen to the many drafts of your *d'var Torah.* You will become closer as a family as they join in your preparation and *shepp nachas* with you as you celebrate this achievement.

A group celebration vs. an individual one

This is usually determined by the circumstances at your synagogue. If you are in a large congregation, the chances are that you will join a group of other people who are also preparing for this special moment. This can be a wonderful experience. It affords you an opportunity to meet and befriend others who share the same goal, to strengthen your relationship with other members of your synagogue, to have a support group around you throughout the process, and to learn with others in a stimulating and enriching environment. However, it can also be difficult, as you may be asked to accommodate the wishes of others in setting the tone for the day. You may all be of different abilities, and it may not be possible for you to do everything you feel you are capable of doing when others must be accommodated as well. You may also not have the luxury of total flexibility in choosing the elements of the service, due to time constraints or the customs of your congregation.

✡ ✡ ✡

Sally: *"The 10 months I spent studying prior to my becoming a Bat Mitzvah at the age of 56 were one of the most exhilarating experiences of my life. Thirteen very diverse individuals came together to study with the rabbi every Sunday morning. We were diverse in many respects: Our ages ranged from late twenties to middle age. We were predominately female and all came from various backgrounds. Five of the group were Jews-by-choice. Some in* the group were observant Jews, and some (myself included) were previously Jewish in name only, so to speak. We all entered the year at different stages of our religious life, and we all completed the year of study at different place. But I feel one thing was for sure: Judaism had become a stronger part of each of our lives. Had I listened to my fears and hesitations when I started, I would have missed out on something that was so special and so meaningful to me that I cannot even begin to properly be able to put it into words. I am a Jew. I am proud to be a Jew. I am proud to be part of a heritage that is thousands of years old. I am even prouder now that I am a more observant Jew who is able to help conduct a service and represent my religion and my heritage in a more meaningful way."

What if you need extra help?

Your rabbi and/or cantor can be of enormous help to you in preparing for this moment. However, they are very busy people, and they may not always have the luxury of meeting with you as often as you would like. If you feel you need extra assistance, here are some suggestions:

- If you have a child who is studying to become a Bar Mitzvah, ask him to help you. Your child can be a wonderful resource for you—after all, he is going through the same process. If your child has already completed a Bat Mitzvah, you have even more help available to you. She is now a pro and can really help you.

- If you know other adults in your congregation who have gone through this process, contact them. Perhaps they will be willing to tutor you during the more difficult stages of your preparation.

- If your synagogue uses a Hebrew tutor, contact this person. While there may be a fee for their time and expertise, it is often well worth the investment. The Hebrew tutor is usually a patient, non-judgmental, experienced professional educator.

- Ask your husband or wife to help you. If your spouse is patient and fairly knowledgeable in Hebrew, you have a live-in resource.

- Use the audiotapes from your teacher to practice your Torah portion and *Haftarah*. Practice at a set time every day.

If you're not a member of a synagogue or there's no rabbi in your community

If at all possible, join a synagogue. If you live in a small Jewish community without a resident rabbi, here are some suggestions:

- Find out if there is someone in your community who knows some Hebrew. (Try the older generation.) Ask this person if he or she would be willing to help you study. Usually, this is such a special request that the person will be delighted.

- If you have a family member living in another town who knows how to read Hebrew and is willing to help, see if you can arrange regular lessons by phone.

- You can also call the nearest board of rabbis for the name of a rabbi in a nearby town. When you call the rabbi, explain your situation, and ask if he or she would be willing to work with you on a regular basis either by phone or e-mail. Begin by working together to create a course of study. Stay in contact with him or her for discussion of the material. Also, well in advance of your date, ask for a tape of the Torah portion and *Haftarah*. This way, you can study on your own and then check in with the rabbi as necessary. (Find out if there is a fee for the rabbi's time. Even if there is none, plan to make a donation to his or her discretionary fund or other suitable *tzedakah* to show your appreciation.)

- Make arrangements for your service with the help of knowledgeable Jews in your community, the local board of rabbis, and friends who may have done this before. Keep it simple. (It may be helpful to you to follow some of the guidelines offered in Chapter 2.)

The adult service

The service may be scheduled for Shabbat morning; late Shabbat afternoon, concluding with *Havdalah*; on a special weekday, such as Thanksgiving; or close to a Jewish holiday.

The time and date chosen may also depend upon the number of people participating, the custom of the individual synagogue, and such practical matters as when the sanctuary will not be reserved for other religious observances—including other Bnai Mitzvah, holiday celebrations, and so on. Many congregations like to schedule adult Bnai Mitzvah in conjunction with some special event in the life of the synagogue.

✡ ✡ ✡

Jane: *"The Torah, I've discovered during our wonderful Shabbat morning Torah study, is all about journeys. Seems to me that someone, or some large group of people, is always on the move: going somewhere, turning around, going back, getting lost, getting stuck, getting scared, finding wonderful places, trusting the wrong people, trusting the right people. As a child of the sixties, I've spent a lot of time doing just that. My great grandfather, Benjamin Papermaster, was the first Jewish rabbi in the Northwest Territory, bringing with him from Russia, at various times, many family members. Now, there's a journey! As our family spread throughout the country pulled by careers or love or adventure, our culture within a culture experienced its own Diaspora....It has been a long journey for me...the trouble I've found with life's journey is that there is no map. I've been reading a book on the life of Moses. On the inside cover there's a map of the wanderings in the desert and the final path to Sinai and into the Promised Land. As in this case, the map is often drawn after the journey. So, as I stand here, I try to look ahead. Above all else, I would like to move forward in life with courage, accepting what is, trusting that the universe is a good and happy place, grateful that I have in my life wonderful companions in whose eyes I see God. I pray today for the courage to make my life a blessing."*

✡ ✡ ✡

What is included in the service?

As noted in Chapter 5, there are certain basic elements of a worship service. These include: *Bar'chu*, the *Sh'ma* and its blessings, the *Amidah*, a Torah service, the reading or chanting of the *Haftarah*, *Aleinu*, and *Kaddish*. In addition, there may be a chanting or recitation of the *Kiddush* and *Ha-Motzi*. They may be abbreviated, with passages given to the individuals taking part so that everyone has a chance to participate in some way. To allow the congregation to join in, some of the prayers may be recited in English, rather than in Hebrew, and some portions may be sung, rather than recited.

Besides the traditional prayers and blessings, each participant will give a *d'var Torah* based upon the week's Torah portion and may also include personal thoughts about this important moment. Presentations are made from the congregation to the group, and tributes are expressed to each participant. Additional songs and/or meditations may be added to heighten the feeling of this special occasion.

With a large group of participants and all the elements of a normal Shabbat service, adult Bnai Mitzvah services can take two or three hours. Because of this, the service is sometimes tailored a bit to make allowances for time.

Sharing the *bimah* with others

At adult Bnai Mitzvah, there are many people on the *bimah*, all taking part in the service. This means that people must share the responsibility for the prayers. Sometimes this is a blessing because it takes some of the pressure off of each individual. But it can be difficult if everyone wants to be a star.

Those who choose to become adult B'nai Mitzvah come from many backgrounds. Some people, as we have seen, have never been exposed to Hebrew before; others have forgotten whatever they learned as children or are timid about taking on another language. Still others are frightened about public participation in any language! Therefore, when people volunteer to take part in the service and learn the necessary prayers and blessings, it is important to accept them where they are. That means that others must be patient and realistic in their expectations. Allowing people to participate based on their own capabilities makes the process more pleasant and more feasible in the long run.

✡ ✡ ✡

Leslie: *"When I began to chant my Torah portion, it was mine! I was there with the Torah, and all else dimmed. I chanted with a depth of feeling and no concern for mistakes. My previous nervousness became irrelevant. I learned the magic of Torah, its beautiful graphics, its words from God. It reached out to me, and I felt serene. When my daughter and sister joined me for their aliyot, I brought them into my heart in a new way. Who can explain this phenomenon? It's like childbirth: It cannot be explained or described; it must be experienced. I am a Bat Mitzvah—a 'Daughter of the Commandments.' I live my life with a deeper meaning and purpose, and I consciously attempt to be a Jew in the deepest sense of the word."*

✡ ✡ ✡

Some participants can read in English, and some in Hebrew. Some prayers can be chanted and some simply read. Some people can be soloists, while others may feel more comfortable participating in pairs or small groups. In the end, it comes down to allowing people to do what they are capable of , assisting them in their preparation, supporting them in their efforts, and applauding their achievements on the big day.

Crafting your own service

Most of the time, when adult Bnai Mitzvah are held on Shabbat, the synagogue will use the format and structure of a regular Shabbat service as found in the *siddur*. But if there are many people taking part, and there are to be several speeches, readings, and presentations, the participants may decide to write their own service. This will allow them to shape it to their specific needs, time limitations, and special circumstances. Using the *siddur* as the basic guide, they may then write their own interpretations of the prayers, include some much-loved poems or readings, and put together their own prayer book.

Such services are inspirational and unique, but they require advance planning to put the elements together in a meaningful way. Readings may come from contemporary Jewish sources, Biblical or rabbinic texts, or even non-religious writings. Whatever is chosen should be in harmony with the customs of the particular synagogue.

The service may then be printed in a booklet and distributed to all the guests at the service. Depending upon the funds available, it may be printed professionally or done on a computer and printer or copy machine. The booklet should contain a short message of welcome from all the adult Bnai Mitzvah students (along with their names), the names of the rabbi, cantor, and/or Bnai Mitzvah specialist, the service itself, a copy of the Torah portion and *Haftarah* for the day, and any special blessings and songs to be included. Depending upon the particular situation, appropriate additional messages and/or prayers may also be printed in the service booklet. This makes a wonderful keepsake for the occasion and involves everyone on a deeper level because it calls upon each student to take an active part in making the service personal and special.

The adult celebration

Unlike children's Bnai Mitzvah, adult celebrations are usually rather low-key. This does not mean they are not filled with joy and meaning, but it does mean that the party is a bit simplified. It is frequently held in the social hall of the synagogue, with all the families hosting the *oneg Shabbat* or *kiddush*-luncheon. The refreshments may be home-made or may be provided by a caterer. In many cases the reception consists of coffee and tea, wine, *challah*, pastries, and fruit.

Each participant may decide to hold a private family gathering after the public celebration. This may take the form of an intimate family dinner at home, a festive meal at a local restaurant, or a reception elsewhere.

Usually, gifts are not part of adult Bnai Mitzvah. When the invitations are sent out, the text can specify "No gifts, please." Sometimes, however, family members establish a fund, create a unique gift, or give donations in the person's honor to charitable organizations or the synagogue.

Making adult Bnai Mitzvah meaningful

There are several ways to add significance to adult Bnai Mitzvah that will not add to the cost or make things more complicated. Here are some suggestions:

- Take an active role in the preparation, creating the service and planning the celebration.

- Keep in mind your reasons for becoming a Bar or Bat Mitzvah at this time of your life. Being clear about your objectives will crystallize your thinking and help you pay attention to what is really important about this moment.

- If there are other people in the adult Bnai Mitzvah class, get to know them and become friends with them. The new friendships will add joy to your lives.

- Be kind and help others in the group. When you exercise your own *menschlicheit* (humanity), you grow in understanding, and your soul will blossom. Helping others will also help you to master difficult parts of the service, the Torah portion and *Haftarah*, or other elements of the event. Often, through teaching comes learning.

- Set aside quiet time every day to focus on this commitment; explain your study schedule to family and friends so they will understand and respect your time limitations.

- Allow others to share your joy all along the way by including them in significant moments of learning and understanding.

- Make a commitment to *tzedakah* and include this in your ongoing *mitzvah* regimen.

- Say a blessing before you study words of Torah. The appropriate *b'racha* to recite is:

  Ba-ruch a-ta Adonai, Eh-lo-hei-nu meh-lech ha-o-lam, a-sher ki-d'sha-nu b-mit-vo-tav, v-tzi-va-nu la-a-sok b'div-rei To-rah.

  Blessed are You, Eternal our God, Ruler of the Universe, Who has sanctified us by His commandments and commanded us to engage in words of Torah.

- Make serious study of Judaism part of this process. Extend your studies beyond the required prayers and blessings. Delve into Torah and text; explore many sources of Jewish knowledge; make continuous learning part of your daily life.

- The women in one class made a joint decision to immerse in the *mikvah* the week before their Bat Mitzvah. While each woman went into the bath individually, they were all there at the same time, sharing the important moment as a group. The youngest member of the class was 16 and the oldest was 62. It was an unforgettable experience for all of them.

After adult Bnai Mitzvah

There was a disagreement between Rabbi Akiba and the other great rabbis of the first century. They asked: Which comes first, the doing or the learning? Many felt that doing was the way to start. Rabbi Akiba disagreed. His response to the question was, "You learn in order to do." And now that you have learned, it is time to do. Here are a few suggestions for how you can extend your Bar Mitzvah experience by fulfilling it with action:

- Start a Torah study group at your synagogue.

- Speak to the rabbi or cantor about being available to read from the Torah when needed on a Shabbat morning.

- Offer to give the *d'var Torah* occasionally at services.

- Offer to lead services regularly at Jewish convalescent hospitals or senior care facilities.

- Share what you have learned by volunteering as a tutor/mentor for others who are embarking upon this process. Now that you have the necessary Hebrew skills, you can assist others by sharing your knowledge with them, and you can become a valuable resource in your local Jewish community.

- Increase your activity and involvement in the life of the synagogue and larger Jewish community. Becoming a Bar or Bat Mitzvah, especially as an adult, makes you a visible role model for others. Show by your actions that you are a living example of the essence of Jewish living, and go on to show others how to do the same.

You have accomplished a wonderful thing. One should feel proud of becoming a Bar or Bat Mitzvah at any age, and especially as an adult. *Mazel-tov!*

PART FIVE:

AFTERWARDS

Chapter 12

Jewish Life After Bnai Mitzvah

After all the guests have left, after the candles have died down, and after the gifts have been opened and the acknowledgments written, you need not let go of all that you have learned and accomplished in preparing for this moment in your life and that of your child.

Here is what usually takes place: Immediately after the party, you will feel exhilarated and on an emotional high. This is wonderful and is as it should be. After all, a great deal of time, effort, and energy went into this event. You have every right to feel on top of the world. When you have said your last goodbye to the family, packed away the last of the party favors, and put the leftover cake in the freezer, you may feel a slight let-down.

What you can do to extend the moment

Ironically, the most important part of the Bat Mitzvah experience begins after it has occurred! The focus changes, but not the importance or the impact of the experience.

✡ ✡ ✡

Cantor Doron Shapira: *"The real challenge in what we teach and model for our youth begins the day after the celebration. If we sincerely strive to make the Bar/Bat Mitzvah a beginning to Jewish adulthood (and not an end to Jewish involvement), the entire Jewish community must take part. Parents: Keep coming to services with your children. Rabbis and cantors: Let students lead services rotationally, join adult choirs, become liaisons to synagogue boards. Religious schools: Incorporate mitzvah and tikkun Olam programs in adult programming. Families: Find ways to truly treat Jewish children differently after their Bar or Bat Mitzvah. Then, this life passage will not be the end of anything, but rather the beginning of a meaningful adult Jewish life."*

✡ ✡ ✡

How can you extend the satisfaction, warmth, and love you feel beyond the Bat Mitzvah day? Even more important: How can you carry over the feelings of Jewish connection into Jewish adulthood?

Here are some suggestions:

∠ Sit down with your child and relive the most memorable parts of the weekend. Take notes of your conversation, and place them in a journal or your keepsake album. Years from now, you'll be able to remember the event more clearly with these impressions and recollections.

∠ Make notes of what you might have done differently. This will be very helpful if you have other children who will be becoming Bnai Mitzvah in the future.

∠ Go to synagogue on a regular basis. Bring your child with you whenever possible. Don't lose the momentum or the connection you have made during the time of preparation; carry it forward with you into the future.

∠ If you took candid photos and/or videos of the celebration, make copies of them. Send them to all your relatives and close friends. Schedule an evening when you can have people over to enjoy the celebration all over again through the pictures. Arrange a special showing for your youngster and his/her friends. They will have a great time reliving the experience.

∠ If you have centerpieces or other decorations left from the party, take these to a convalescent center for the elderly or the children's ward of your local hospital.

∠ Write letters of thanks to all who made the occasion so special. This goes beyond thanking the caterers and other service providers. These letters should be sent to family and friends whose presence was vital to the celebration of this moment in your lives. It is especially meaningful if your child can do this with you, as appropriate.

∠ Make donations to your synagogue and/or other agencies in your Jewish community. In your letter accompanying the monetary gift, explain why you are making this contribution and what you hope to accomplish by giving it. This will help you articulate what you feel and will make the recipients feel a part of your happiness.

∠ Make an appointment with your rabbi and/or cantor to ask what you can do to help in the life of the synagogue. You may specifically suggest ways to assist others who are becoming Bnai Mitzvah and their families. Now that you have gone through the experience, you can give practical advice to others with this ahead of them. Some possibilities might be helping a working mother with her carpool during the hectic last weeks of preparation, baking cakes or cookies for another family's celebration, or helping put together the *oneg Shabbat* or *kiddush*-luncheon for a family who has few relatives to help them. Articulate why you are doing this. You will reap great emotional rewards by volunteering to help others in this way.

∠ Initiate a mentor program for families in your congregation or community. You can get the names from your synagogue secretary or from local Jewish agencies. Reach out to immigrant Jewish families, people who have relocated from other parts of the country, and those who have no family or friends in your town. Offer to bring Shabbat to them by taking candles, wine, and *challah* to their home in time for the Sabbath. Bring these families with you to services and introduce them to others in the congregation.

∠ Continue to study. There is no end to Jewish learning. Arrange a parents' post-Bnai Mitzvah Torah study group or Judaica class. Find things on the Internet having to do with Jewish learning. Immerse yourself in serious study. Enjoy Jewish theatre, books, movies, and so on. These activities will broaden your knowledge base incredibly and will further enhance your Jewish identity and that of your family.

∠ If you are able, offer to teach religious school or Hebrew school. Your presence and experience can greatly benefit those in your congregation.

What your child can do

From the synagogue's point of view, post-Bnai Mitzvah students can provide a wealth of knowledge and assistance to the congregation and especially to the religious and/or Hebrew school. They can also be wonderful resources in the larger Jewish community.

Here are some ways your child can be of help:

- Start a youth congregation at your synagogue (if you don't already have one).

- Lead regular or youth services once every few months.

- Offer to read Torah and/or *Haftarah* at least once a year. Some congregations encourage this on the anniversary of Bnai Mitzvah celebrations. Other synagogues extend the privilege of an *aliyah* to post-Bnai Mitzvah students on the High Holy Days. In any event, it is always beneficial to use Hebrew skills throughout the year, and whenever your child is given the privilege of reading from the Torah or chanting the *Haftarah*, it is truly an honor.

- Offer to give the sermon or *d'var Torah* during regular Shabbat services.

- Become a teacher's aide in the religious school.

- Become a peer-tutor for others who are beginning their Bnai Mitzvah preparations.

- Assist in the religious school office.

- Help out as a camp counselor or group leader for your synagogue or other Jewish youth organization.

- Come to synagogue board meetings to give valuable input from a teen/young adult perspective.

- Assist your rabbi and/or cantor in setting up a Torah-readers' group of those who can be called upon to read from the Torah when needed.

- Volunteer to lead Shabbat services with others who have become Bnai Mitzvah at your local Jewish Home for the Aged. The residents will be deeply appreciative of your efforts.

✡ ✡ ✡

Rabbi Elka Abrahamson: *"It is difficult for people to comprehend that Bar/Bat Mitzvah is a process, not a service, not a single event, not a culmination. It is but one step in the evolution of an emerging Jewish identity, an expanding sense of oneself as a spiritual person, a partner with the Holy One. It is leading the community, and it is the knowledge that the bimah is shared sacred space, a place of honor earned not for one day only, but for life.... Ah, if we could but make it clear to every person that the Shabbat when one is called to the Torah is not the summit! It is a beautiful and long cherished traditional cliff upon the mountain of Jewish learning. It is a place to savor and celebrate the goodness of becoming. Then, we must teach and model for our children as we continue with our study."*

✡ ✡ ✡

The rewards of engaging in the study of Torah—at any age—are very great. As it is written in a tractate of the Talmud called *Pirke Avot* (Ethics of the Fathers) 7:1:

> Rabbi Meir said, Whosoever labors in the Torah for its own sake, merits many things; and not only so, but the whole world is indebted to this person: he is called 'friend, beloved, a lover of the All-present, and a lover of humankind'; it clothes him in meekness and reverence; it fits him to become just, pious, upright and faithful; it keeps him far from sin, and brings him near to virtue; through him the world enjoys counsel and sound knowledge, understanding and strength.

As you plan for the Bar or Bat Mitzvah of your child, yourself, or another loved one, may you continue to grow in love of Torah, observance of *mitzvot,* and performance of *chesed* (acts of loving kindness). May you go from strength to strength, and may this celebration lead you to many more beautiful Jewish experiences in your life, the life of your family, and the life of the Jewish people.

Appendices

Appendix A

Resources

Contacting the movements

You may contact the offices of any of these to obtain information about religious, educational, and communal services and resources in your local Jewish community.

Aleph: Alliance for Jewish Renewal: 7318 Germantown Avenue, Philadelphia, PA 19119. Phone: (215) 242-4074 or (215) 247-9700.

Jewish Reconstructionist Federation: 7804 Montgomery Avenue, Suite #6, Elkins Park, PA 19027. Phone: (215) 782-8500.

The Orthodox Union: 333 Seventh Avenue, New York, NY 10001. Phone: (212) 563-4000.

Union for Traditional Judaism: 811 Palisade Avenue, Teaneck, N J 07666. Phone: (201) 801-0707

United Synagogue of Conservative Judaism: 155 Fifth Avenue, New York, NY 10010. Phone: (212) 533-7800.

Union of American Hebrew Congregations (Reform): 633 Third Avenue, Seventh Floor, New York, NY 10017. Phone: (212) 650-4000.

Children with special needs

The Jewish Education Service of North America, Inc. (JESNA) provides resources for children with special needs through its Consortium of Special Educators in Central Agencies for Jewish Education. Rabbi Martin Schloss is director of the Special Education Center of the Board of Jewish Education of Greater New York. Sara Rubinow Simon directs the Special Needs Department of the Board of Jewish Education of Greater Washington.

To reach either of these professionals, contact Caren Levine, Director, Media, Technology, and Networks, at JESNA, 730 Broadway,

New York, NY 10003. Phone: (212) 529-2000, ext. 1312. FAX: (212) 529-2009. E-mail: info@jesna.org.

The following communities are represented in the consortium and can be reached through JESNA: Atlanta, Cleveland, Dallas, Denver, Detroit, Florida, Houston, Kansas City, Los Angeles, the greater New Jersey area, New York, Philadelphia, Phoenix, St. Louis, San Francisco, and Washington, D.C.

If your child has a visual disability, contact:

The Jewish Heritage for the Blind: 1655 East 24th Street, Brooklyn, NY 11229. Phone: (718) 338-5385.

The Jewish Braille Institute of America: 110 East 30th Street, New York, NY 10016. Phone: (212) 889-2525.

Families living in Israel who have children with learning disabilities may contact Judith Edelman-Green, director of the Masorti Bar/ Bat Mitzvah Program for the Special Child, at Masorti Movement, 13 Ben Yehuda Street, P.O. Box 7559, Jerusalem 91074, Israel. Phone: 011-972-2-678-2433.

Here are just a few of the resources available on the World Wide Web to parents, educators, and children with special needs. You may contact them directly for specific publications and additional teaching/ learning tools to help your child.

Center for the Study of Autism: www.autism.org

CH.A.D.D. (Children and Adults with Attention Deficit Disorders): www.chadd.org

Deaf Resource Page: www.darwin.clas.virginina.edu/~tms4s/deaf.html

Gallaudet University: www.gallaudet.edu

Gifted and Talented Resources Page: www.eskimo.com/~user/kids.html

Internet Resources for Special Children: www.one.net/~julio_c

Jewish Education Service of North America (JESNA): www.jesna.org

Shema Yisrael Torah Network: Special Education Resources: (under construction) www.pirchei.co.il/specl_ed/index.html

Toys, Etc. for Kids With Special Needs: www.nas.com/downsyn/toy.html

Bnai Mitzvah in Israel

The more liberal branches of Judaism, especially Reform and Conservative, will be of help to you. You may contact them locally or at the national level, or you may get in touch with them in Israel.

The U.S. offices of ARZA (The Association of Reform Zionists of America) and **The World Union for Progressive Judaism** (both under the auspices of the Reform movement): 633 Third Avenue, Seventh Floor, New York, NY 10017. Phone: (212) 650-4000.

The U.S. offices of the World Council of Conservative/Masorti Synagogues: 155 Fifth Avenue, New York, NY 10010. Phone: (212) 533-7693.

The Shirley and Jacob Fuchsberg Center for Conservative Judaism in Israel: 2 Agron Street, P.O. Box 7456, Jerusalem 94265, Israel. Phone: 011-972-2-625-6386.

The Israel Movement for Progressive Judaism, Hebrew Union College/Jerusalem Campus: 13 King David Street, Jerusalem 94101, Israel. Phone: 011-972-2-620-3447.

Some Jewish philanthropic and social service organizations also conduct and facilitate Bnai Mitzvah in Israel. They have tours that focus on the student, who, in many instances, travels for free if there is a ceremony in Israel. One possibility is:

American Jewish Congress, International Travel Program, 15 East 84th Street, New York, NY 10028. Phone: (800) 221-4694 or (212) 879-4588.

Congregations in Israel that may be of help to you

Orthodox:
Hechal Shlomo Synagogue: 56 King George Street, Jerusalem 94262, Israel. Phone: 011-972-2-622-3312.

Conservative:
Moreshet Yisrael Conservative Synagogue: 1 Agron Street, Jerusalem 94265, Israel. Phone: 011-972-2-625-3539.

Reform:
Beit Daniel: 62 B'nei Dan Street, Tel Aviv 62305, Israel. Phone: 011-972-3-544-4030.

Kol HaNeshama: 1 Asher Street, Baka, Jerusalem 93740, Israel. Phone: 011-972-2-672-4878.

Reconstructionist:
Congregation Mevakshei Derech: 22 Shai Agnon Street, Jerusalem 92586, Israel. Phone: 011-972-2-679-2501.

Tour companies that arrange Bnai Mitzvah trips to Israel

These tour companies will make all the travel arrangements for you. Some of them will take care of all the other details, which may include:

- Engaging the services of a rabbi.
- Helping you choose a site.
- Hiring a florist, musicians, videographer, and photographer.
- Customizing the trip for you.

Abrams Travel, Inc.: 2909 Friendlywood Way, Burtonsville, MD 20866. Phone: (800) 338-7075. Also at 55 West 39th Street, Suite #707, New York, NY 10018. Phone: (800) 377-6740. Contact Leila Abrams.

Ayelet Tours, Ltd.: 21 Aviation Road, Albany, NY 12205. Phone: (800) 237-1517 or (318) 437-0691.

InStyle Events: 44/28 Tagore Street, Tel Aviv 69341, Israel. Phone: (800) 349-5286 or 011-972-3-643-1704.

Israel Discovery Tours, Inc.: 5230 Monroe Street, Skokie, IL 60077. Phone: (800) 362-8882 or (847) 677-5624. Contact Ilene Wallerstein.

Israel Tour Connection: 107 East Mount Pleasant Avenue, Livingston, NJ 07039. Phone: (800) 2-Israel or (973) 535-2575. Attention: Barney Ross.

Margaret Morse Tours: 17070 Collins Avenue, Suite 262, Miami Beach, FL 33160. Phone: (800) 327-3191.

Rainbow Travel and Tours, Inc.: 1801 Avenue of the Stars, Suite 260, Century City, CA 90067. Phone: (800) 647-0402 or (310) 552-0977 or (213) 879-3365.

Tova Gilead, Inc.: 938 Port Washington Blvd., Port Washington, NY 11050. Phone: (800) 242-TOVA.

For more complete information about Bnai Mitzvah experiences in Israel, see *Bar/Bat Mitzvah in Israel: the Ultimate Family Sourcebook*, by Judith Isaacson and Deborah Rosenbloom, Israel Info Access, 1998.

Some families choose to hold Bnai Mitzvah in their own synagogues in the United States, and then, as part of the celebration of the event, travel to Israel as a family. It is a wonderfully unifying experience to be with those you love on such a trip. The memories are irreplaceable and the sights are unforgettable. Any of the travel agencies listed above can arrange such a pilgrimage. You can consult your local travel agent, but it may be best to work with someone who is especially knowledgeable about Israel. *N'siah tovah!* (Have a good trip!)

Educational Resources

These Jewish publishing houses provide materials specifically for Bnai Mitzvah students.

Shilo Publishing House, Inc., 73 Canal Street, New York, NY 10002. Phone: (212) 925-3468. Shilo offers audio cassettes and booklets for every week of the annual Torah cycle, each containing the portion and *Haftarah* with *trope* and vowels, as well as the accompanying blessings. There is also an expanded series called *My Bar Mitzvah Book*, which offers additional information on the Torah portions and *Haftarot*.

The Union of American Hebrew Congregations (UAHC), 633 Third Avenue, Seventh Floor, New York, NY 10017. Phone: (212) 650-4000. The Reform movement publishes booklets for each Torah portion and *Haftarah*, with additional ones for special observances and holidays. In addition to the *trope* and vocalization, each booklet includes extensive commentary about the portion, based upon *The Torah: A Modern Commentary*, by W. Gunther Plaut.

If you are comfortable with computer technology, contact:

Davka Corporation, 7074 Northwestern Avenue, Chicago, IL 60645. Phone: (312) 465-4070 or (800) 621-8227. Davka puts out an extensive catalogue of Hebrew software and learning aids suitable for IBM and Macintosh, including the Torah portions and *Haftarot*.

Lev Software, 693 Racquet Club Road, #2, Weston, FL 33326. Phone: (800) 776-6538. The BMitzvah program provides help with a specific Torah portion and *Haftarah*, while BMitzvah-Pro contains the entire set of 81 *Haftarot* and 54 Torah portions. The programs also have additional features to assist in learning Hebrew. Software is geared for IBM compatibles or Macintoshes with a virtual PC option.

You might also want to contact companies that produce general Hebrew educational materials, such as:

A.R.E. Publishing, Inc., 3945 South Oneida Street, Denver, CO 80237. Phone: (800) 346-7779.

Behrman House, 235 Watchung Avenue, West Orange, NJ 07052. Phone: (800) 221-2755.

KTAV Publishing House, Inc., 900 Jefferson Street, Hoboken, NJ 07030. Phone: (201) 963-9524.

Melton Research Center for Jewish Education, The Jewish Theological Seminary of America, 3080 Broadway, New York, NY 10027. Phone: (212) 678-8031.

Torah Aura Productions, 4423 Fruitland Avenue, Los Angeles, CA 90058. Phone: (800) 238-6724.

UAHC Press, 633 Third Avenue, Seventh Floor, New York, NY 10017. Phone: (212) 650-4000.

Extra Touches

Here are some helpful resources to make your celebration special. While this list is not exhaustive, hopefully it will provide you with inspiration to elevate your *simcha* in a significant way.

Software that uses Hebrew fonts is useful for creating personalized service programs, prayer books, and other materials. One such program is available from **Davka**, 7074 Northwestern Avenue, Chicago, IL 60645. Phone: (800) 621-8227.

Jewish mail-order catalogues: There are several to choose from. One of the best is **Hamakor Judaica, Inc.**, P.O. Box 48836, Niles, IL 60714. Phone: (800) 426-2567.

Judaica designs in glass: The Glass People, Inc., 6836 Lake Avenue, Elyria, OH 44035. Phone: (440) 324-7598. There are dozens of Judaica items, some serious, some whimsical. Handcrafted glass cartoons make unusual gifts and special tributes or favors for your party. Especially delightful are the "personal protectors." For information and a catalogue, contact Carl Goeller, head glass cartoonist.

Party favors: To choose from a wide variety of unusual and inexpensive party favors, contact **The Oriental Trading Company, Inc.**, P.O. Box 2318, Omaha, NE 68103. Phone: (800) 228-2269. They advertise themselves as "the world's biggest toy box," and they aren't kidding!

Party-planning and decorating: The Basket Tree, Inc., P.O. Box 7017, West Orange, NJ 07052. Phone: (973) 731-2377. Basket Tree president Heidi Sussman offers a comprehensive service, adaptable to your individual needs. Sussman provides balloon decorating, centerpieces, sign-in boards and books, party favors, interesting and unusual place cards, imprinted balloons and napkins, photo collages, memory books, hotel amenity baskets, decorated *yarmulke* baskets, and kosher gourmet gift baskets. She works locally, nationally, and internationally and offers planning/consulting via telephone (with a written follow-up), fax, mail or e-mail. She also sells a party-planning guide.

Personalized and custom embroidery: MDS Discount Embroidery, P.O. Box 150790, Cape Coral, FL 33915. Phone: (941) 574-6622. Nannette Shapiro Palumbo, MDS president, offers *kippot, tallitot, tallit bags*, and other gifts embroidered in Hebrew and English.

Personalized prayer books and keepsake booklets: Special Simchas, 4736 Park Granada, Suite #236, Calabasas, CA 91302. Phone: (877) 774-6242. Owners Franci Goldberg and Diane Townsend are Jewish educators who create custom prayer books and memento booklets for Bnai Mitzvah and other life-cycle events.

Professional tapes of family interviews and personal tributes: Living Legacies Productions, 3134 Greenfield Avenue, Los Angeles, CA 90034. Phone: (310) 473-4513. Ellie Kahn, a professional oral historian and award-winning documentary filmmaker interviews grandparents and older relatives to preserve their memories about your family's history. These guided interviews are transformed into either a hardcover book of family photos and documents or a video documentary. Also, for Bnai Mitzvah, Kahn produces a short video about the child's life and family history, which may be shown at the party.

Specialty *Yarmulkes* (*Kippot*): For unique skullcaps and other head–coverings, available in any color, print, or trim, call **J. Lowy, Manufacturers of Suede and Leather Yarmulkas**, 940 East 19th Street, Brooklyn, NY 11230. Phone: (718) 338-7324.

Video Montages: Howard Wallach will see to it that your family photos are transformed into a creative video montage to be shown at the reception. Contact **A-Z Entertainment, Ltd.**, 600 Northgate Parkway, #L, Wheeling, IL 60090. Phone: (847) 537-5100.

On the Internet: You will find endless resources on the Internet. Using any of the search engines, simply type in "Bar Mitzvah."

Appendix B

A Bar/Bat Mitzvah Contract

This details the student's obligations and is reprinted with permission from Peninsula Sinai Congregation, Foster City, California.

Pirke Avot (The Ethics of the Fathers) states: The world rests on three foundations: on Torah, or learning; on *avodah*, or prayer; and on *gemilut chasadim*, or bestowing deeds of kindness.

1. Torah
   a. Read your Torah portion completely in English.
   b. Study one part of the reading in depth with a commentary provided by the rabbi.
   c. Write a *d'var Torah* based on the materials, stressing how they apply to you.
   d. Read your *Haftarah* fully in English.
   e. Know who was the prophet who wrote it, when he lived, which major events in Jewish history happened in his lifetime, or what is important about the event or person described in the *Haftarah*.
   f. Write a one page summarizing the message of the *Haftarah*.
2. *Avodah*
   a. Attend Shabbat services, both Friday night and Shabbat morning, at least twice a month for the six months prior to your Bar or Bat Mitzvah.
   b. Learn how to perform the mitzvah of *tefillin*.
3. *Gemilut Chasadim*
   a. Undertake at least one of the following projects:
      • Collect canned goods for a local food bank.
      • Adopt and correspond with a Righteous Person who saved Jews during the Holocaust. (The rabbi will help you get the name.)
      • Collect money or earn money to give to a charity of your choice.
      • Visit a Jewish patient at a convalescent home under the direction of the rabbi.
      • Another creative idea of service to others approved by the rabbi.
   b. Write a brief summary of what you have done and how you feel about it.
   c. Give some of your gifts to *tzedakah*.

_____   _____
Bar/Bat Mitzvah   Rabbi

_____
Date

Appendix C

Excerpts from one synagogue's handbook

Reprinted in abbreviated form with permission from Peninsula Temple Sholom, Burlingame, California.

A date for the ceremony should be scheduled with the rabbi three years ahead of the time selected and can be arranged by calling the Temple office. Students should begin studies with the cantor 10 months before the date of the ceremony.

A ceremony is usually held on Shabbat morning during part of the congregation's Shabbat worship.

The candidate, accompanied by at least one parent, must attend 10 Shabbat services during the year preceding the ceremony.

Although the student begins the preparation with the cantor, it is not an automatic guarantee that he or she will qualify for the ceremony unless he or she fulfills the requirements:

- Enrollment in the religious and Hebrew schools.
- Attendance at 10 services as noted above.
- Mastery of material assigned by the cantor.
- Lessons with the cantor.

Students should plan on studying an average of 20 minutes a day for 10 months before the ceremony. Under certain circumstances, the cantor may recommend additional private tutoring.

The assistant rabbi will meet with the student and at least one parent for approximately three half-hour appointments, beginning four months before the ceremony, to study the Torah portion and *Haftarah* in depth.

Beginning approximately two months before the ceremony, the student will meet with the senior rabbi for help writing the sermon and to reflecting on learning experiences and plans for the future.

The family generally meets with the cantor for a complete practice run-through of the service in the sanctuary from 1:15 to 3 p.m. the Sunday preceding the ceremony.

On Saturday morning, the student should come to the rabbi's study to meet with him at 9:30 a.m. for a walk-through of the service and for answering last-minute questions.

The service will be one and a half hours, concluding at noon. Following the service, the family is requested to provide a *kiddush* reception for the congregation; usually *challah* and wine.

The Elijah Program at our synagogue allows the Bar or Bat Mitzvah to become a Son or Daughter of the Commandment on the day of the ceremony. The celebrant will be able to fulfill the *mitzvah* of aiding the poor: It is suggested that the prophet Elijah (in Jewish legend, the heavenly emissary sent to earth to combat social injustice), be invited to attend the reception. The family should calculate what the cost would be for this one extra guest. That amount of money should go to aid those who need food. The check should NOT be made out to the Temple. Instead, the young person who is to become the bearer of the commandments should take that money, go to the supermarket, and purchase canned food. The package of groceries should be brought to the sanctuary on the day of the ceremony and placed on the *bimah*. The food then will be taken by a Temple representative to a community agency that distributes food to the poor. The gift of food will be Elijah's Gift.

Our students are expected to continue their religious studies and become confirmed. We hope that they will then participate in the Summer in Israel youth program, together with the confirmands of all the other synagogues in the area.

Appendix D

Sample Bar/Bat Mitzvah preparation timeline

Reprinted with permission from Peninsula Temple Beth El, San Mateo, California.

End of 6th grade

Students are tested.

**Summer before 7th grade
Circle of Success program**

Students who test well at the end of their 6th grade years may attend. All other students are required to attend.

**Summer before 7th grade
Tutoring**

Students who are within six months of their service begin with temple tutors.
Students who test poorly, no matter when their services are scheduled, are required to meet with a temple tutor a minimum of four times, and are reevaluated. If they are still behind, the family will be asked to hire a tutor to bring the student up to standards to enter the 7th grade.

**One month
before the service**

Student has a complete run-through in the sanctuary with the cantor. Meetings with the cantor continue, if necessary, for two more weeks.

**Three months
before the service**

Students leave the tutor and begin to see the cantor; Torah and Haftarah are prepared.
If students are not well prepared, temple tutors may still be recommended.

**Six months
before the service**

Students begin to meet with temple tutors one-half hour each week.
Material for the service is mastered, and Torah portion may be started.

**Wednesday, the week
BEFORE the service**

Student meets with the rabbi in the sanctuary. Student reads and chants the service. Student no longer sees the cantor.

**Wednesday, the week
OF the service**

Student meets with the rabbi in the sanctuary Student reads and chants the Torah service, Torah and Haftarah portions, and sermon.

**Thursday, the week
OF the service**

Complete run-through of the service with the student, parents, and siblings.

Appendix E

Do a *mitzvah!*
Some suggested *tzedakah* organizations

Note: Although this is not an exhaustive list, it is meant to be a first step for students and their families to become involved in *tikkun olam*.

ARMDI: American Red Magen David for Israel, 888 Seventh Avenue, Suite #403, New York, NY 10106. Phone: (212) 757-1627. Israel's version of the Red Cross. Provides emergency medical supplies.

Bay Area Council For Jewish Rescue and Renewal, 106 Baden Street, San Francisco, CA 94131. Phone: (415) 585-1400. Project Director for Bar/Bat Mitzvah Twinning: Marina Ostrova. Office Manager: Larisa Margulis. Connects students in the United States with Jewish children of the same age in rural town in the former Soviet Union.

B'nai B'rith, 1640 Rhode Island Avenue, N.W., Washington, DC 20036. Phone: (202) 857-6633. The oldest Jewish philanthropic organization in the United States. Raises money for youth projects, humanitarian efforts, and Jewish relief worldwide.

Hadassah, 50 West 58th Street, New York, NY 10019. Phone: (212) 355-7900. The world's largest Jewish women's Zionist organization. Funds medical research and care in Israel, especially through the Hadassah hospital in Jerusalem.

Jewish Foundation for the Righteous, 165 East 56th Street, New York, NY 10016. Phone: (212) 421-1221. Provides ongoing funding for Christians who saved Jews during the Holocaust, many of whom are now elderly and without financial means. It also oversees a Bar/Bat Mitzvah twinning program.

Jewish National Fund, 42 East 69th Street, New York, NY 10021. Phone: (212) 879-3000. The Israeli organization known for its tree-planting. Develops land and forests and oversees infrastructure, parks, playgrounds, water development, and natural resources in Israel.

Mazon—A Jewish Response to Hunger, 12401 Wilshire Blvd., Suite 303, Los Angeles, CA 90025. Phone: (310) 442-0020. If you give three percent of the cost of your celebration, Mazon will donate that money to relieve hunger all over the world.

North American Conference on Ethiopian Jewry, 132 Nassau Street, Room #412, New York, NY 10038. Phone: (212) 233-5200. Director of Bar/Bat Mitzvah Twinning Program: Miriam Weissman. Assists in educational opportunities and materials for Ethiopian Jews now living in Israel.

The United Jewish Appeal, 99 Park Avenue, New York, NY 10016. Phone: (212) 818-9100. The umbrella organization for Jewish monetary contributions worldwide. Gives money for social services on international, national, and local levels, with special allocations to Israel.

Ziv Tzedakah Fund, 384 Wyoming Avenue, Millburn, NJ 04041. Phone: (973) 763-9396. Administrator: Naomi Eisenberger. An independent fund-raising organization, founded by author and activist Danny Siegel, supporting worthwhile causes and *mitzvah* heroes in the United States and Israel.

Appendix F

Sample requirements for students with no synagogue, school, or resident rabbi

Reprinted with permission from Rabbi Arlene Schuster, Bellevue, Washington.

In all areas of study, requirements will be adjusted to meet the needs and particular situation of each student and their family. Exceptions to requirements are at the discretion of the teacher. Additions to these requirements may be added by the teacher or student, if special areas of interest are desired.

Hebrew

Basic reading skills: Ability to read with reasonable fluency, not slowly sounding out words. Demonstrate an understanding of the *shoresh* (root of the word) and how it works. Be able to translate all words in a basic *bracha* (blessing) and explain the difference between *brachot* over *mitzvot* (blessings over commandments) and other blessings.

Read fluently: The blessing over the candles on both Shabbat and holidays, Kiddush, Ha-Motzi, Shema and Baruch Shem, Mi Chamocha, V'ahavta, Avot, Oseh Shalom, Aleinu, V'shamru, Sheh-hechiyanu, Sheh-asah Nissim (on Chanukah), brachot for foods, the tallit bracha, Torah and Haftarah brachot.

Optional: *Kaddish, Birkat Ha-Mazon, Brachot* for Passover, the four questions, blessings of appreciation, *Havdalah brachot* and *Eliyahu Ha-Navi,* and *brachot* for Torah study, *lulav* and *etrog, shofar,* and the *megillah.*

History

Demonstrate a basic understanding of the course of Jewish history. Text: *Amazing Adventures of the Jewish People,* by Max Dimont.

Values

Demonstrate a basic understanding of Jewish values. Text: *It's a Mitzvah: Jewish Living Step by Step,* by Bradley Shavit Artson.

Holidays, rituals, and life cycle

Demonstrate a basic understanding of the cycle of Jewish holidays, holy days, and life-cycle events. Text: *Seasons of our Joy*, by Arthur Waskow. Life-cycle materials to be provided. Resource: *The Jewish Home*, by Daniel Syme.

Mitzvot

Torah: In the area of study, the student will, in consultation with the teacher, choose an area of study on which to become a mini-expert. Study will be pursued in that area, and the student will be able to teach the subject to others and to talk about it comfortably, without notes.

When feasible, student will tutor or teach younger students.

Student will be able to define *Tanach* and to describe the three sections of it.

Avodah: Student will be able to define "*siddur*" and to describe the basic order of the service.

Student will describe the wearing of *kippah, tallit,* and *tefillin*. Consideration will be given to making one's own *tallit*.

Student will be able to describe the procedure of the Torah service.

Student will take responsibility for conducting all or part of a worship service and/or a regular home ritual.

Student will introduce into the home an observance not currently practiced.

Student will make a traditional Jewish dish for a holiday or Shabbat meal.

Student will help conduct a *seder*.

Gemilut chasadim: Student will define *tzedakah*, explain how it differs from charity, and memorize and explain the eight steps of *tzedakah*. Resource: *Tzedakah, Gemilut Hasadim and Ahavah*, by Joel Lurie Grishaver and Beth Huppin.

Student will work for a worthy cause in the congregation and/or general community for ten hours.

Student will explain the Mazon organization to his or her family and two other adults.

Klal Yisrael: Student will identify Israel on a map and define *Yisrael* as a people and as a country.

Student will follow current events pertaining to Jewish affairs and be able to give a regular summary of events.

Report

Student will write a report on a subject approved by the teacher.

Students writing biographies should include: a paragraph on where the person was born, lived, immigrated to, and died, and on his/her family. Explain the person's main contribution(s) to the Jewish people: changes made and where; what led them to their work; when and with whom they worked; how what they did changed our lives today; problems they had. If writing about a woman, note whether her work was affected by being a woman, that is, did this cause any problems or make any difference? Also, do you think the person felt a sense of accomplishment about this work while alive? Explain your answer.

Appendix G

Calendar of Shabbat Torah readings through 2005

Note: The last portion of the Torah, *Ve-zot Ha-Bracha*, is not listed, because it is only read on Simchat Torah and not on Shabbat.

Parasha	1999-2000	2000-2001	2001-2002	2002-2003	2003-2004	2004-2005
Bereshit	10/9/99	10/28/99	10/13/01	10/5/02	10/25/03	10/9/04
Noah	10/16/99	11/4/00	10/20/01	10/12/02	11/1/03	10/16/04
Lech Lecha	10/23/99	11/13/00	10/27/01	10/19/02	11/8/03	10/23/04
Vayera	10/30/99	11/18/00	11/3/01	10/26/02	11/15/03	10/30/04
Chaye Sarah	11/6/99	11/25/00	11/10/01	11/2/02	11/22/03	11/6/04
Toledot	11/13/99	12/2/00	11/17/01	11/9/02	11/29/03	11/13/04
Vayetze	11/20/99	12/9/00	11/24/01	11/16/02	12/6/03	11/20/04
Vayishlach	11/27/99	12/16/00	12/1/01	11/23/02	12/13/03	11/27/04
Vayeshev	12/4/99	12/23/00	12/8/01	11/30/02	12/20/03	12/4/04
Miketz	12/11/99	12/30/00	12/15/01	12/7/02	12/27/03	12/11/04
Vayigash	12/18/99	1/6/01	12/22/01	12/14/02	1/3/04	12/18/04
Vayechi	12/25/99	1/13/01	12/29/01	12/21/02	1/10/04	12/25/04
Shemot	1/1/00	1/20/01	1/5/02	12/28/02	1/17/04	1/1/05
Va'era	1/8/00	1/27/01	1/12/02	1/4/03	1/24/04	1/8/05
Bo	1/15/00	2/3/01	1/19/02	1/11/03	1/31/04	1/15/05
Beshalach	1/22/00	2/10/01	1/26/02	1/18/03	2/7/04	1/22/05
Yitro	1/29/00	2/17/01	2/2/02	1/25/03	2/14/04	1/29/05
Mishpatim	2/5/00	2/24/01	2/9/02	2/1/03	2/21/04	2/5/05
Terumah	2/12/00	3/3/01	2/16/02	2/8/03	2/28/04	2/12/05
Tezaveh	2/19/00	3/10/01	2/23/02	2/15/03	3/6/04	2/19/05
Ki Tisa	2/26/00	3/17/01	3/2/02	2/22/03	3/13/04	2/26/05
Vayakhel	3/4/00	3/24/01	3/9/02	3/1/03	3/20/04	3/5/05
Pekudei	3/11/00	3/24/01	3/9/02	3/8/03	3/20/04	3/12/05
Vayikra	3/18/00	3/31/01	3/16/02	3/15/03	3/27/04	3/19/05
Tzav	3/25/00	4/7/01	3/23/02	3/22/03	4/3/04	3/26/05
Shemini	4/1/00	4/21/01	4/6/02	3/29/03	4/17/04	4/2/05
Tazria	4/8/00	4/28/01	4/13/02	4/5/03	4/24/04	4/9/05
Metzorah	4/15/00	4/28/01	4/13/02	4/12/03	4/24/04	4/16/05
Achari Mot	4/29/00	5/5/01	4/20/02	4/26/03	5/1/04	4/23/05
Kedoshim	5/6/00	5/5/01	4/20/02	5/3/03	5/1/04	5/7/05
Emor	5/13/00	5/12/01	4/24/02	5/10/03	5/8/04	5/14/05
Behar	5/20/00	5/19/01	5/4/02	5/17/03	5/15/04	5/21/05
Bechukotai	5/27/00	5/19/01	5/4/02	5/24/03	5/15/04	5/28/05

Parasha	1999-2000	2000-2001	2001-2002	2002-2003	2003-2004	2004-2005
Bamidbar	6/3/00	5/26/01	5/11/02	5/31/03	5/22/04	6/4/05
Naso	6/17/00	6/2/01	5/25/02	6/14/03	5/29/04	6/11/05
Behaalotecha	6/24/00	6/9/01	6/1/02	6/21/03	6/5/04	6/18/05
Shelach-Lecha	7/1/00	6/16/01	6/8/02	6/28/03	6/12/04	6/25/05
Korach	7/8/00	6/23/01	6/15/02	7/5/03	6/19/04	7/2/05
Chukat	7/15/00	6/30/01	6/22/02	7/12/03	6/26/04	7/9/05
Balak	7/15/00	7/7/01	6/22/02	7/12/03	7/3/04	7/16/05
Pinchas	7/22/00	7/14/01	6/29/02	7/19/03	7/10/04	7/23/05
Matot	7/29/00	7/21/01	7/6/02	7/26/03	7/17/04	7/30/05
Masee	7/29/00	7/21/01	7/6/02	7/26/03	7/17/04	8/6/05
Devarim	8/5/00	7/28/01	7/13/02	8/2/03	7/24/04	8/13/05
Vaetchanan	8/12/00	8/4/01	7/20/02	8/9/03	7/31/04	8/20/05
Ekev	8/19/00	8/11/01	7/27/02	8/16/03	8/7/04	8/27/05
Re'eh	8/26/00	8/18/01	8/3/02	8/23/03	8/14/04	9/3/05
Shoftim	9/2/000	8/25/01	8/10/02	8/30/03	8/21/04	9/10/05
Ki Teze	9/9/00	9/1/01	8/17/02	9/6/03	8/28/04	9/17/05
Ki Tavo	9/16/00	9/8/01	8/24/02	9/13/03	9/4/04	9/24/05
Nitzavim	9/23/00	9/15/01	8/31/02	9/20/03	9/11/04	10/1/05
Vayelech	9/23/00	9/22/01	8/31/02	9/20/03	9/11/04	10/8/05
Haazinu	10/7/00	9/29/01	9/14/02	10/4/03	9/18/04	10/15/05

Appendix H

Torah portions and their *Haftarot*

The Torah consists of the first five books of the Jewish Bible. It is some-times called the Pentateuch (from the Greek, meaning five). In Hebrew, the portions are called either *parashiyyot* (selections/divisions) or *sidras* (orders/arrangements). The two terms may be used interchangeably, although usu-ally Ashkenazim use *sidra/sidrot* and Sephardim use *parasha/parashiyyot*. They are read throughout the year on a set schedule, according to the Jewish calen-dar. The cycle of Torah readings begins on the holiday of Simchat Torah (Rejoicing in the Torah), which falls a few weeks after Rosh Hashanah, and concludes just before Rosh Hashanah the following year.

In addition to the weekly Torah readings, there is a related portion called the *Haftarah* (conclusion), taken from the section of the Jewish Bible called *Nevi'im* (Prophets). If you have questions about variations between Ashkenazic and Sephardic customs, special *shabbatot* on holidays or *Rosh Chodesh*, or other related matters, consult a rabbi. The Torah portions are listed here with their accompanying *Haftarot*. The *Haftarot* read in Sephardic services are indicated by an asterisk (*).

Genesis

Torah		Haftarah	
B'raysheet	1.1 - 6.8	Isaiah	42.5 - 43.11
			*42.5 - 21
Noach	6.9 - 11.32	Isaiah	54.1 - 55.5
			*54.1-10
Lech-Lecha	12.1 - 17.27	Isaiah	40.27 - 41.16
Vayera	18.1 - 22.24	II Kings	4.1 - 37
			*4.1 - 23
Chaye Sarah	23.1 - 25.18	I Kings	1.1 - 31
Toledot	25.10 - 28.9	Malachi	1.1 - 2.7
Va-yetzeh	28.10 - 32.3	Hosea	12.13 - 14. 10
			*11.7 - 12.12
Va-yishlach	32.4 - 36.43	Hosea	11.7 - 12.12
		*Obadiah	1.1.-21
Va-yayshev	37.1 - 40.23	Amos	2.6 - 3.8
Mikketz	41.1 - 44.17	I Kings	3.15 - 4.1
Va-yiggash	44.18 - 47.27	Ezekiel	37.15 - 28
Va-yechi	47.28 - 50.26	I Kings	2.1 - 12

Exodus

Torah		Haftarah	
Shemot	1.1 - 6.1	Isaiah	27.6-28.13; 29. 22, 23
		*Jeremiah	1.1 - 2.3
Va-ayra	6.2 - 9.35	Ezekiel	28.25 - 20.21
Bo	10.1 - 13.16	Jeremiah	46.13 - 28
Be'shallach	13.17 - 17.16	Judges	4.4 - 5.31
			*5.1 - 31
Yitro	18.1 - 20.23	Isaiah	6.1 - 7.6; 9.5, 6
			*6.1 - 13
Mishpatim	21.1 - 24.18	Jeremiah	34.8 - 22; 33.25, 26
Terumah	25.1 - 27.19	I Kings	5.26 - 6.13
Tetzaveh	27.20 - 30.10	Ezekiel	43.10 - 27
Ki Thissa	30.11 - 34.35	I Kings	18.1 - 39
			*18.20 - 39
Va-yakhel	35.1 - 38.20	I Kings	7.40 - 50
			*7.13 - 26
Pekudey	38.21 - 40.38	I Kings	7.51 - 8.21
			*7.40 - 50

Leviticus

Torah		Haftarah	
Va-yeekra	1.1 - 5.26	Isaiah	43.21 - 44.23
Tzav	6.1 - 8.36	Jeremiah	7.21 - 8.3; 9.22, 23
Shemini	9.1. - 11.47	II Samuel	6.1 - 7.17
			*6.1 - 19
Tazria	12.1 - 13.59	II Kings	4.42 - 5.19
Metzora	14.1 - 15.33	II Kings	7.3 - 20
Acharay Mot	16.1 - 18.30	Ezekial	22.1 - 18
			*22.1 - 16
Kedoshim	19.1 - 20.27	Amos	9.7 - 15
		*Ezekial	20.2 - 20
Emor	21.1 - 24.23	Ezekial	44.15 - 31
Be-Har	25.1 - 26.2	Jeremiah	32.6 - 27
Be-chukkotai	26.3 - 27.34	Jeremiah	16.19 - 17.14

Numbers

Torah		Haftarah	
Bamidbar	1.1 - 4.20	Hosea	2.1 - 22
Naso	4.21 - 7.89	Judges	13.2 - 25
Be-ha'alotecha	8.1 - 12.16	Zechariah	2.14 - 47
Shelach-lecha	13.1 - 15.41	Joshua	2.1 - 22
Korach	16.1 - 18.32	I Samuel	11.14 - 12.22
Chukkat	19.1 - 22.1	Judges	11.1 - 33
Balak	22.2 - 25.9	Micah	5.6 - 6.8
Pinchas	25.10 - 30.1	I Kings	18.46 - 19.21
Mattot	30.2 - 32.42	Jeremiah	1.1 - 2.3
Massei	33.1 - 36.13	Jeremiah	2.4 - 28; 3.4
			*2.4 - 28; 4.1, 2

Deuteronomy

Torah		Haftarah	
Devarim	1.1 - 3.22	Isaiah	1.1 - 27
Va-etchanan	3.23 - 7.11	Isaiah	40.1 - 26
Ekev	7.12 - 11.25	Isaiah	49.14 - 51.3
Re-'eh	11.26 - 16.17	Isaiah	54.11 - 55.5
Shoftim	16.18 - 21.9	Isaiah	51.12 - 52.12
Ki Tetzeh	21.10 - 25.19	Isaiah	54.1 - 10
Ki Tavo	26.1 - 29.8	Isaiah	60.1 - 22
Nitzavim	29.9 - 30.20	Isaiah	61.10 - 63.9
Va-yelech	31.1 - 30	Isaiah	55.6 - 56.8
Ha'azinu	32.1 - 52	II Samuel	22.1 - 51
Ve-zot Ha-bracha	33.1 - 34.12	Joshua	1.1 - 18
			*1.1 - 9

Appendix I

Example of a Bar/Bat Mitzvah service booklet

NOTE: This is only one example of a service booklet to use as a guide. There may be other pieces of information you would like to include. A short biography of the Bar/Bat Mitzvah student, the history of the synagogue, a copy of the Torah portion and Haftarah to be chanted, special prayers and/or meditations, a message from the student—all are possibilities to help you create a personalized keepsake for the day.

CONGREGATION
BETH AMI

[Secular Date]   [Hebrew Date]

Inside first page:

Congregation Beth Ami
Rabbi
Cantor
Synagogue Administrator
President

Welcome to our synagogue

Congregation Beth Ami is a liberal Jewish congregation. In Hebrew, our name means "house of my people." The sanctuary in which we are gathered is built to resemble the *ohel moed* (the tent of meeting) that the Israelites carried throughout their journey from Sinai to the Promised Land. The stained glass windows remind us of sun, sand, wind, and sky, which surrounded them in the desert. The large window in the back of the sanctuary is blue, to represent life-giving water. The Torah scrolls are kept in the *Aron Ha-Kodesh* (the holy ark), which is the centerpiece of the synagogue. The Hebrew inscription on the carved wooden doors of the ark read, "Holy, Holy, Holy is the Lord of Hosts! The whole earth is full of God's glory!" The Torah mantles were woven in Jerusalem using threads in many shades of green; they symbolize flourishing vegetation in "the land of milk and honey." The Torah finials are all of hand-wrought Yemenite silver. The *bimah* (raised pulpit area) represents the altar that stood in the tabernacle.

The ceremony

On this Shabbat morning we welcome a young member of our congregation as an adult in the eyes of the Jewish community. [Name of student] will lead the congregation in the service, chant from the Torah, and give words of commentary on the portion. [Name of student] will also chant a *Haftarah* from one of the books of the prophets. The preparation for this day has been long and intense. From this day on, [name of student] will accept the adult obligations of a Jew: the wearing of the *tallit* (the prayer shawl), the laying of *tefillin* (the phylacteries), being counted as part of a *minyan* (a quorum of ten for prayers), having the honor of being called up to the Torah, and being responsible for his or her individual acts of *tzedakah* (giving to those less fortunate).

Inside second page:

[name of student]
[student's Hebrew name]
[secular date]   [Hebrew date]

Parashat [name of parasha]
[book, chapter, and verse]

Haftarah
[book, chapter, and verse]

Handing down the Torah
[names of those honored]

Aliyot: The honor of being called to the Torah
[names of those honored]

Hagbahah and *Galilah:* Dressing and raising the Torah
[names of those honored]

Opening and closing the Ark doors
[names of those honored]

Shabbat Shalom

Please join our family for *Kiddush* and *Ha-Motzi* in the social hall
immediately following the service.

Back of service booklet:
Transliterated lyrics of songs to be sung by the congregation during
the service

Appendix 3

Sample letter to friends of the student

This letter is printed here with permission from Leslie Reisfeld of Burlingame, California, who created this in preparation for her daughter's Bat Mitzvah:

Dear friends of Stephanie,

We are so glad that you will be able to celebrate Steph's Bat Mitzvah with us. Your support means a lot to Steph!

Many of you may have been to Bat or Bar Mitzvahs before and may know a lot of what happens in the service. Many of you may have never been to a Bat Mitzvah before, and we wanted to give you some information ahead of time. What follows is just some general info on Steph's Bat Mitzvah service and also on her party Saturday night. Please feel free to call us with any questions.

- The service begins PROMPTLY at 10 a.m. It would be a good idea to get to the Temple by 9:45 or 9:50. Once you arrive, please come into the sanctuary, where Steph's school friends will sit together.
- Please try to be quiet and respectful during the services. Steph really needs your support, attention, and participation. Please do not go in and out during the service, as that can be distracting to those around you.
- Girls should wear nice dresses with no bare shoulders or really short skirts. Boys should wear nice pants, a nice shirt, a tie, and a jacket or a suit.
- The service lasts about two hours. Steph will lead almost the entire service.
- After the service is a light buffet luncheon. Please stay and enjoy the lunch. Your parents may pick you up any time between 12:45 and 1:15 p.m.
- Saturday night's party at the hotel is dressy. Girls should wear fancy dresses and shoes they can dance in. Boys should wear nice pants, a nice shirt, a tie, and a jacket or a suit. Boys are welcome to take their jackets off during dancing.
- The party Saturday night begins at 6:30 p.m. From 6:30 to 7:30, the kids will be in a room next to the ballroom while the adults have cocktails in the foyer. At 7:30, the kids and adults will all go to the ballroom for a party together, which will include folk-dancing, dinner, lots of dancing, and games.
- The party will end at 11:30. Please ask your parents to pick you up between 11:15 and 11:30.

We appreciate your being with us to celebrate this important day with our family. Thanks for coming. We'll see you on Saturday, November 7!

Sincerely,
Leslie and Bob Reisfeld

Bibliography

Balka, Christie, and Andy Rose. *Twice Blessed: On Being Lesbian, Gay, and Jewish.* Boston: Beacon Press, 1989.

Birnbaum, Philip. *Encyclopedia of Jewish Concepts.* New York: Hebrew Publishing Company, 1964.

Brown, Joni Bass. "Children With Special Needs." In *The Jewish Principal's Handbook*, edited by Audrey Friedman Marcus and Raymond A. Zwerin. Denver: Alternatives in Religious Education, 1983.

Brown, Steven M., and Stephen Garfinkel, eds. *Higher and Higher: Making Jewish Prayer Part of Us.* New York: United Synagogue of Conservative Judaism, 1980.

Davis, Judith. *Whose Bar/Bat Mitzvah is This, Anyway? A Guide for Parents Through a Family Rite of Passage.* New York: St. Martin's Griffin, 1998.

Donin, Hayim Halevy. *To Be A Jew: A Guide to Jewish Observance in Contemporary Life.* New York: Basic Books, 1972.

Gilbert, Beth. "Judaism Found." *Reform Judaism*, spring 1999.

Gillman, Neil. *Conservative Judaism: The New Century.* West Orange, N.J.: Behrman House, 1993.

Glaser, Gabrielle. "Can a Gentile Wife Raise Jewish Kids?" *Moment Magazine*, April 1999.

Hertz, J.H. *Pirke Avot: Sayings of the Fathers.* New York: Behrman House, 1945.

Hertz, J.H., ed. *The Pentateuch and Haftorahs.* 2nd ed. London: Soncino Press, 1977.

Hirsch, Samson Raphael. *T'Rumath Tzvi.* Translated by Gertrude Hirschler. New York: The Judaica Press, 1990.

Isaacs, Ronald H. and Kerry M. Olitzky. *Doing Mitzvot: Mitzvah Projects for Bar/Bat Mitzvah.* Hoboken, New Jersey: KTAV, 1994.

Isaacson, Judith, and Deborah Rosenbloom. *Bar and Bat Mitzvah in Israel: The Ultimate Family Sourcebook.* Baltimore: Israel Info. Access, 1998.

Jaffe-Gill, Ellen. "Patrilineality: Creating a Schism or Updating Judaism?" *Moment Magazine*, December 1998.

Kadden, Bruce and Barbara Binder Kadden. *Teaching Tefilah: Insights and Activities on Prayer.* Denver: A.R.E. Publishing, 1994.

Kolatch, Alfred J. *This Is the Torah.* New York: Jonathan David Publishers, 1988.

Leneman, Helen, ed. *Bar/Bat Mitzvah Education: A Sourcebook.* Denver: A.R.E. Publishing, 1993.

Leneman, Helen. *Bar/Bat Mitzvah Basics: A Practical Family Guide to Coming of Age Together.* Woodstock, Vermont: Jewish Lights, 1996.

Lerner, Michael. *Jewish Renewal: A Path to Healing and Transformation.* New York: J.P. Putnam's Sons, 1994.

Lewit, Jane, and Ellen Epstein. *The Bar/Bat Mitzvah Planbook.* Lanham, Maryland: Scarborough House, 1982.

Marcus, Audrey Friedman, and Raymond A. Zwerin, eds. *The Jewish Principal's Handbook.* Denver: A.R.E., 1983.

Nulman, Macy. *Concise Encyclopedia of Jewish Music.* New York: McGraw-Hill, 1975.

Olitzky, Kerry M., and Ronald H. Isaacs. *Rediscovering Judaism: Bar/Bat Mitzvah for Adults-A Course of Study.* Hoboken, New Jersey: KTAV, 1997.

Olitzky, Kerry M., and Ronald H. Isaacs. *The How-To Handbook for Jewish Living.* Hoboken, New Jersey: KTAV, 1993.

Olitzky, Kerry M., and Ronald H. Isaacs. *The Second How-To Handboook for Jewish Living.* Hoboken, New Jersey: KTAV, 1996.

Plaut, W. Guenther. *The Torah: A Modern Commentary.* New York: Union of American Hebrew Congregations, 1981.

Reider, Frieda. *The Challah Book.* Hoboken, New Jersey: KTAV, 1988.

Sage, Linda Seifer. *The Complete Bar/Bat Mitzvah Planner.* New York: St. Martin's Press, 1991.

Salkin, Jeffrey K. *Putting God on the Guest List: How to Reclaim the Spiritual Meaning of your Child's Bar or Bat Mitzvah.* Woodstock, Vermont: Jewish Lights, 1996.

Siegel, Richard, Robert Strassfeld, and Sharon Strassfeld. *The Jewish Catalogue,* vol. 1. Philadelphia: Jewish Publication Society, 1973.

Stern, Chaim, ed. *Gates of Prayer: The New Union Prayerbook.* New York: Central Conference of American Rabbis, 1975.

Stern, Chaim, ed. *Gates of Prayer for Shabbat and Weekdays.* New York: Central Conference of American Rabbis, 1994.

Wertheimer, Jack. *A People Divided: Judaism in Contemporary America.* Hanover, N.H.: Brandeis University Press/University Press of New England, 1997.

Glossary

Adonai: My lord. One of the Hebrew words for God.

Ahavah Rabbah: Paragraph recited before the *Sh'ma*, acknowledging God's love for the people of Israel. Recited in the morning.

Ahavat Olam: Evening version of *Ahavah Rabbah*.

Amidah: Literally, standing. Central prayer of the worship service. Also referred to as *Ha-Tefillah* (the prayer) and the *Shemonah Esray* (eighteen benedictions).

Aleinu: Closing prayer of the service, which announces the unique destiny of the Jewish people and the sovereignty of God, looking forward to the time of peace on earth.

Aliyah (pl. **aliyot**): Literally, going up. Being called up to the Torah to say the blessings and/or to read the Torah portion during worship services. It also means immigrating to Israel.

Arbah Kanfot: Four-cornered garment with fringes worn by observant Jewish males under their shirts. Also called *tzitzit*.

Aron Ha Kodesh: Holy Ark in which the Torah scrolls are kept.

Ashkenazim: Jews of Central and Eastern European descent.

Ashrei: Psalm 145, part of the worship service.

Atarah (pl. **atarot**): Decorative neckband of the *tallit*. Also sometimes indicates a half-*tallit*.

Avodah: Literally, worship or work. In ancient days denoted the sacrificial Temple service. Today means public prayer.

Avot [v'Imahot]: Literally, fathers [and mothers]. The first paragraph of the *Amidah*, acknowledging ancestors.

Ba'al Koreh: The Torah reader.

Bar'chu: Call to worship which initiates each Jewish worship service in the morning and evening.

Bar Mitzvah (pl. **bnai mitzvah**): Son of the commandment. A Jewish boy after his 13th birthday, when he reaches religious maturity. Also, the ceremony that celebrates achievement of this status.

Baruch atah Adonai eloheynu melech ha-olam: Blessed are You, O Lord our God, King of the Universe. Hebrew phrase that begins every Jewish blessing.

Bat Mitzvah (pl. *bnot mitzvah*): Daughter of the commandment. A Jewish girl after her 12th or 13th birthday, when she reaches religious maturity. Also, the ceremony that celebrates achievement of this status.

Beit Ha-Knesset: Literally, house of assembly. Synagogue.

Beit Ha-Midrash: Literally, house of study. Synagogue.

Beit Ha-Tefillah: Literally, house of prayer. Synagogue.

Besamim: Spices, especially used in the *Havdalah* ceremony.

B'racha (pl. *b'rachot*): Blessing.

Bimah: Raised area in the sanctuary from which the Torah is read and from where the services are led.

Birkat Ha-Mazon: Grace after meals.

Birkot Ha-Shachar: Morning blessings; the first part of the Shacharit service.

Brit: Covenant, referring to the covenant between God and the Jewish people.

Brit Milah/ Bris: Covenant of Abraham; circumcision of a Jewish boy on the eighth day after birth.

Chai: Alive.

Challah (pl. *challot*): Traditional braided egg bread eaten on Shabbat.

Chanukah: Literally, dedication. The Feast of Dedication or the Feast of Lights, an eight-day festival commemorating the Jewish victory over the Syrian-Greeks in 165 B.C.E., in which the Maccabees re-dedicated the Temple to God.

Chesed: Lovingkindness.

Chumash (pl. *Chumashim*): Book containing the Torah, *Haftarot*, and commentaries.

Daven: Yiddish word for pray.

D'var Torah: Literally, a word of Torah. Commentary or sermon on the Torah portion.

Drash: From the word *Midrash*, to expose, expound. Words of insight, commentary on the Torah portion.

Emet: Truth.

Etz Chaim: Literally, tree of life. Wooden rollers to which the Torah scroll is attached.

Gabbai (pl. *gabbaim*): Person responsible for logistics of the synagogue and services.

Gartl: Torah binder.

Gemilut Chasadim: Deeds of lovingkindness.

Get: Jewish bill of divorce.

Gevurot: Literally, greatness. Second paragraph of the *Amidah*, referring to the greatness of God.

Hachnasat Orchim: Hospitality to guests.

Halachah: Jewish law.

Haftarah/Haftorah (pl. *Haftarot*): Reading taken from the Prophets or Writings, linked to the subject matter of the Torah portion.

Hagbahah: The honor of raising the Torah scroll for all the congregation to see after the reading.

Hakafah (pl. *hakafot*): Circle made when carrying the Torah around the synagogue.

Hallel: Psalms of praise recited during the service on certain holidays.

Ha-Motzi: Blessing recited over bread.

Hashkiveinu: Second blessing after the *Sh'ma* in the evening service.

Havdalah: Ceremony concluding the Sabbath and festivals, separating them from the rest of the week.

Hazzan/Hazzan Ha-Knesset: Literally, one who oversees the assembly. The cantor.

Hiddur Mitzvah: Enhancing the observance of a *mitzva.*

Gelilah: The honor of rolling the Torah scroll back together after the Torah reading.

Golel: One who performs *gelilah.*

Kabbalat Shabbat: Friday night prayer service welcoming the Sabbath.

Kaddish: Prayer of praise to God that requires a *minyan* for its recitation. There are different forms of the *Kaddish,* including one said by mourners.

Kasher: To make something kosher.

Kashrut: Jewish dietary laws.

Kavannah: Intent and concentration during prayer.

Kedusha: Part of the *Amidah* recalling the angels' praise of God.

Keter Torah: The crown on the Torah, usually made of silver.

Ketubah: Jewish marriage contract.

Ketuvim: Writings. The third section of the *Tanach.*

Kiddush: Literally, sanctification. The blessing said over wine.

Kippah (pl. *kippot*): Skullcap traditionally worn by Jewish males. Also referred to by its Yiddish name, *yarmulke.*

Klal Yisrael: The entirety of the Jewish people.

Kohen (pl. *Kohanim*): Priest, descendant of a subgroup of the tribe of Levi. Called first to the Torah in traditional synagogues.

Korban: Sacrificial offering brought by the *kohanim* in Temple days.

Kosher: Ritually fit. Usually used to describe foods that conform to Jewish dietary laws.

Kotel: Western wall of the Second Temple in Jerusalem, still standing today. Traditionally the holiest site in Judaism.

Lag B'Omer: The 33rd day of the counting of the *omer*, a sad period between Passover and Shavuot.

L'Chaim: To life. Toast of good wishes offered at Jewish celebrations.

Levi (pl. ***Levi'im***): Descendant of the tribe of Levi, called second to the Torah in traditional synagogues.

Ma'ariv: Evening worship service.

Ma'ariv Aravim: First paragraph before the *Sh'ma* in the evening service, praises God for bringing on evenings.

Machzor (pl. ***machzorim***): Prayer book used for the High Holy Days.

Maftir: The last section read from the Torah portion of the week.

Magbihah: One who performs *hagbahah*.

Mashgiach: One who supervises the preparation of kosher food.

Mechitzah: Divider separating men and women in a traditional synagogue.

M'eel: Mantle covering the Torah scroll.

Mezuzah: Literally, doorpost. A small case affixed to a doorpost, containing a parchment with the first two paragraphs of the *Sh'ma*.

Midrash: Commentaries by the rabbis on Biblical texts.

Mincha: Afternoon service.

Minhag Ha-Makom: Literally, the custom of the place. The prevailing custom one should follow.

Minyan: Quorum of 10 adult Jews required to recite certain prayers. In Orthodox Judaism, only men are counted.

Mi Shebayrach: Prayer asking God's blessing for those who are ill.

Mitzvah (pl. ***mitzvot***): Commandment, sometimes interpreted as good deed. There are 613 *mitzvot* in the Torah.

Mizrachi: Literally, eastern. Refers to Middle Eastern Jews.

Musaf: Additional service following *shacharit* on Shabbat and festivals.

Nefesh: Soul.

Ner Tamid: Light that is kept burning continually above the ark that holds the Torah scrolls.

Nevi'im: Prophets. Second section of the *Tanach*.

Nusach: Musical style of the service.

Oneg Shabbat (pl. ***Ongai Shabbat***): Reception on Shabbat, often held following a Friday evening service.

Oseh Shalom: Literally, creator of peace. Title of a prayer/song.

Parashah (pl. ***parashiyyot***): Weekly Torah portion.

Parochet: Drape covering the holy ark.

Pesach: Passover. Jewish holiday celebrating the Exodus from Egypt.

Pesukei De'Zimra: Passages of song; introductory portion of a worship service.

Pirke Avot: Collection of rabbinic teachings from the Talmudic period, 200 B.C.E. to 500 C.E.

Retzay: A prayer that is part of the *Amidah.*

Rimmonim: Literally, pomegranates. Torah finials.

Rosh Chodesh: Holiday celebrating the new month.

Rosh Hashanah: Jewish New Year.

Seder: Festive ritual meal held on the first two nights of Passover.

Sefer Torah (pl. **Sifrei Torah**): Torah scroll.

Sephardim: Jews whose ancestors came from Spain and Portugal.

Shabbat: Sabbath.

Shacharit: Morning service.

Shaliach Tzibbur: Person who leads the worship service.

Shalom: Hello; goodbye; peace.

Shalom Rav: Final blessing of the evening *Amidah.*

Shemonah Esray: Literally, 18. Another name for the *Amidah,* which has 18 benedictions.

Sheh-hecheyanu: Blessing recited for new and happy moments and to mark the first night of every festival.

Sh'ma: Central prayer of Jewish belief in one God.

Shomer Shabbat: Sabbath-observant.

Shul: Yiddish word for synagogue.

Siddur (pl. **siddurim**): Prayer book.

Shabbat Shalom: Traditional greeting for the Sabbath.

Shavua Tov: Good week. Greeting given following the *Havdalah* ceremony.

Shepp Nachas: Feel a sense of satisfaction and pride in the accomplishments of a loved one.

Simcha: A joyful celebration.

Sim Shalom: Morning *Amidah* prayer for peace.

Sofer: Scribe who writes sacred texts, including the Torah scroll.

Synagogue: From the Greek "to assemble." The place where Jews come together for prayer and study.

Tallit: Prayer shawl.

Tanach: Hebrew Bible, consisting of three sections: *Torah* (the Five Books of Moses), *Nevi'im* (Prophets), and *Ketuvim*(Writings).

Tefillah: Prayer.

Tefillin: Phylacteries. Leather boxes containing passages from the Torah, worn by adult Jews on the arm and head during weekday morning prayers.

Tikkun: Text used in training one to read from the Torah, using two columns of Hebrew—one with vowels and *trope* and one without.

Tikkun Olam: Repairing the world; making the world a better place through good deeds.

Tisha B'Av: The ninth of the Hebrew month of Av. Commemorates the destruction of the First and Second Temples and other calamities that befell the Jewish people throughout history.

Torah: Literally, instruction; direction. The Five Books of Moses. First section of the *Tanach*.

Trope: Signs above and below the Hebrew text indicating the musical melody to be chanted when reading Torah and *Haftarah*. Also known as *Ta'amei Ha-Mikra*.

Tu B'Shevat: Jewish Arbor Day, the 14th of the Hebrew month of Shevat.

Tzedakah: Literally, righteousness. Giving money to those in need.

Tzitzit: Fringes on the four corners of a prayer shawl, reminders of the 613 *mitzvot* in the Torah.

V'Ahavtah: Part of the *Sh'ma*. Paragraphs from Deuteronomy exhorting Jews to follow the commandments on a daily basis.

Yad: Pointer used by the Torah reader to follow the text while reading.

Yahrzeit: Anniversary of a death.

Yisrael: Israel.

Yamim Nora'im: Days of Awe. Rosh Hashanah and Yom Kippur.

Yasher Koach: May you be strengthened. Sentiment expressed by well wishers after the performance of a *mitzvah*, such as an *aliyah* to the Torah.

Yizkor: Memorial service held on Yom Kippur, Pesach, Shavuot, and Sukkot.

Yom Ha-Shoah: Holocaust remembrance day.

Yom Ha-Zikaron: Memorial day for soldiers killed in Israel's wars.

Yom Kippur: Day of Atonement.

Yotzer Or: Morning prayer praising God for creating light.

Zichronam L'vracha: May their memories be for a blessing.

Index